Discourse Analysis as Sociocriticism

Discourse Analysis as Sociocriticism

The Spanish Golden Age

Antonio Gómez-Moriana

University of Minnesota Press

Minneapolis

London

Published by the University of Minnesota Press
2037 University Avenue Southeast, Minneapolis, MN 55455-3092
Printed in the United States of America on acid-free paper

Library of Congress Cataloging-in-Publication Data

Gómez-Moriana, Antonio.
    Discourse analysis as sociocriticism : the Spanish Golden Age /
Antonio Gómez-Moriana.
        p.   cm.
    Includes bibliographical references and index.
    ISBN 0-8166-2072-5 (hard : alk. paper)
    ISBN 0-8166-2073-3 (pbk : alk. paper)
    1. Spanish literature—Classical period, 1500-1700—History and
criticism.   2. Discourse analysis, Literary.   I. Title.
PQ6066.G66   1993
860.9'003—dc20   92-34790
                                                                          CIP

Contents

Preface

The studies collected in this book are the result of a decade's research in critical theory and methodology and in the traditional ways of reading (and interpreting) some of the classical texts of Hispanic literature. Special attention has been paid to *Lazarillo de Tormes* (in an attempt to clarify the origins of the picaresque novel), to *Don Quijote* (considered as the dialogical space in which the transition from the epic to the novel took place — i.e., the confrontation between medieval feudal and modern bourgeois thought), and to *Don Juan* (which witnesses the ongoing conflict between modernization and antimodernization in Spain after the Council of Trent). The always lively and intense reception of these texts, above all after the so-called Generation of 1898, proves that this debate continues into the twentieth century. Thus, I consider that these texts are still relevant today and demand to be reread. From the perspective of 1992 I have also included two studies on the chronicles of the "discovery" of the New World.

Versions of some of these studies have been published in Spanish, French, or both in the following periodicals: *Nueva Revista de Filología Hispánica* (Mexico), *Dispositio* (United States), *Revista de Occidente* (Spain), *Imprévue, Cotextes*, and *Poétique* (France), *Revista Canadiense de Estudios Hispánicos* and *Canadian Review of Comparative Literature* (Canada). Four articles appear as a book in French, under the title *La Subversion du discours rituel* (Longueuil, Quebec: Les Editions du Préambule, 1985). In English, one of my studies of this material appears in *Sociocriticism*, one in *Critical Studies*, and two in *Hispanic Issues*. I am grateful to the editors of all of these publications.

I am also grateful to the Social Sciences and Humanities Research Council of Canada (SHRC) and to the Fonds pour la Formation de Chercheurs et l'Aide à la

Recherche (FCAR), Quebec, for the grants that made possible this research and the presentation of its results for discussion at national and international conferences, and to the Université de Montréal for continuous support and especially for giving me the opportunity to focus only on research during my sabbatical year, 1985-86. Many thanks also to Alice Monty-Diry, James V. Romano, Jane E. Gregg, and Marie Lessard for their collaboration in preparing the English version of these often-difficult texts. Throughout the book, when no published English translation is cited with a quotation, responsibility for the translation is mine. Special thanks to Craig Ireland for his help in converting a series of articles into a book, and to Karin G.-M. for the compilation of the bibliography.

Montreal
Fall 1991

Introduction
Semiotics and Philology in Text Analysis

Although the *illusion* of the literary text's autonomy as well as that of the work of art in general arises from the Enlightenment's emancipatory project (that is, the attempt to establish a science, morality, and art answerable respectively only to scientific, ethical, and aesthetic norms), literary criticism did not begin to isolate its object of study until very recently. Such has been, since the European Renaissance, the influence of historicism, in its various modalities, and the identification of philology with its objectives and methods. It was thus in the twentieth century—and under the impact exerted almost simultaneously by structural linguistics, semiotics, and Russian formalism—that literary studies focused on the text's so-called literariness or on its forms conceived of as structures, that is to say, on the principles governing the composition of the text as a whole rather than on the origins and historical development of its components.

In their first encounter, then, semiotics and philology face one another as irreconcilable enemies. Semiotics presents itself as synchrony, a system of signs organized according to oppositional axes (such as Saussurian phonology); philology seeks the diachrony of isolated elements whose study ignores the totality in which these elements are inscribed (as the phonetics, always diachronic for Saussure). A misunderstood and uncontested opposition between diachrony and synchrony[1] marks the first steps in the renovation of literary studies—a renovation based on the linguistic model and within the framework of cultural semiology envisioned by Saussure as a kind of universal science capable of accounting for all the sign systems by virtue of which human beings communicate with one another. Abandoning this project that recognized, parallel to the more ontological concepts of "system" or "structure," the more sociohistorical concepts of

1

"communication" and "convention," structuralism then became the champion of the immanent study of literary texts — the so-called synchronic study — whereas philology had fallen into the undeniable excesses of historicism and nationalism during the last decades of the nineteenth century and the first of the twentieth. It was indeed during this period that philology served more than ever to bolster nationalism (particularly in Europe) by insisting on the "creative genius" of a group or nation and by orienting historical research — in an extraordinary deployment of scholarly data and historical scholarship — toward the apologetic defense of the own creation. Later creations of others were thus reduced to copies or continuations of the first, according to the universally accepted principle *post hoc, ergo propter hoc*. Let us recall, to take an example from the field of Hispanic studies, Menéndez y Pelayo's "literary" investigations, which we can now see as a project of retracing the history of the contributions of (Catholic) Spanish genius to universal history — a project that reveals Menéndez y Pelayo as both author and scholar (the famous controversy about "Spanish science") and leaves its mark on all of his later work and that of many of his followers, even to this century.[2] Texts were henceforth ignored in the name of a preoccupation with external factors, such as their "sources."

In addition to such nationalist projects, the traditional search for "sources" fragmented the text by isolating the elements (motifs, sayings, actions, situations, and so on) to be studied. Hence the inability to account for the text as a coherent and articulated whole in the interaction of those very elements (identifiable, to be sure, in previous and contemporary works, only now converted into functions within the new totality, which appropriates and integrates them). These oversights on the part of philology may perhaps explain the violent reaction of structuralism against all diachronic considerations. Yet "immanent" — or synchronic — study sets the literary text in a timelessness that fails altogether to take into account the mark or semantic load carried by the elements integrated into the new whole or text by the mere fact of having previously belonged to other texts or to an entire textual tradition. For this reason, I have elsewhere qualified as achronic an approach that ignores both the tradition in which is inscribed every sign and the selective restrictions imposed upon it by social conventions.[3] Such an approach indeed isolates the artistic text from all spatial, temporal, and social anchoring, thereby transforming it into a self-sufficient and autotelic entity. In order to do this, it reduces the text, in the manner of neopositivist scientism, to its quantifiable (verbal) materiality and ignores the social convention within which all texts operate — whether through the faithful reproduction of stereotypes or their transgression or, at any rate, through dialogue with social convention.

The possible tension between system and event, tradition and act (of writing as well as of reading), norm and use escape the reach of both historicist philology and immanentist structuralism. These two approaches therefore remain incapable of accounting for historical processes and changes (including those that affect systems, norms, the temporal forms of the realization of dynamic structures), as well as for the aesthetic effects that the dialectical tension between norm and transgression will produce in every speech act and text that does not limit itself to the purely mimetic reproduction of a (socially) regulated discursive model. In order to grasp this aesthetic dimension of language games and the historical processes in which they participate, one must thus pay greater attention, in addition to the study of sign systems, to the signifying processes in which those signs are involved. What I propose here is a twofold functional study of the sign—as a system and as a (historical) process—within diachronically, diatopically, and diastratically marked subsystems (dialects, sociolects, and jargons) and within the interaction of those subsystems (intertextual borrowings, interdiscursive calques), and all uses or abuses of what Bakhtin calls "the other's discourse" (*chushaia riech*).[4]

The issue here is no longer one of mere historicist pleasure or of a return to scholarly positivism. Over and above the satisfaction provided by erudition in revealing the origins of something (a purely historicist satisfaction characteristic of the traditional search for sources), what is at hand here is a study of the text that focuses on the mark or semantic load carried by the text's components and that can thus account for the inflections or mutations to which these components are possibly subjected in the new entity or text. It is a matter, then, of duly considering the twofold referentiality postulated by the two dimensions—system and process—of all semiosis, but particularly of literature. Aside from enhancing our knowledge of the historical evolution of the elements concerned (the object of traditional philology), the consideration of this double referentiality (to their original mark and to the new text; to the associative relations of the paradigm or paradigms from which they proceed, and to the syntagmatic relations established by the new text that integrates them) allows us to understand any work in that dynamics of signification that historically organizes it as an intersection of texts and discourses in (often conflictual) dialogue, rather than as the finished product of a particular author.

By substituting for the research object's "sources" (in the traditional sense of an isolated element's historical origin and influence, the *Wirkungsgeschichte*) the dual dialogue established by the components (that is, their own history and the new whole into which they are now integrated), I propose nothing less than a synthesis of diachrony and synchrony. Such a synthesis has already been attempted by diachronic structuralism, yet the results led only to a literary aestheticism severed from any dialogue with the nonliterary and, a fortiori, with the socioaesthetic dimension of transgression. In order, then, to situate my position vis-à-vis this proposed synthesis, I will first have to expand the horizon against which the preceding considerations have been made. This horizon has in fact been limited so far to the paradigmatic and syntagmatic axes, that is to say, to the signs' relations between themselves, along with that more or less constant tension, particularly in literature, between the system of virtualities and that of concrete realizations. It is what Charles Morris (1938) calls the "syntactic dimension" of semiosis. What I propose now is that we include in the study of texts the other relations pointed out by Morris—relations to be also considered as dimensions of semiosis: the semantic and pragmatic dimensions that are indispensable complements to the syntactic dimension in any communicative process.

Whereas the inclusion of the semantic dimension will force us to revise the concept of literature as autonomous and autotelic (a common denominator of all schools of diachronic structuralism that proclaim autoreferentiality as the mark of specificity of literary language), the inclusion of the pragmatic dimension will force us to consider the sociohistorical implications of literary practices as opposed to the claim of literature's ideological "innocence" and neutrality. I am thus opposed to those who deny literature its social contingency in the name of an aseity that disavows its continuous dialogue with the outside world. I propose, in other words, that we study literature as a discourse among the discourses produced and consumed by given societies, and that we investigate in textual analysis the confluence of all the agents of the literary phenomenon as a *communicative semiosis, situated at a given time and in a given society and participating in that society's channels of verbal (and nonverbal) interaction.* The consideration of literature as but one of the discursive practices of a particular society strips away its transhistorical attributes and reduces it to the social, the conventional, and the arbitrary, thereby leading us along with Jacques Dubois (1978, 11) to the discovery that "literature does not exist; there are only specific practices that work simultaneously on language and on the collective imagination."

This "working on language and on the collective imagination" is perhaps what defines the specificity of literary discourse, its social dimension, and its historical role in the collective imagination. By defining the function of literature as a "working on language," I concur with those who consider poetic language as artifice—a view held by New Criticism and by the various European stylistic schools, as well as by Russian formalism and several of its branches of recent decades. I do not agree with these critics' view of literary evolution, however. The definition of literary language as a transgression, to be sure, is nothing new; rhetorical treatises from every period serve as inventories of the most diverse linguistic anomalies, which they arrange under rubrics such as "tropes" and "figures." Although I acknowledge that inventiveness, or artifice, and rule transgression are basic components of the working of literature upon language, I can subscribe neither to the predominant view of literary history as the history of the construction, dismantling, and reconstruction of rhetorical devices, nor to the notions that the literary work is definable and analyzable merely as a "set of devices" or that genres are only "specific types of such sets," a definition that is applied to schools, movements, and literary generations alike.

The philology proposed here along with the semiotics that I associate with it cannot be limited to the description of literary traditions that feed upon themselves and are linked historically. Nor will it suffice merely to place the literary work in the context of (intra)literary history. What the new philology—what diachronic semiotics—must study is the dialectic interaction between what is intrinsic and extrinsic to every text considered as a kind of transtextual anaphora, inasmuch as it is a dialogue with stimuli of various origins. The study of the text as a dialogical space, to use Julia Kristeva's (1969a) expression inspired by Bakhtin, thus appears as a true challenge to both philology and semiotics, which must henceforth account for the manner in which the text both reads history and is inscribed in it. This is what I call interdiscursive reading, and this is the object of sociocriticism and discourse analysis as I intend to apply it in the field of literary criticism.

A literary text works upon and thereby modifies not only the literary system but also language as such and the verbal or nonverbal, artistic or nonartistic interactive devices available to the society in which it is produced. In our culture, such a text occurs mainly in literary (especially narrative) practices. But in its disregard for linguistic rules (the system's grammar) and the limits imposed by the "order of discourse" (Michel Foucault) on all social discursive practice, the literary text operates within a paradoxical communicative frame. Because it is circulated beyond the borders of the immediate context in which it is produced, the literary text, in the course of its history, filters through perpetually renewed contexts of reception that do not match the original conditions of its production— that is, the informational assumptions or objectives that surrounded it at the time of its production. As the surroundings in which the text circulates change, the traditions and practices of reception also change, as does the evocative power of the textual elements that affect individuals and groups of diverse cognitive and affective backgrounds. In this manner different readings, translations, and imitations arise, and just as they eliminate from the text certain evocative references, they also add to it new and unexpected meanings. This institutional reality of literary discourse is also a challenge to textual analysis: if it cannot be reduced to the archaeological study of the context of production and the original meaning of the text, it will have to be accounted for in the process of its reading or reception through space, time, and the various groups that accept or reject it. In short, what is needed is the complementing of the diachrony, diatopy, and diastraty of production with those of the reception processes. Indeed, the history of the literary text is exhausted neither by the intertextual and interdiscursive study of its origin and production (the problem of textual genetics), nor by statistical accounts of editions, translations, or reader typologies (the reception being understood as distribution and consumption). Also to be included is the study of all the uses, ab-uses, re-uses, and amalgamations, along with other types of discourses, that new practices—literary or other—will impose on it.

Two examples from my recent investigations will illustrate the twofold approach that I propose. *Lazarillo de Tormes* (chapters 1 to 3) originally functioned, I propose, as a grotesque replica or parody of a discursive practice prevalent at the time of its production: the autobiographical confession addressed directly or indirectly to the Inquisition tribunal and produced upon the latter's demand. *Lazarillo*'s agrammatical discursive calque of that ritual-discursive practice gave rise to a new practice: the fictional autobiography, which was to play an important role in the origins of the modern novel. That which at first was a subversive text later became a model of writing intended for the entertainment of an idle public; it eventually became an institutionalized genre—now referred to as the picaresque novel—from whose viewpoint we have learned to read *Lazarillo*, the very text to which the genre owes its origin.

If my reading places Lázaro de Tormes's "account" of his life in interdiscursive contiguity with the various autobiographical confessional practices prevalent in the Spain of his time, I do not claim to have discovered new sources for the text, whether as a whole or in terms of its components. At stake here is not a comparison of *Lazarillo*, or of one of its fragments, with a particular autobiographical text or some of its fragments. Coincidences at lexical, situational, or other levels reveal nothing more than the connection between texts (or their fragments) and the discursive framework of which each is an echo in its own way. And the way in which *Lazarillo* becomes an echo of this discursive framework and of its practices is by the unmasking of the latter through a subversive or agrammatical imitation of its working rules. In later readings, several of the text's allusions will be forgotten, along with its intertextual and interdiscursive dialectical tension with the aforementioned practices. This is precisely what will make it possible for the picaresque novel to appear as belonging to an autoreferential tradition. The philologist's semiotic work on the text, then, should address not only the text's genesis but also the subsequent historical process of its reading and reception.

My second example (chapters 5 and 6) is taken from *Don Quijote*. Rather than subscribe to its usual reading, which would have Cervantes's work reflect the struggle between (sound) realism (the presentation of things "as they are") and the excesses of idealism (the protagonist's antics as inspired by imaginative readings on chivalry), I propose instead that we study the text as an interdiscursive crossroads, that is, a mise-en-scène of an entire repertory of regulated and accepted modes of speaking, of discourses—some obsolete, others still in force—of the various social milieus represented in the work: the country and the court, peasantry and nobility, the inns and country roads (the latter already traveled more by merchants than by wandering knights). These discourses contrast with one another in their different modes of representation whenever each describes the same object from its own perspective or when the same story is narrated repeatedly but with substantial variations. Seen in this manner, *Don Quijote* becomes an experimental interdiscursive test tube, so to speak, in which the literary genres of Cervantes's time (the epic, popular epic, courtly novel, chivalric novel, eclogue and pastoral novel, Moorish novel, Byzantine novel, picaresque novel, comedy, and so on) are weighed and tested. To these genres can be added the prevailing discursive formations contemporary with *Don Quijote*: medical, psychological, theological, and literary critical discourses. The complex and contradictory picture of an age in crisis and epistemological rupture is offered by the dialogue that the text of *Don Quijote*, as dialogical space, conjures from the disparate and conflicting discursive elements of the society from which it emerges. In Cervantes's novel, elements pertaining to a recent past (but already sensed as anachronic) coexist with others that point to a nearby future (but are still not accepted by the hegemonic discursive system). The issue is not only that of the hidalgo's archaic arms, dress, or language clashing with the expectations of the "women of the town," the innkeeper, and the muleteers whom he encounters during his wanderings; it is also that of different world perceptions and irreconcilable logical stands confronted with one another to the extent that any dialogue between the characters becomes impossible.

Rather than attempt the difficult—if not unfeasible, within the limits of my proposal—task of studying the numerous interpretations of *Don Quijote* made over the years, I will limit myself to establishing a possible parameter for systematizing them. Depending on whether it identifies itself with one mentality or another represented in the dialogical space that is *Don Quijote*, a society or group will make of its (problematical) hero a figure to be admired, although not imitated—as was the case, for instance, in the interpretations of the epic found in German Romanticism as well as in the Spanish Generation of 1898; or it will see the hero as the expression of the Spanish knight's enslaving intransigence—the equation with the Spanish *conquistador* (*"matamoros"* or *"mata-indios"*) found in the Amerindian iconography of *Don Quijote*; or finally, it will simply see in the hero a dreamer unable to adapt to the modern world—a representation found in many European manuals of the history of Hispanic literatures. These as well as many other interpretations of *Don Quijote* share the biased perspective of an ideology that one wishes to see excluded from literature but paradoxically almost always unconsciously projects on the literary work. The placing of the "hero" into the plural and contradictory frame of the discourses integrated in Cervantes's text might very well give rise to a different understanding of the text's genesis, thereby allowing for the systematization of the history of its reception—a task yet to be accomplished.

In chapters 6 and 7 I deal with the problem of intervention of literature in the collective imaginary through the appropriation of socialized linguistic practices. The oaths in *Don Quijote* and *Don Juan* function quite differently: in *Don Quijote*, Cervantes demystifies this practice as a residual element of the feudal social "order," Tirso de Molina in *Don Juan* tries to reestablish this order on the basis of the theological doctrines of the Counter-Reformation. This opposition between two conceptions of society and two ways of literary intervention in the discursive practices that emerge in this frame give place to the long historical tension between modernization and antimodernization of Spain. It is within this same frame that I approach both the chronicles of the New World, proposing a new reading in an attempt to revise the Spanish (auto)historiography (chapters 8 and 9), and the autobiographical writing as such (chapters 3 and 4). The final chapter of the book comes back to the theoretical discussion to which this introduction is but the overture.

Chapter 1
The Subversion of Ritual Discourse:
An Intertextual Reading of *Lazarillo de Tormes*

Working with the hypothesis that only the existence of a discursive correlate in sixteenth-century Spain could explain the irruption in *Lazarillo* of the autobiographical fiction characteristic of the narrative mode of the picaresque novel, and given that not only the communication circuit that frames this narration but also its lexical chart and narrative program point to the practice of confession (whose addressee is God, the confessor or spiritual director, or a tribunal—perhaps that of the Inquisition), I began searching a few years ago for autobiographical texts that might document such a practice.[1] My hypothesis was confirmed by the discovery of three autobiographical discourses that merged—and this is my thesis—in the composition of *Lazarillo* (although the manner in which *Lazarillo* uses these almost ritualistic discursive practices is entirely subversive). These discourses are: the soliloquy, addressed to God or Jesus Christ, in which an account of God-given favors predominates (favors for which gratitude is expressed and with which one's worthlessness is contrasted); the general life confession—an autobiographical account addressed to and written at the behest of the confessor or spiritual director, in which a predominantly internal itinerary is described; and finally, the more or less "spontaneous" confession, oral or written, intended for the Inquisition tribunal. In the latter practice, where a mostly external itinerary is sketched as an explanation for or justification of a given situation and in which a juridical discourse predominates, we also find elements pertaining to the first practice (invocations to God, to Jesus Christ) and to the second (references to one's inner life, to intimate spiritual experiences). Conversely, elements of the third type of confession can be found in the first two. If *Lazarillo* is considered as a "reading" of this kind of contemporary discourse,

9

then this reading undoubtedly consists precisely of the disarticulation of its auto-biographical value: the subversive (ab)use of the aforementioned practices brings out the nonauthenticity of the autobiographical discourse intended directly or indirectly for the inquisitorial tribunals and produced upon their request. Before I analyze in detail those practices and their relationship with *Lazarillo* and the picaresque novel (chapter 2), let us retrace the path that has led me to these conclusions.

It should first of all be pointed out that the search for a discursive correlate to the autobiographical "confession" of *Lazarillo* has nothing to do with the traditional search for literary sources. The latter isolates the elements under study (motifs, actions, sayings, situations, and so on) without taking into account that these elements (identifiable perhaps in previous texts), integrated into a new whole, become functions that complement (or oppose) other components in the new whole. It is precisely the interaction of these parts that creates this new whole. Understanding the functioning of a text as a whole coherent in itself and as structured according to a principle of correspondence between its elements consequently depends considerably more on understanding the formal (functional) aspect of the elements that compose it than on the purely scholarly (material) information on the origins or sources of those elements. By neglecting this aspect, traditional literary studies provoked the violent reaction of structuralism against historical or diachronic methods, with the result that immanent literary study and an emphasis on synchronic considerations have been opposed to these methods. Because an emphasis on the synchronic isolates the literary text from temporal considerations and thus severs it from the contemporary systems of signification to which it is linked, it is essentially achronic. Even in its initial stages, literary structuralism followed the same path as linguistic structuralism: the latter also began with a rejection of diachrony, which it confused with historical phonetics or the study of the evolution of sounds (phonetic rules), in favor of phonology or the synchronic study of the system in which these sounds are inscribed and function as basic units, or phonemes.

My research is also opposed to this achronic approach to texts characteristic of immanent structuralism. The simultaneous grasp of the functioning of each element of a text in its new whole on the one hand, and in the whole or wholes in which it was originally organized on the other, by a kind of cross-referentiality allows for a better understanding of the process of signification. The study of texts, then, must take into consideration the mark or semantic load that its components, as well as all signs, carry merely by having been integrated into other systems during their cultural past. This integration of components into a new system (here, the text we are about to study), however original the new purpose and function assigned to them, will not allow for the oversight of what might be called the sanction by use that weighs — as does any tradition — upon the elements that compose the text.

Signs are defined by selection restrictions or rules of grammaticality that limit their use, opposing them at the same time to other signs of the same system. This is a convention that acts upon any writing, inasmuch as it limits the combinatorial possibilities of elements that make up the available resources in the paradigmatic axis, the code shared by the writing's transmitter and receiver. To be sure, not all writing restricts itself to an accurate reproduction of that convention; yet such a convention cannot be overlooked, not even (and perhaps even less) when it is a matter of subverting its use in order to lead the code into delirium. Reading must therefore also take into account the elements' mark so as to be able to recognize possible mutations or even alienating violations to which the new text sometimes submits those elements (motifs, actions, sayings, situations, and so on) taken from another text or textual tradition. As pointed out in the introduction, this multiple referentiality (to the mark as well as to the whole, to the paradigmatic and syntagmatic axes) must be taken into consideration if the text is to be understood within the dynamics of signification or meaning-producing processes that (historically) organize it as a crossing or intersecting of texts in dialogue. This consideration led Kristeva (1969a) to speak of the text as *espace dialogique*.

The element integrated into such a dialogical text changes with it into a connotative sign because of its multiple referents (as opposed to the purely denotative character of the monologue). The text itself, capable of functioning in various isotopies simultaneously connoted by its polysemous components, may generate different (if not conflictual) readings. The comprehension, then, of such a text requires an intertextual reading that takes into consideration the cross-referentiality that transforms the text into a crossroads where joining or bifurcating "allusions" breach the syntagmatic linearity of its reading by introducing, without the need for explicit development, the stories, ideas, and myths that the text evokes in the reader as the result of the semantic load of the text's components in their cultural past. These components function as anaphoric elements — not in the transphrastic but in the transtextual sense — and thus transform the reference text into a *cotext* indispensable for the understanding of the dialogical text in question. If the study of the cotext uncovers in the mark of its cultural past the selection restrictions or rules of grammaticality that restrict its use, it will then be possible to evaluate the degree of faithfulness or unfaithfulness to convention on the part of the new text, whose purpose may range from simple reproduction to distance-creating irony, to parody, or to total subversion.

An example is the anecdote usually told to illustrate both the sexual ambiguity and the cunning attributed to Don Jacinto Benavente by literary criticism. We are told that upon meeting him at a fiesta, Doña Emilia Pardo Bazán greeted him with these words: "Your head is lovely, but sexless."[2] Don Jacinto answered: "Said the fox to the bust after sniffing at it." Let us consider for a moment these two sentences. Both are almost literal replicas of passages from a text — the fable of the fox and the bust — which is not only the inspirational source but also the shared code that makes communication possible between the speakers. The substitution of the phoneme /ks/ for /s/ in the passage reproduced by Doña Emilia Pardo Bazán substantially alters the original text without, however, erasing its identification mark—its belonging to the fable. The new referentiality created by the communicative circuit in which Doña Emilia utters her textual sequence also promotes an important change in the referent of the possessive adjective: the possessor becomes Don Jacinto in lieu of the bust. The substitution of a phoneme and of the possessive adjective's referent, even as it reminds the listener of the fable and respects the fragmentary nature of the sequence, has the latter say something that was not registered in its former tradition. These are meaning-producing alienations, and the result is that what in a first reading might have seemed a mere "rhetorical recital" has been transformed into an ambiguous play of words palliating the insult. The ambiguity created by the alienating use of the passage from the fable and Don Jacinto's immediate recognition of the cotext afford him a brilliant exit line. Because the atemporal character of the statement as it appears in the fable is made explicit, Don Jacinto distorts the change of referent brought about by Doña Emilia. This is the first effect of Don Jacinto's quote of the passage corresponding to the narrator's presentation: "Said the fox to the bust." Although the verb "said" itself designates the atemporal enunciation of the fable, it also connotes the utterance just made by Doña Emilia, with the result that "fox" and "bust" are understood as interchangeable with "Doña Emilia" and "Don Jacinto."

The short analysis of the anecdote must be completed by considering the functioning of the fable when it is told today. Assumed is the listener's knowledge not only of the fable as evoked by the text as cotext, but also of Don Jacinto Benavente's sexual inclination as presented by a literary criticism that deems a sensitivity to the feminine soul present in Benavente's dramatic work. The anecdote thus turns out to be a transtextual anaphora, a text understandable only by transtextual recourse to the fable of the fox and the bust and to the literary criticism on Benavente. These cotexts are acting components of the text of the anecdote by virtue of the cross-referentiality mentioned earlier, and they constitute the information without which communication would remain blocked by the absence of a shared code between narrator-transmitter and listener-receiver.

This same ambiguity that results from the alienating use of an intertextual referent can be found in *Lazarillo*. When Lázaro, for instance, in the first *tractado* (chapter) says of his father that he "confessed . . . denying nothing," the same two verbs with which the gospel describes Jesus' attitude upon being interrogated by the high priest with regard to his messianic calling are used to refer to the miller of Tormes's having "shamefully cut the seames of mens sacks" (i.e., his having stolen). As if the first scriptural citation were not sufficiently suggestive, the text immediately adds another: "wherefore he was persecuted" [*por justicia*].[3] With this allusion to the Sermon on the Mount, Lázaro comes to the conclusion that his father must be in heaven, as the cotext explicitly declares: "For the *Gospel* calls them blessed" (those suffering that particular persecution). Nonetheless, the sentence is ambiguous. Justice, in the interpretation of the Beatitudes sanctioned by catechism, is a cardinal virtue. In *Lazarillo*, however, by appearing in the sequence of events as a subsequent step to and logical consequence of confessing to larceny, this sentence means that his father was prosecuted for reasons precisely contrary to the virtue of justice. The preposition *por*, with its double function (*por* means both "by" and "for" and thus functions both in the passive voice and as an indicator of final cause), and the polysemy of the word justice produce the ambiguity of the sentence whose meaning will be clarified in the last *tractado*, when Lázaro describes his occupation as town crier—an occupation that consists, among other things, of escorting "any [who] suffer persecution by justice . . . declaring with loud voyce their offence."

In other instances, Lázaro uses lexical items or fixed syntagmas (sanctioned by use as belonging to the spiritual—ascetic and mystic—tradition) to express his most elemental material needs. In the second *tractado* the tale of the stratagems that Lázaro deploys when in the service of the cleric from Maqueda in order to enter the bread coffer tells us of the comfort he experiences by looking at the coffer when hunger gnaws at him most. Lázaro borrows from the spiritual literature: "I opened the saide coffer to comforte my selfe a little, and beholding the bread, which I durst not touch, but worshipping it" (29). To interpret this example, we now have to pass from the paradigmatic axis—the selection axis—to the syntagmatic axis—the combination axis—in order to clarify a new dimension in my study of texts, which I call *interdiscursiveness*.

We have so far seen how, in textual analysis, we may single out elements that one text borrows from others by insisting on the meaning-producing mechanism of those elements that are in a dialectical tension between their original mark and their functioning in the new syntagma incorporating them. By generalizing, I think it can be declared that all texts are constructed as a kind of mosaic in which are organized disparate elements taken from the cultural legacy of a social group or cultural community. Each new writing, of course, submits these elements to a new purpose; yet it cannot thereby ignore their origins. Following the terminology commonly accepted in historical linguistics and in the study of interlinguistic contacts, I will call this phenomenon a *borrowing*; in order to distinguish it from the lexical borrowing of one language from another (the subject of interlinguistic studies), I will add the qualifier *textual*. This term designates both the nature of the exchange—the intertextuality—and the object of the exchange, the unit that is called text because it is a whole unto itself. This unit may consist of a lexeme or a fixed syntagma, a sentence or group of sentences, a situation or motif more or less elaborated or indirectly evoked by allusion. Finally, the term intertextual reading will refer to the identification of textual borrowings in the new unit or text that assimilates them, to the study of possible interferences in the new function of the semantic load (mark) of their cultural past, and to the mutations, if not violations, of these textual borrowings that the adoption of the new function may bring forth in the new unit or text.

In addition to incorporating elements of the surrounding cultural patrimony, a text will use the combinatorial rules or discursive practices in force in the cultural community in which it is produced; only in this manner can it be elaborated and accepted as such by the addressee presupposed by every textual production. Interdiscursiveness, to be sure, does not consist only of adherence to the discursive rules of a given model; along with the realization of the model can be found its modification and transgression, its mingling with other models, its alienation and parody, its total subversion. The point here is to ascertain the presence of discursive models, whether they be servile copies or radical oppositions. Indeed, even when it is a matter of a specific discursive practice's code being led into delirium by subversive use—as seems to be the case in *Lazarillo*—the object of the parodic manipulation, or of the subversive countermanipulation, is to be found in the laws or precepts that define the discursive code. The exaggerated faithfulness to such precepts or their demotivation ridicules a discursive practice, just as the deconstruction or the transcodification of that practice consists precisely of a disarticulation of precepts, which will thus serve as the basis for the formation of a new type of discourse.

An interdiscursive reading must also bring out the reality of intersecting codes or discursive practices in a text by identifying what will be called discursive calques, to complete the analogy with textual borrowing. The term calque is also taken from interlinguistics, where semantic calque indicates the type of lexical construction adopted by one language from another through the translation of its components. The Spanish words *balompié* or *baloncesto* are semantic calques of the corresponding English words football and basketball. By analogy, discursive calque stands for the adoption of one or more discursive practices by a text in the strategic ordering of its components.

Let us return to the quotation from the second *tractado* of *Lazarillo*, which is still in need of clarification: "I opened the saide coffer to comforte my selfe a little, and beholding the bread, which I durst not touch, but worshipping it." To find comfort through worship when one dares not receive the Eucharist because one finds oneself unworthy (whether as a result of a spiritual disposition or of being in a state of sin) is one of the recommendations frequently found in Counter-Reform spiritual treatises. What is involved here is a bringing out of the multiple effects of the true, real, and substantial presence of Christ in the eucharistic bread and wine along with the legitimacy of adoring the reserve of eucharistic bread kept in the tabernacle, two practices challenged by the Protestant Reform. The text can thus be identified as a borrowing from ascetic and mystic literature if we heed those words in the large sense under which they appear in the terminology of literary and historical studies of Hispanic literature.

This textual borrowing in *Lazarillo*, however, goes beyond the mere quoting or appropriating of lexical elements. By using the first person, Lázaro incorporates the verbs of this sentence into a personal experience of which he gives an account by adopting the code pertaining to the discursive practice of confession.

The discursive calque reinforces so strongly the lexical mark of eucharistic spirituality by relating the words coffer and bread to open, behold, and receive (all of which are framed by the verb to comfort and its counterpoint, not to dare receive) that the sequence of events in which it appears in *Lazarillo* is forgotten once the text is taken out of its real context. Having noticed the disappearance of some bread rolls from his chest (to which Lázaro had obtained a key), the cleric from Maqueda counts them and takes good note of his reserves. Lázaro, famished, is left with no recourse but to open the chest and comfort himself by looking at the bread, which he dare not eat lest his master discover the shortage. The ambiguity of the text is perfect, as both isotopies can arrange all the components. Yet the opposition of the readings is such that one cannot understand the use of the discursive practice of confession as anything but a rupture of the syntagmatic linearity in which the events are chronologically ordered, with the result that attention is drawn more toward the discourse itself than toward the narrated events. If we reread the *tractado* in its entirety with this highlighting by the discursive calque in view, we will discover in it the convergence of a series of indicators that make of the *tractado* a discursive transposition converting the festive and jovial tone of the folkloric anecdotes about the Lázaro-blind man pair (object of the first *tractado*) into a kind of mystical delirium in which the hunger-related stratagems are arranged into a confessional discourse giving testimony to a series of inner incidents, spiritual states, and crises according to external events that appear to occur on the double level of the providential and the ill-fated.

> At such times I found ease in nothing but in death. And being in such
> affliction (God of his grace deliver every faithfull Christian from the
> like) not knowing how to counsell my selfe, my misery dayly
> increasing, upon a day . . . there arrived by chance to the dore a tinker,
> which I believe was an Angel disguised, sente from God . . . (by divine
> inspiration) I saide unto him . . . the heavenly tinker began to assay,
> nowe one key, now another, of his great bunch, and I helped him with
> my prayers, so that immediatly before I was aware, he opened it:
> whereof I was so gladde, that mee thought I did see in figure, (as they
> say) the face of God, when I beheld the bread within it. . . .
> Incontinently after, who commeth in, but my unhappy master, and as
> God would, he never tooke heed of the loafe, which the heavenly tinker
> had borrowed. The next day after, as soone as he went abroade, I began
> to open my paradise of bread, and what betweene my hands and teeth,
> with the twinkling of an eye I made a loafe invisible, forgetting in no
> wise to lock the chest againe: then I began cheerefully to sweepe the
> house, judging that by such remedy I might ease my sorowfull life. So I
> passed that day and the nexte. . . . But my contrary Fortune went
> aboute to hinder mee to enjoye suche pleasure long. (28-29)

We have here some of the indicators preceding the text. After this we read:

I was almost dead . . . wherefore being alone, I did nothing but open
and locke againe the coffer, beholding alwayes the bread as God. And
God himself which succoureth those that are afflicted, seeing me in
such necessitie, brought a little remedie to my memorie. (29)

The well-known "little remedy"—to feign that mice are entering the chest
and gnawing at the bread—does not last long, given the cleric's diligence in
blocking all possible entry for the presumed mice. Before such diligence, Lázaro
exclaims:

Lord God, unto howe many perils and calamities of Fortune are
humaine creatures subject? how short a time doe the pleasures of our
troublesome life rest? lo where I am now, whiche trusted by this my
poore remedie, to ease my miserie, being in beste hope of good
adventure, my evill lucke would not consent, but opened the sighte of
my covetous maisters understanding, causing him to have more subtile
wit than he had given him by nature, although such wretches are
commonly subtile enough. When he had summed up the holes, I
thought his chest shoulde bee shutte to my comforte, and opened to my
paine. (30-31)

Lázaro will try once again to maintain the illusion of mice penetrating the
chest by perforating the chest himself with a knife. His comment on opening a
"wound on the side" of the coffer wavers between erotic insinuation—as does
the entire motif of the mice—and the conjuring of Christ's Passion, whose rec-
ollection is brought about precisely by the (symbolic) meaning of "breaking the
bread" in the eucharistic celebration:

I gave the assault with my rustie knife, which served my tourne wel for
a wimble: but the chest by reason of good yeeres, beeing weake,
without strength, very softe and tender, did straight wayes render and
consent that I should make for my commoditie a good hole in the side
of it, and that done, opening the wounded chest, and knowing everye
loafe severally by the touch, I did as I had done before, and by that
meanes beeing somewhat comforted, having locked the chest againe, I
returned to my pallet, whereupon I slept little. (31-32)

In the majority of cases, intertextual reading reveals a correspondence between the conveyed elements and the type of discourse that conveys them. The
textual borrowing and the discursive calque thus usually go hand in hand in a
coherent complementarity. But it is not always so. The subversion of one or the
other (or of both at the same time) can indeed rest on the nonconformity of the
text's two levels. This nonconformity, for instance, makes Fray Gerundio's sermons seem grotesque. There is no correspondence between the ritual discursive
practice of predication and the information given in this predication. If, in the
example taken from *Lazarillo*, the series of indicators presented as signs uphold-

ing the spiritual tone in Lázaro's confessional discourse give the impression of perfect coherence, a series of allusions to mundane things intermingling in the text with borrowings from the spiritual lexicon will help us see that they serve as counterpoints and thereby create a double tension in the text: on the one hand between the components themselves, and on the other between these components and the discourse that assumes them. One need only fill in the suspension points with which the quoted text has been cut to reveal that the "death" in which Lázaro finds respite is none other than the death of his neighbors in the village—a death Lázaro beseeches of God, having become himself "an enemy to humane nature" because "at burials and dirges . . . wee shoulde fare well, and have meate at libertie" (26). The contemplation of the bread consoles Lázaro for his "former diet," which had begun to make his "stomake rive for hunger." We have already seen, in the mice's skirmishes, the tension produced by the play between the erotic and the sacred. All these tensions, which forge a kind of *contradictio in terminis*, undermine the sacred nature of the textual borrowings from the spiritual lexicon and completely alienate the discursive calque, thereby showing how it is agrammatically (ab)used.

Edmond Cros (1975, 63-73) has dedicated an interesting study to what he calls "le discours usurpé." Relying on Bakhtin's study on Rabelais, Cros distinguishes two discourses in *Buscón* ("discours qui masque" and "discours qui démasque") upon which he lays the foundations of his work's basic thesis: *Buscón* consists of two texts that "dans certains cas se juxtaposent et, dans d'autres, se recoupent" (in certain cases they are juxtaposed, and in others they are superimposed). As a first example of the superimposition of the two texts, Cros singles out the parodic glosses introduced by copulative conjunctions whose function is to make explicit the polysemy of the preceding proposition: "In my youth, I always went to church, and not only as a good Christian," says Pablos of himself; "They say he was from good stock, and from the amount he drank, it had to be true," says Pablos of his father. In his commentary on those texts, Cros takes the viewpoint of Francisco Rico (1970), who considers the glosses psychologically implausible because, so he tells us, the statement made in the second segment of these sentences could not have been uttered by one who precisely tried to deny his blood ties. Rico compares Pablos's "jokes" with Lázaro's "subtleties":

Lázaro would have simply insinuated: "they say he was of good stock." But Pablos does not appreciate the kind of subtlety which makes the *Lazarillo* a masterpiece of ironic truth: he cannot abide that the least crumb escape us and he hurries to gloss the joke with an addition that makes it transparent, even at the cost of robbing all plausibility from his stated intention of "denying his blood ties." This happens to him as writer and as personage. A striking example. When, dressed as the King of Roosters with a feathered hat, stall-holders and youngsters assail him with "carobs, turnips, eggplants and other vegetables," as would have happened to a publicly shamed sorceress, Pablos starts yelling: "Sisters, although I wear feathers, I am not Aldonza de San Pedro, my mother.'' Absurd. More or less amusing, but incredible. Nobody would say such a thing under such circumstances, and Pablos, least of all. Here, one hears but his master's voice. (127)

By "master's voice" Rico means the voice of the author, Francisco de Quevedo, as he says explicitly a few lines after the quoted passage, repeating once more that these words coming "from the Buscón's mouth are impossible."

Basing his analysis on Rico's observations, Cros exposes the nerve center or "centre of gravity" (as he calls it) of *Buscón* by bringing to the fore the fact that all the superimpositions of both texts function around lexicalized expressions (to go to church, to be of good stock) that on first reading denote social values such as piety and nobility. But once integrated into the textual flow, "dans le réseau sémantique allusif du second texte" (in the semantic allusive network of the second text), each set phrase or lexicalized expression "éclate et se délexicalise" (explodes and becomes delexicalized).

What Rico criticizes, then, in the *Buscón* text is—to use the terminology proposed above—the following: the sentences coordinated with and following the textual borrowings bring about the destruction of the borrowings' marks in their traditional and popular usage, that is, the cultural repertory from which they have been taken. According to Rico, an attentive reader is capable of inferring such a destruction. In reply to Rico, Cros appeals to the problem's discursive dimension and makes discourse the object of the demystification characteristic of the functioning mode of the carnivalesque system in *Buscón*: "But in truth, the lexicalized expression is itself seen as an element of a mystifying discourse whose denunciation must be explicit" (65-66).

I do not agree with what Rico says of *Lazarillo*. We have already seen how the *Lazarillo* also explicitly brings about, in the same lexical flow, the neutralization of borrowed elements by means of a contextual alienation that simultaneously denounces the disproportion between the text's components and the discourse that conveys them. Furthermore, Rico's reading seems to be a typical example of the superficial reading of a literary work's ideological dimension. He lingers on social elements that surface in the materiality of the text—the purity of caste in *Buscón*, the case of dishonor in *Lazarillo*—to which he applies, moreover, a criterion of plausibility not necessarily that of the speaker but our own, and this in a monologism that Bakhtin so rightly describes and to which he opposes the dialogism specific to the polyphonic novel. Rico overlooks the discursive calque, the actualization or possible denunciation of the very discourse that is used.

As Michel Foucault (1971) pointed out, discourse, in addition to being both (1) the medium that discloses (or conceals) the drive (desire) for power and (2) the representative of struggles or systems of domination, is also precisely the object of the desire for and the practice of power. This is why far more important than the anecdotic surface of any work of art (outlines of customs, the characters' representation of the social strata, and so on) is the discourse that is used and its mark, as well as the degree of submission or subversion enacted by the text being studied. It is indeed not only the textual elements borrowed by a text that carry a mark: the discourse also has its own, which consists of the ideology that upholds the discursive practice as it imposes selection restrictions that regulate its usage. This is a sociocultural variable that must be taken into account when interpreting a discursive calque.

Foucault (1971) tells us that "in any society, discursive production is at the same time controlled, subject to selection, organized and allocated according to a number of procedural rules whose function is to ward off its power and threat, to subdue the unforeseen occurrence, to elude its weighty, fearsome materiality." Foucault summarizes here the discourse-society relationship—an issue I will briefly examine in order to clarify what is meant by "subversion of ritual discourse." The control exercised by any society over the discursive production that takes place within itself—whatever the type of discourse involved—can be studied in a double dimension:

1. Society dictates precepts—an apparently positive aspect—that are actually restrictions on usage: they specify the subject, object, and circumstances through which each type of discourse gains legitimacy. Foucault thus speaks of a threefold prohibition or exclusion and refers to the "taboo object," the "ritual of circumstance," and the "subject's privileged or exclusive right" as the external boundaries of discourse.
2. In the name of what Foucault calls the "will to truth," society rejects "fraudulent" discourse, thereby creating the internal boundary or operating law for each type of discourse.

It is within the limits of these two coordinates, wherein each component functions as a variable of the *épistème* in force, as Foucault (1966) states, that the changing criteria of verisimilitude in occidental literary discourse (in its various forms) are to be accounted for according to each literary or discursive genre's specific laws and according to the "illusion of truth" to which its addressee (the audience or the reader) lends itself. Scientific discourse also has its laws, although the issue is more a matter of being true to a discipline than of telling the truth. Even economic and juridical discourses, by imposing norms, endeavor to legitimize their methods as "truth criteria" (the former with wealth and production theory; the latter with legal, sociological, and medical theories). Rhetorical precepts, "decorum" or observation of poetic norms and censorship, the legitimacy of the speaking subject and his relation to the object and the circumstances of his utterance, the act of communication itself, all answer to a kind of ritual that in every society distinguishes the true from the untrue.

If we consider all the restrictions imposed by society on the use of a specific type of discourse as criteria of its suitability, any discourse's grammaticality or agrammaticality will then be the result of its concurrence or the nonconcurrence to them in a given situational context. This is what I will call the discursive norm, against which the discursive calque in question may be judged as using or abusing the chosen discursive model.

When I speak here of the adoption by a text of operating discursive models — even if the theory I am attempting to elaborate has as its primary objective the understanding of the literary text's functioning — I am not necessarily referring to models condoned by rhetoric, or to literary genres. On the contrary, it can be readily seen that all literary texts use and abuse discursive models taken from colloquial, scientific, or technical language by having either the fundamental speaking subject or various characters produce theological, juridical, economic, or administrative discourses. Furthermore, I believe that the genetic explanation of literary genres — if their linguistic roots are studied in depth — will perforce be found in the potential for expansion inherent in structures or syntactically simpler communication units belonging to the everyday use of language. Transformations made possible by what Greimas (1966, 72-73) calls "the semantic expansion principle" must account for the formation of more complex communication structures on the basis of less elaborate ones — a maneuver already at work in Aristotle's deduction of the major literary genres (epos and drama) from the inclusion of new episodes in the narrative schema of a simple story or anecdote, where the epic technique is distinguished from the dramatic according to whether different stories were or were not integrated into a single common axis.

In the study of the subsequent evolution of an established literary genre, one must also bear in mind not only the boundaries drawn by the precepts that define it, but also the potential for expansion inherent to the dynamic structure that is the genre in evolution, along with its power to generate infinite combinatorial possibilities from those precepts (with the restrictions they impose taken into account).

An adequate explanation of a literary genre's genesis and an authentically historicoliterary account of its subsequent evolution require a profound reformulation of the precepts and their interpretation as transformation rules defining and conditioning the generative mechanism of texts. The acceptability or unacceptability (agrammaticality) of texts, as pointed out earlier, will depend on the correct use of rules or on the transgression of the selection restrictions defining the components of a text. This agrammaticality, far from signifying, in literature, the rejection of the result thus obtained, can on the contrary point to the subversion of ideology or the rebellion against the conditions imposed by the society in which this phenomenon is produced. Here, perhaps, we may find one of the characteristics of "literariness" or the specificity of literary practices as opposed to the discourse of everyday communication. It is in this context, so it seems, that one should interpret the "originalidad artística" that María Rosa Lida de Malkiel discovers in *Celestina*. *Celestina*'s rupture with the noble tradition—it raises to the status of poetic object ruffians and whores integrated into the text and treated with the depth and seriousness heretofore reserved for noble heroes and their "lofty deeds" (Aristotle's expression in his *Poetics*)—is a type of creative agrammaticality that opens new vistas to literary expression by breaking the taboo described some pages ago, following Michel Foucault.

This reading of *Lazarillo* also brings out a transgression, although it encompasses at the same time the poetic object, the narrator-subject himself and, more particularly, the "ritual of circumstance" and the "will to truth" of its autobiographical confessional discourse. I will call this total transgression the "subversion of ritual discourse."

Before studying in detail each of the circumstances of the discursive calque's "agrammaticality" as it appears in *Lazarillo*, the mode of reading the interaction discourse-society must first be elaborated—a mode situated (as pointed out earlier) between discursive practice and the ideology, or sociocultural variable, sustaining that practice and dictating the norms of its use. The Russian formalists had already considered the immanent analysis of literary works as but a point of departure for further detailed study. In addition to the internal functioning and interrelation of the work's components, their research had to take into account the relation of the latter to the work in its entirety and the work's relation to the national literature, to the genre, and to the global system with which any genre is correlated. Just as isolating an element during the analysis of a work—a necessity brought about by the discrepancy and inequality of a text's components—is but a working procedure (because in reality, one has to search for the meaning of each element in its relationship with its constituents), so isolating a work while studying its components is but a first step toward the subsequent understanding of its relationship with other systems, including other series of systems of signification. Only in this way can the work be understood as a "differential sign," as Tynjanov defines it (1965; see also Todorov [1971a], 9-31).

Julia Kristeva (1970) proposes the substitution of a *typologie des textes* for classical rhetoric's classification of literary genres. By such a typology, Kristeva means defining different textual organizations to situate them in the general text of the culture of which they are part; the general text, in turn, belongs to these textual organizations. The discovery of the mutual relation between text and sociohistorical coordinates, "materialized at different levels of the structure of each text", is the function of intertextuality. Kristeva calls this mutual relation *idéologème*, a term borrowed from Medvedev and defined as "the nucleus where rational consciousness grasps the transformation of utterances (to which the text is irreducible) into a *whole* (the text), as well as the insertion of this whole into the historical and social text." I think it is possible to read this convergence in the different modalities of the discursive calque, at which level I would situate the text's "idéologème," because I consider the discursive level as the privileged locus in which the text's laws (all laws are the expression of an ideology) converge with the symbols that every society gives itself (visualization of the ideology). The discursive calque is always a "reading" of the laws and symbols it reproduces (by more or less consciously paying a tribute to the ideology) or opposes (by rejecting it). Hence the great care taken by all societies to control the discursive production, as Foucault pointed out, and hence the questioning of laws and symbols of discursive practices with which all social subversion begins. For insofar as the most elemental structure of human communication takes shape by finding its expression in discourse—a necessary step for any deep structure that manifests itself only through the superficial textual structure—it is already implicated in a concrete social and cultural reality. This dimension of the discursive production has not always been taken into consideration by the generative school, although its importance appears to be decisive not only for literary production but also for all discursive uses.

Here is the source of the preoccupation shown by some generativists who, trying to cope with sociocultural reality when defining linguistic competence, have developed the concept of "communicative" or "pragmatic competence." This component of generative grammar considers psycholinguistic and sociolinguistic aspects of the relationship between competence and performance—beyond the rules of grammaticality dictated by syntax, morphophonology, and semantics—and proposes to account for the rules underlying the use and acceptance of relevant elements and discursive practices at the correct time and in the appropriate situation. With a consideration of this component (by transferring generative grammar terminology of the phrase to textual production), I have insisted on the sociocultural variable that determines the selection restrictions or discursive mark in the discursive norm. In an attempt to go further in this direction, I have ventured to include those components essential in all discourses into the grammaticality of the latter. Indeed, the discourse's grammaticality cannot be systematized by the mere application of the linguistic categories mentioned above: the pertinence of a discourse depends in any society primarily and essentially on the "ritual of circumstance" in which it is produced, that is, on its appropriateness to a given time and situation.

Any application of generative grammar to discourse analysis will thus have to bear in mind the various sociocultural situations liable to explain the appearance of particular types of discourse at a given time, their success, disappearance, or reappearance at a certain moment, as well as the circumstances of their modification by way of reduction or elimination of their elements through expanding or inserting new elements and substituting or transforming others.

An example of a practical and global application of the principles set forth here can be found in the inclusion in *Lazarillo* of the folkloric motif of the blind man-youth pair. By being integrated into a syntagmatic axis—the narration of Lázaro de Tormes's life of which they are part—those elements taken from the folkloric tradition become purely functional, syntactic elements with no other meaning than that of their relation to the development and finality of the story in its entirety. They have become the arbitrary props of a "function," defined by Propp (1970, 31) as "a character's action interpreted from the point of view of its significance in the unfolding of the plot."

The perception as such of the inserted motif nevertheless forces upon us an intertextual reading that by identifying the motif accounts for its different uses and meanings, for the tradition to which it belongs on the diachronic axis, and for the cultural marking or "myth" that the pair brings to mind. The new appearance of the theme will not merely enrich or sustain its traditional signifieds, just as its recognition in *Lazarillo* will not merely afford us scholarly data on the elements that constitute it. By bearing in mind in our reading the double referentiality previously mentioned, we cannot but perceive a dialectic tension between the poles.

As Edmond Cros (1976) has demonstrated, a comparison between the blind man-youth pair in *Lazarillo* and the same couple in medieval farces and in the illustrations of *Decretales*, discovered by Foulché-Delbosc at the end of the nineteenth century, exemplifies the evolution, through the intervening centuries, of Christianity's view of poverty, begging, and almsgiving. Whereas the medieval church, by exalting scorn for worldly goods, makes of the poor Christ's living image and of poverty the highest of virtues, the poor appear at the beginning of the sixteenth century—above all for Protestantism—on a par with the insane and the demonically possessed. To give alms is no longer to give succor to God but to feed the devil. Cros explains this evolution, which makes of poverty a social illness instead of a virtue, by the appearance of new socioeconomic structures. Above all precapitalistic production's need for an abundant labor pool, together with the struggle against vagrancy, will determine the attitude change toward the poor and the underprivileged. Vives states in his treatise *De subventione pauperum* that "not even the blind should be allowed to be idle or wander aimlessly; there are many tasks they are capable of undertaking."[4]

With this change in perspective Cros explains the appearance of the blind man in *Lazarillo* as a diabolic character and Lázaro's passage from innocence to knowing "a bit more than the devil" (as he shows when he takes leave of the blind man with a final blow to the latter's head). The blind man-Lázaro interrelation is indeed presented in the text by means of a whole range of diabolical connotations, as Cros observes. The escalating contest between them throughout the first chapter or *tractado* especially constitutes, in Cros's words, "a duel of diabolical characters, explicitly manifested by the convergence of expressions qualifying the antagonists' respective aggressions" (1976, 15-16).

If the change in socioeconomic and religious perspectives explains the insertion of the motif into a specific tradition and the time frame of this tradition echoed by *Lazarillo*, a transition to the discursive level will deepen our understanding not only of the function performed by these borrowings from folkloric tradition in the development of the story of *Lazarillo* (for these borrowings are part of the life experiences narrated by Lázaro), but also of the tension created between the discourse selected to narrate these experiences and the changing signified of the folkloric short stories—that is, between the discursive calque and the textual borrowing that constitute the text dealt with here.

If there is a point on which modern criticism of *Lazarillo* is in complete agreement, it is in considering the work as autobiographical fiction and in acknowledging—beyond reservations voiced by critics such as Camille Pitollet, Marcel Bataillon, Angel Valbuena Prat, and others—that its unknown author was blessed with what Francisco Rico (1971) calls "the gift of gathering together timeless themes and pretenses, valid in all circumstances, in a construction so skillfully located in time and space, that they gave the impression of being indissolubly linked to them." Such are, in Rico's words, the "subtlety and cleverness with which *Lazarillo* re-elaborates extraneous motifs" that they "have become . . . the narrative's flesh and blood, integrated into a living organism whose members are mutually implicated, and where setting aside any one of them would lead to a disastrous mutilation" (13). This is how Rico explains the critics' delay in acknowledging the independence of the folkloric motifs borrowed by *Lazarillo*. From this Rico infers (as Américo Castro [1935, 1948], Claudio Guillén [1957], and Fernando Lázaro Carreter [1970, 1972] had before him), what he calls *Lazarillo de Tormes*'s "singular transcendency in the history of the modern novel," which consists precisely of "the art of selecting and conjoining pieces of various origins in order to give them a unity and meaning under the authority of the central figure brilliantly depicted and—above all—individualized" (1971, 13).

Can one imagine a more perfect harmony? From entertaining serious doubts about the integrity of the text that has reached us, critics have come to recognize the exemplary architecture of *Lazarillo*. Let us return for a moment to Cros's thesis on the evolution of the signified of the blind man that converts him into a diabolic personage. The change in socioeconomic and religious views at the time of the writing of *Lazarillo* allows for its inclusion in an autobiography that wishes to give an account of the school in which its cynical (naive-cunning) narrator made his way in life. Against Baader's (1964) scruples about the ethical content of a narrative that, according to him, requires the use of the first person because an external observer would have no choice but to condemn such infamies, the new social attitude allows Lázaro to treat the blind man as he does while removing much of the cruelty from the final retaliation: the victim of the vengeance is, in the last analysis, the devil himself.

But what of the acceptance of the ideology on the part of *Lazarillo*? We face here a double-edged blade. If we maintain that *Lazarillo* really accepts the ideology of poverty's diabolic character (at which point Lázaro's attitude toward the blind man would be justified ethically), then with the problem of ethical verisimilitude resolved, we would have to come to the realization that Lázaro, also a beggar, could not be an aesthetic object according to this ideology. According to Américo Castro, the use of the first person is thus justified—but this solution further complicates matters because along with the object we would also have to justify the speaking subject himself. Lázaro Carreter would perhaps answer that *Vuestra Merced*'s making Lázaro the butt of a joke by asking him an account of his case is precisely that which explains why this poor devil speaks out or puts pen to paper. Such a clever device, however, is not without its problems. My study of the proceedings of the Inquisition kept in the Archivos Históricos Nacionales of Madrid suggests that to demand, by means of monitions, that an individual living on the fringe of society give an account of his life and thereby to wring from him a confession was a frequent enough occurrence in the Spain where *Lazarillo* was produced; but because of its ritual character and given the "circumstances" in which it occurred—in the juridical and religious confines of the Inquisition—the matter was far too serious to be anything but the object of a simple joke.

The only way, then, to answer the three requirements of the type of discourse that is the calque-object in *Lazarillo* would be to map it on the true biographical act of confession. The subject who speaks—and who speaks unacceptably within the frame of literary autobiography of the era (the decorum then in force was indeed hardly respected)—would be legitimated by the judge interrogating him. Likewise, the object, hardly edifying from an ethical standpoint and excessively nonheroic in terms of the epic norm inherited by the Spanish Renaissance novel (and thus an object all the more unethical and nonrhetorical), would be legitimated by the fact of its conversion into an object of confession. In this hypothesis, the ritual of circumstance completely legitimates both the subject of the enunciation and the enunciated object of Lázaro's confessional discourse. But it is precisely here that the folkloric anecdotes surface, within the frame of this hypothesis, with an entirely new signified as evidence of the untruth of ritual discourse—the confession—whose highest virtue is truthfulness before God and man. Any autobiographical discourse would be revealed as spurious, as fiction, by the mere fact of including the narration of folkloric (i.e., well-known) anecdotes that irremediably destroy the individual, unique, and nonrepeatable character specific to the type of experiences that are the object of autobiographical narrative. Fiction here simply means "literature," and autobiographical fiction is not necessarily excluded in European Renaissance literature, except that, as shown earlier, neither subject nor object answer to the rhetorical norms of such a fiction. Furthermore, if we add that we are dealing with an autobiography of a confessional nature—and the passages taken from *Lazarillo*'s second *tractado* (and analyzed rather extensively as examples of interdiscursiveness) are eloquent enough as evidence of this—the folkloric anecdotes are not a sign of the alienation of autobiographical discourse in the sense of its being declared fictitious or literary but are rather a radical subversion of autobiographical confession as a discursive practice.

If we consider, then, *Lazarillo* as a "reading" (for being a discursive calque) of the ritual discursive practice that was the autobiographical confession spoken before (or written for) the Inquisition tribunal, and given all the contradictions and problems of agrammaticality presented by this calque, we cannot but maintain that such a "reading" consists precisely of the disarticulation of its autobiographical value, of its truthfulness, by means of a subversive use that makes conspicuous the nonauthenticity of such ritual discursive practice, and perhaps also of the value of all biographies. Intimate discourse that is confidentially intended for a single person but that will be brought to the attention "of al men" is not feared if there are hopes of being rewarded by being read and praised : "If the worlde were otherwise, very fewe would take pen in hand to pleasure one man only, seing that they can not bring their workes to ende without great travell" (5). In a word, the addressee's ambiguity is underlined by the instituting subject's ambiguity. Lázaro's very name is the condensation of a complete narrative program: it embodies not only the poverty of the beggar at the door of the wealthy Epulon in the gospels, but also the artistic tradition that echoes this motif and that has in the text its lexical correlation in the words—meaning all manners of misery—so frequently used in *Lazarillo*: "lacerated" (*lacerado*), "lacerate" (*lacerar*), "laceration" (*laceria*). The selection of this name for the subject who institutes an autobiographical discourse is thus at the same time a negation of such a discourse and the prefiguration of the character's fortune, given the horizon of expectations it creates in the reader. The signified that Edmond Cros discovers in the folkloric anecdotes is thus easily linked as a correlative with the name Lázaro.

The two correlatives are nevertheless the reverse side of the historical individuality and identity that autobiography requires between author and narrator, as it does between the speaking and the spoken subject. Under these conditions, their function is none other than to unmask the sham: the "things so worthy of memory, peradventure never heard of before," that are about to be narrated are short stories known from folklore. The "I" that assumes them declares itself inauthentic simply by assuming them and by having an equally well known name—a kind of *mise en abyme* that at the same time creates and destroys that contrivance of the illusion of identity between author, narrator, and personage that characterizes *Lazarillo*'s anonymity—perfect contrivance and perfect strategy that convince with the same force with which they declare themselves as contrivance and strategy. While creating the illusion of movement, they reveal the puppet strings of the farce along with the external hand manipulating them.

Truth here is thus pure verisimilitude. The "contradictio in terminis" that brings the three elements of this discourse (subject-object-circumstances) into presence enables readers who would delve deeper into the matter (those who do not will have to content themselves with "pleasure") to see that ritual discourse, marked by the rules of its rhetorical convention, cannot be a true autobiography, just as an autobiographical confession does not reconcile itself well with a court as receiver. The Sophists well understood the real function of rhetoric—already lamented by Plato—and its means of persuasion, whose force before the juridical courts outweighed the innocence of the accused. Indeed, to establish the truth in legal proceedings is pure chimera. In reality, it is a question of the illusion of truth, of verisimilitude. This is the subversion I believe *Lazarillo* carries out by disrupting ritual discursive practice and, with it, the ideology that is its foundation.

Chapter 2
Intertextuality, Interdiscursiveness, and Parody: On the Origins of the Narrative Form in the Picaresque Novel

In his 1968 address to the Third Congress of the International Association of Hispanists in Mexico, Fernando Lázaro Carreter (1970, 1972) proposed a review of the concept of "picaresque novel" starting with the "processes of its creation and formation." Only by carefully establishing (1) the distinctive features outlining the morphology of a literary genre from its very first historical manifestation and (2) its generative power, as manifested by the various transformations giving rise to subsequent imitations, can we actually reach a definition of the genre's dynamic structure—a definition that will in turn make possible the historical ordering of texts as manifestations of discursive models. An examination of the *Lazarillo de Tormes-Guzmán-Buscón* interrelation (as has been frequently proposed) and a contrastive study of past and synchronic texts (as I propose) will help to establish the distinctive features of the picaresque novel in its genesis and in its historical development as a literary genre.

Many works in recent years have created a perception of the picaresque novel in terms of narrative form rather than in terms of the character of the "pícaro," the view long shared by critics. Judging by the uniformity, not to say the monotonous repetition, of the conclusions reached, one might conclude that the subject has been exhausted. If I venture, in spite of these circumstances, to undertake a study dealing once again with the origins of picaresque discourse, it is because I believe that a new link should be added to the chain in order to satisfactorily answer Lázaro Carreter's question about the genesis and evolution of the picaresque as a literary genre. The point of departure for this study will thus not be *Lazarillo* but the discourse that made possible the emergence of what I consider to be Lázaro de Tormes's "antidiscourse" along with, through imitations of *Lazarillo*, picaresque discourse as a genre. My objective is not to search for new sources in the traditional sense but to scrutinize the concourse of elements that allows for the possibility of textual production and defines it as a redistribution or reworking of preexisting materials (the selection axis) and as a faithful reproduction, modification, or subversive (ab)use of the prevailing discursive practices in the sphere of its production (the combination axis) (see chapter 1).

In recent decades, studies of the picaresque novel in general and of *Lazarillo* in particular have been so preoccupied with the work's organization (or lack thereof) that they have questioned its integrity. It is said that the text of *Lazarillo* handed down to us is but a collection of (altered) fragments of the (missing) original text. This conclusion is maintained, for instance, by Camille Pitollet (1946) in the prologue to his edition of *Lazarillo*. His thesis is based on the unfortunate disproportion between what he calls "the work's original plan" (evident, according to him, in the first three chapters) and its whole. Marcel Bataillon (1954, 21) agrees with Pitollet, pointing out a certain artistic unity in the first three chapters as opposed to the others, which he describes as "an insecure stride through a series of bare-boned episodes in which the story of the distributor of papal bulls looms as an excrescence, almost as a foreign body." From the same point of view, Angel Valbuena Prat (1958) distinguishes two forms of construction in *Lazarillo*. He finds the first episodes perfect chapters of a novel: Lázaro's adventures as a blind man's servant, as the curate's altar boy, and as the squire's page—to which Valbuena Prat would add the episode about the distributor of papal bulls. The rest of the book consists of "quick references" to the friar, the clergyman, the constable—all of them Lazarillo's masters and only the character of the friar fully depicted. According to Valbuena Prat, the other masters in the second series are "mere outlines or allusions" (36).

In addition to this yearned-for symmetry between the elements of *Lazarillo*, critics have dealt at length with the picaresque genre's (apparent) lack of thoughtful order and organization. At the end of the nineteenth century, Frank W. Chandler (1899) considered the picaresque novel an open series of adventures in which the hero acts only to ease the transition between one adventure and another; he observed that a "formless plan" (243) was the genre's major drawback. Half a century later, Juan Chabás (1953) shared Chandler's view, stating that because such novels had no architectural links, one could add or suppress episodes or alter sequences without prejudice to the narrative (128). Jules Romain, who expressed himself in almost identical terms in the Introduction to his edition of Lesage's *Gil Blas*, went so far as to add that the picaresque novel's characteristic lack of logic and of internal guidelines correlates with its lack of organization and structure.

Critics who disagree with these perceptions have searched for the cohesive elements that fashioned *Lazarillo* as a whole—a flimsy whole perhaps, but one capable of establishing the modern novel's foundation. Américo Castro (1948) contrasts the biographical form of *Lazarillo* with that of the tales of Boccaccio and other forerunners whose characters' lives are elaborated and conveyed directly by the author. Castro shows the extent of the innovation in narrative technique brought about by *Lazarillo*: where the traditional storyteller was given a framework into which to weave happenings involving love, virtue, treachery, guile, vengeance, and so on into a coherent and well-connected whole, *Lazarillo* presents itself as a fragmentary and open narrative—as if life, by the very fact of being told, must produce a fluctuating and inconclusive narrative. The narrative fashioned on the common denominator of a flow of incidents is replaced by one that attempts to establish itself on one's own experience, and out of which new possibilities are opened, rather than foreclosed. By this maneuver, *Lazarillo* contributed to the creation of the literary genre of the modern novel.

Claudio Guillén (1957) considers Lázaro's narration of his life an "account" (*relación*) rendered from a perspective through which the apparent lack of continuity ceases to be an imperfection. The selective process to which Lázaro submits his existence reveals that which is important for him to display: the fundamental features of his person. Guillén notes that the culminating moments in *Lazarillo* coincide with matters of conscience and with the essential components of Lázaro's memory. We cannot speak, then, of blanks or interruptions in the narrated events, as those events are of interest only from the perspective of the nearby conscience observing them. Guillén thus speaks of "arrangement" (*disposición*) and calls *Lazarillo* an "arranged novel" (*roman disposé*), a concept he opposes to the *roman composé* and the *roman déposé*, following Albert Thibaudet's (1938) well-known classification. Lázaro's autobiographical account consists of disclosures of and expansions on that which he understands as forming part of his present (that is, the moment of writing) life and self. Arranged and selected are those occurrences that elicit his interest as he recounts his past from the perspective afforded him at the time of writing.

Some years ago, Fernando Lázaro Carreter (1969) completed a major study on the construction of *Lazarillo* in which he distinguishes two structural frameworks: the first, in the first three chapters, follows the triptych rule of the epic; the second, less elaborated and not internally articulated, follows the model of the tales in Apuleius's *Golden Ass*. Both frameworks, according to Lázaro Carreter, reveal an attempt to create a new narrative architecture. Without denying the traditional folkloric elements in the work's construction, we must discover the new relations that organize and link those elements in original ways and that thus prepare the ground for what will be later called the novel. Lázaro Carreter believes that in this manner he can "historically" explain away the "imperfections" he deplores in *Lazarillo*—imperfections justified, he believes, because they are specific to the moment of transition from the traditional narrative model, the folktale, to the new narrative model characteristic of the modern novel. *Lazarillo* appears at this junction as a testimonial to its author's bid to transcend one form while creating another.

Lázaro Carreter (1969) summarizes in four points *Lazarillo*'s "initiatives" in going beyond what he considers its model, the old technique employed in *The Golden Ass* that attributed various folkloric adventures to a single character.

1. The adventures, far from being ordered into a disconnected sequence, are interconnected and do not elude the character's mind: they are occasionally referred to and can even condition the character's later behavior.
2. The themes are subjected to a design: the author does not merely collect them and connect them to one another but selects them from the prevalent cultural patrimony in order to subordinate them to set purposes.
3. Because structures and folkloric elements do not necessarily conform to the author's designs, the author must adapt or reformulate them or give them other meanings; in very difficult cases, the author must resort to inventiveness.
4. This process of adaptation or invention, important to the history of the novel, is complemented by another: all of the more or less stray elements that make up the character's life are presented to illustrate or justify the circumstances of his life at the moment of the account.

Beginning with F. Courtney Tarr (1927), critics, in their search for thematic units spanning the whole of *Lazarillo*, have insisted on the first point emphasized by Lázaro Carreter. In addition to the chronological succession of disparate adventures or episodes, critics discovered a series of axes imparting consistency and structural articulation to the text. Tarr points out, for example, the theme of hunger and the reiteration of the "joining [oneself] with those that are good" motif at the beginning and end of *Lazarillo*. In spite of his insistence on the "composition flaws" of *Lazarillo*, Marcel Bataillon (1968) also acknowledges various thematic units in the text: Lázaro remains a disciple of the blind man throughout the work; the prophecy of the wine links the first chapter to the last; the first chapter's opening scene of the stone bull corresponds to the closing scene of the vengeance with the pillar; a parallelism exists between Lázaro's various masters, between his mother and his wife, between the cleric's and the squire's house, between father and son. Oldrich Belic (1969, 19-60), Francisco Rico (1970), and Charles Minguet (1970) have undertaken an exhaustive investigation of the motifs that span the diverse narrative segments of *Lazarillo* and have orchestrated them around the process of "apprenticeship for Life" (Belic), the "case" of dishonor (Rico), or a cluster of conceptual axes that expose the "sordid society" faced by Lázaro as a "problematic hero" (Minguet).

The other three points noted by Lázaro Carreter must be considered in terms of intertextuality and interdiscursiveness, that confluence of textual elements from prior texts (the diachronic dimension) that a new text reelaborates or redistributes (the synchronic dimension), subjects to a new purpose (the teleological dimension), and organizes according to a discursive strategy appropriate to that purpose (the pragmatic-discursive dimension of textual production). The interference of an element's previous paradigm in the new organizing syntagma creates a type of cross-reference whose understanding is crucial in any intertextual reading, but more crucial still to an intertextual reading of parody. Indeed, the inclusion of a borrowed element in the new text does not always respect the earlier text's selection restrictions validated by the mark or ''sanction by use'' that—as with any tradition—weigh on it. But we saw earlier how a text, in addition to incorporating elements from the surrounding cultural patrimony (which either respects their operating rules in varying degrees or which imposes on them alienating inflections), must also function within a discursive practice or code shared by the transmitter and the addressee. Furthermore, the discursive practice to which the production of the new text is subjected also carries its mark (the convention that allows for this activity while imposing selection restrictions that limit its acceptability or grammaticality); from this mark one may judge the text's stance vis-à-vis the ideology sustained in the discursive practice it reproduces. Distancing irony, parody, and outright subversion shows that the attitude of the new text toward its adopted discursive models is not always that of a simple mimetic reproduction.

Literary criticism of *Lazarillo* has persisted above all in investigating the mostly folkloric sources of the elements incorporated into Lázaro's narrative and has paid less attention to the identification and origins of the discourses used. It has noted the work's originality and its contribution to the modern novel without troubling itself over the discursive models imitated, parodied, or subverted—the very discursive models, in other words, that could help account for the emergence of a new conventional model or genre. Critics—Guillén (1957), Lázaro Carreter (1969), and Rico (1970)—have at most suggested the epistle as a model for the narrative's circumstances. For their part, Margot Kruse (1959) and Lázaro Carreter (1972) refer to Apuleius's *Golden Ass* in order to explain how the various anecdotes of folkloric origin are linked.

Hans Robert Jauss (1957), in an article in *Romanistisches Jahrbuch*, ventured to present *Lazarillo*'s autobiographical fiction as a parodic derivative of the Christian's confession in its highest literary form—Augustine's *Confessions*. Jauss contended that the use of the first person singular in Lázaro's narrative is not the author's invention. In a later issue of the same publication, Peter Baumanns (1959) and Margot Kruse (1959) were quick to dismiss Jauss's attempt. Although the parallel with Saint Augustine might be somewhat strained, Jauss nevertheless pointed to a new direction ignored by later investigators for whom the originality of *Lazarillo* was an untouchable principle that Bataillon (1968) summarizes ''Any reader of *Lazarillo* knows that these various procedures of the newborn autobiographical fiction have nothing to do with stiffly applying a routine: they are the findings of a writer gifted with a marvelous story-telling instinct'' (55).

Francisco Rico (1971) also insists on this "story-telling instinct" of *Lazarillo*'s author and on the ''subtlety and cleverness with which *Lazarillo* reelaborates extraneous motifs'' and integrates them into the ''living organism'' of the text. From this, Rico once again posits the singular importance of *Lazarillo* in the history of the modern novel.[1] From the serious doubts initially entertained by critics with regard to the completeness and organization of *Lazarillo*, there has been a marked shift to acclaim for the work as an architectural prototype.

I do not subscribe to such notions as "spontaneous generation," To account for the production of a text (and thus all the more for the emergence of a new discursive type or a new literary genre), it is necessary, I believe, both to identify the interweaving of discursive codes or practices to be found in it and to emphasize the text's use or (ab)use both of the mark specific to that discourse and of the ideology underlining it.

In the preceding chapter I detailed the way three practices of autobiographical discourse converge in *Lazarillo* and how their alienating and subversive (ab)use challenged the autobiographical practices that had become rituals in the Spain of that time: the so-called soliloquy (whose addressee is God or Jesus Christ) acknowledging God's blessings; the internally focused general confession written for the confessor or spiritual advisor; and the purportedly spontaneous confession responding to the ''admonitions'' of the Inquisition court.[2] In this last autobiographical practice, usually of a judiciary character, the largely external itinerary is intended to vindicate or explain a given circumstance—the *case*; the accused makes a general life confession with the intent of procuring a so-called reconciliation.[3] These three practices contaminate one another in varying degrees: invocations to God or Jesus Christ appear in thanksgiving prayers as well as in moments of contrite meditation on past sins; external events may form part of the internal itinerary's unfolding, testing it or spurring it onward; and references to intimate spiritual experiences pepper accounts of the external itinerary's progress. The general life confession written at the behest of the spiritual advisor often became part of the investigating declaration upon which the judicial censors carried out an initial evaluation (prima facie) of the accused or suspect. At other times, its purpose was a reconciliation during the so-called grace period established by the *edicto de gracia*. The frontiers between the internal, or sacramental, forum and the external forum, the church as an external and visible society, thus remain nebulous in inquisitorial praxis, and the types of autobiographical discourse reflect this ambiguity. Although one must inspect the manuscript section of the Biblioteca Nacional de Madrid, the cathedral and convent libraries, as well as the Inquisition records in the Archivos Históricos Nacionales de Madrid to grasp the extensiveness of these discursive practices, there is nevertheless enough printed material from each of the three practices to enable us to refer to them without the disadvantage of having to cite only unpublished manu-scripts.[4]

If I maintain the existence of a confluence of contemporary assorted autobio-graphical practices in Lázaro de Tormes's confessional discourse, I do not thereby claim that a particular document might be a source for *Lazarillo*. Neither do I assert that the composition of *Lazarillo* merely follows the organizational rules of those autobiographical models. My point is rather that *Lazarillo* be considered as a (subversive) reading of the discursive organization of such texts. Reading here is called discursive calque because upon reproducing a discursive model, the new text reads and interprets its functional rules. The term subversive reading refers to the agrammatical use of the model; here, the code is led into delirium or is put at the disposal of an ideology in opposition to the one underlying it, thereby breaching the selection restrictions of the elements imparted by the original dis-course.

In the case of *Lazarillo*, the derisive use of a ritual discourse and the ensuing disclosure of its functional rules by means of its use as a disguise (while at the same time unmasking it as such), is a subversive destructive-creative act: it dem-onstrates that the ritual-discursive practices lack authenticity by dislocating their autobiographical value, thus giving way to autobiographical confessional fiction, a new social convention or discursive practice later institutionalized by the genre of the picaresque novel.

Three discourses produced by Lázaro de Tormes confirm this assertion:

1. The prologue, a metadiscourse that accounts for the circumstances of the narration as an act of communication. The narrator appears and informs, publicly and in the present tense, a first immediate and inherent addressee about what, why, and for whom he is writing.
2. The story of his life, a narration where the preterit (epic?) predominates in its dual function of recalling the past and carrying it over to the present in the act of narration. This twofold temporal aspect of the past tense generates a vivid effect when the narrating subject is the subject whose deeds are being narrated, the "Ich-Form."[5]
3. An opinion on the world, expressed by means of digressions where the alternation between past and present reveals changes in the narrator's awareness; the narrator, at the time of writing, can either associate with or divorce from his past vision of the world.[6]

Lázaro's three discourses, along with the elements involving the book's orga-nization (its title and the chapter epigraphs, added by a narrator external to the narrative universe of Lázaro's tale), make up the *Lazarillo* text handed down to us in the Burgos and Antwerp editions of 1554. I consider the interpolations in the Alcalá edition as evidence of a contemporary reading of the original text, although that edition also appears in 1554.[7] The three discourses, flowing smoothly into one another in the text, share a common denominator: the lexicon, the narrated facts, and the underlying scale of values belong to a repertory of rhetorical commonplaces, moral judgments, folktales, and popular sayings. The functions of all these textual borrowings, however, are so well defined in the new text that it is difficult to sense that they are folkloric borrowings or clichés, depending on the case. This subtlety, according to Francisco Rico, explains the critics' belated appreciation of the anecdotes integrated into Lázaro's "life." André Labertit (1972) has shown, in a study on *Lazarillo*'s prologue, that the series of its commonplace components become perfectly coherent, seeming original by the information they convey. Labertit therefore concludes that "all persuasiveness is therefore not missing. Conventional forms are not lifeless forms" (163).

Critics have repeatedly stated that the religious lexicon undeniably present in *Lazarillo* has no significance in Lázaro's mouth because it has been stripped of its meaning through popular usage. One indeed may have reservations about trivial features seemingly imbued with reckonings and premeditation, as is the case with all the components of this text. The recurrent religious and spiritual vocabulary, its ambiguous function in Lázaro's tale (always in contrast with the mundane vocabulary), and the type of discourse that transmits it all seem to support this proposition. The twofold tension in the text lies between its components on one hand, and the whole of these components and the discourse that conveys it on the other. I return to my analysis (see chapter 1) of the fragment from the second *tractado*: "I opened the saide coffer to comforte my selfe a little, and beholding the bread, which I durst not touch, but worshipping it" (29). These are not only lexical borrowings stamped with Counter-Reformation spirituality; Lázaro's use of these verbs in the first person—the discursive code specific to autobiographical spiritual confessions—reinforces to such a degree the symbol of eucharistic devotion to which they pertain that we tend to forget the sequence of events leading to this performance and the secular allusions combining with these borrowings from the spiritual lexicon that Lázaro—not his contemporaries—alienates and profanes. This profanation, typical of "carnivalesque literature," as Bakhtin (1965) has stressed àpropos Rabelais, is not confined to the second chapter but extends throughout *Lazarillo*. Lázaro refers to the gospels when he speaks of his father: "He confessed the whole matter, denying nothing," wherefore he was "persecuted by Justice," and he should thus be in paradise "for the Gospel call them blessed" (those "suffering persecution by Justice") (7). He continually refers in his prayers to God and to divine providence (which guides him from one wretched situation to a worse one) when he chances upon de Toledo's squire and hires himself out to him (the theme of the third *tractado*). At the end of the last *tractado*, Lázaro, upon hearing the rumors ("they ["the evill tongues"] would say this and that") about the wife he shares with his protector, the archpriest of

San Salvador of Toledo, makes the following ambiguous statement emphasized by a sacrilegious oath:

> My wife, which I love better than any thing in this world, considering howe that by her meanes, God hath done more for mee, than I have deserved, and I dare sweare by the holy sacrament, that shee is as honest a woman as any that dwelleth within the foure gates of Toledo. (70).

But above all, the communication situation framing this discourse suffused with profanations should be interpreted as a truly subversive profanation of the autobiographical confessional practices. Although these practices have a very precise addressee whose request induces the narrating subject to write a response, which creates the tone of confidentiality specific to this type of autobiographical discourse, they do not exclude a larger audience, the virtual readers. Occasionally, permission for publication is specifically given. Such is the case of most confessional autobiographies, which were intended primarily for the spiritual director but also for the Inquisition, for the general public, or for both, to serve as the testimony of an inspiring life (see chapter 3). Whatever the actual case, the text's organization reveals that the writer assumes this larger audience. In the case of the soliloquy, always written in the first person, the text's title and the presentation of its chapters or divisions are in the third person. Even those oral confessions submitted to the inquisitorial tribunal and transcribed often literally and in the first person by clerks or notaries are integrated into the trial's records and preceded by epigraphs or presentations in the third person.

It is as if a common deep structure were subtending all of these textual manifestations whose communication circuit splits — double bind — into an enunciating act framed by the communication situation of personal confidentiality (a situation thus located temporally and spatially) and patterned on a fixed institutionalized textual model marked by its own conventional rules of rhetoric (an almost atemporal form external to the discursive universe from which the tale originates). A conscious, if not intentional situation of autonomous and open reception integrated into the written text and regulating its contents opposes the well-defined performance of confidential enunciation (oral or written). The self-image projected by the enunciating subject will thus be delineated according to the account's two addressees.[8] The tension corresponds perhaps to the dual function of these language acts: the first function, immediate and internal, is to give an account of one's life to the tribunal or to the person requesting that information; the second, remote and external, is to give an account to be read by many — or heard, since Lázaro's profession as town crier, as he tells us, includes ''escorting those who suffer persecution by justice . . . declaring with loud voyce their offences'' (69).

In the prologue, Lázaro is explicit about this tension at the very moment when he reveals who the addressees of his account actually are:

Very few would take penne in hand to pleasure one man only, seing that
they can not bring thier workes to en without great travell: And when
they have ended their labor, they rightfully desire to be recompenced,
and not with money, but only that all men with curteous minds will read
and allow their workes. . . . Wherefore nowe that all things passe after
such a sort, I confessing my selfe to bee no holier than my neighbours,
am content that such as finde any taste in this my grosse stile and
noveltie, may pleasure and delight themselves therwith: and they may
percieve how a man liveth, after so many fortunes, daungers and
adversities. . . . Therefore now I beseech your worship, receive with
willing hart this poore token of my true affection, which shuld have
bene much richer. (5-6)

The old question of the function of the narrating "I" in the picaresque novel
(and particularly in *Lazarillo*) becomes highly topical in light of the discourse
pragmatics. One of the basic principles of pragmatics is that textual productions
call for the conjunction of a transmitting author and a receiving addressee in an
enunciating act framed by a communication situation (actual or fictitious, as is
the case with a literary text within an "as if" context). To explain the autobiographical character of *Lazarillo*, Américo Castro (1935) asks rhetorically: "Had
it not been so, who would have paid attention to that life?" Given that any "I"
implies a "you" as Emile Benveniste (1966) pointed out, we must also ask ourselves who might be the addressee interested in learning about that insignificant
life, that "opposite of an accomplishment," as Castro would call it. The principle of verisimilitude underlying Castro's question requires a reconsideration of
the communication situation framing the whole of Lázaro's account.

It seems that Claudio Guillén (1957) was the first to propose the idea that
Lazarillo is a letter—a "spoken epistle," as he called it (268). Fernando Lázaro
Carreter (1969) and Francisco Rico (1970) have suggested that Lázaro's account
of his life is an answer to a letter that he received from his protector's enigmatic
friend who enjoined him to give a detailed account of the case involving his dishonor: "And seeing that you have commanded me to write the matter at length,
I have thought good not to begin the midst of my life, but first to tel you of my
birth, that al men may have ful knowledge of my person" (6). Actually, the text
does not impart as much information as Lázaro Carreter and Rico (as well as the
English translator) have inferred.[9] Jenaro Talens (1975) interprets it very differently: "Lázaro does not write to V.M. because the latter has asked him directly to
do so. V.M. has written to another person, probably the archpriest, Lázaro's superior in the social scale, and through his means, asks that the matter be cleared
up" (91).

To say that Lázaro owes a letter on the basis of "Your Worship commands"
(whom?) is to add information extraneous to the text, though the text may be
ambiguous and may not exclude Lázaro as the direct addressee of Your Worship's
presumed order or letter. Because "Vuestra Merced escribe" does not in six-

teenth-century Spanish necessarily mean "to write a letter"; *escribe* meant also today's "prescribe." Here the English translation "command" is correct. Such readings divert one's attention from the topic of writing in obedience to a command (a directive either coming from the spiritual director or implied by the "admonitions" of the inquisitorial court), a formula common to many confessions or autobiographical reports of that era. In Lázaro's case, it is intimately connected to rhetorical *moderatio* and *captatio benevolentiae*:

> Therefore now I beseech your worship, receive with willing hart this
> poore token of my true affection, which shuld have bene much richer if
> power and abilitie had bene equall with desire. And seeing that you
> have commanded . . . (6)

This is not a mere dedication: The cryptic Your Worship refers both to the instigator and the internal addressee of Lázaro's dedicatory words and autobiographical confession.

> Your worship shal understande before all things, that my name is *Lazaro*
> *de Tormes*, son of *Thome Gonsales* and *Antona Peres*. (7)

Furthermore, *Lazarillo*'s textuality is supported by the recurrent appeal of Lázaro to this personal, concrete addressee. This appeal also frequently both divides and connects the text's narrative units. The tale's opening invocation, "Your worship shal understande before all things," connects the prologue's discourse with that of the autobiography and allows Lázaro to identify himself (a legal convention?) and to present the circumstances of his birth as an explanation both of his nickname and of his family's social condition, which in turn explains why his mother entrusts him to his first master, the blind man. From the account of his hitting his head against the stone bull—Lázaro's first awakening to the ways of the world—to his description of the blind man's shrewdness, Lázaro refers to Your Worship twice, ending one narrative segment and initiating another:

> I rejoyce to declare unto your worship these Childish toyes, that you
> may see how commendable it is for a man of low estate to bee brought
> to authoritie and exalted, and contrariwyse what a shame it is, a man
> for dignitie and estimation to bee pulled downe to wretched miserie. But
> to retourne to my blynde master, and to shew his nature, I assure you
> [your worship] that . . . (11)

Another invocation to Your Worship closes the depiction of the blind man's sagacity and introduces the narration of the justified hoaxes familiar from traditional folklore:

> Yet for all his daily gaines, you [your worship] must understand that
> there was never man so wretched a niggarde. For hee caused mee not
> onely to die for hunger, but also to wante what so ever I needed. And
> therefore to confess the troth, if I had not founde out meanes to helpe

my selfe, I had bene buried long withence. Wherefore oftentimes I would so prevent him of all his crafte, that my portion shoulde prove as good as his: and to bring my matter so to passe I used wonderfull deceits (whereof I will recite unto you some) although sometimes my practising of them did cost mee bitter paines. (12)

The appeal to Your Worship surfaces again in the recounting of the practical jokes (*burlas*), in this instance because Lázaro wishes to emphasize the exemplary value he attributes to the tale of the grape incident:

But now because your worship shal understand how farre his crafte did extende, I will declare one chaunce amongst many, which happened in the time I served him, wherin he seemeth to give full understanding of his subtiltie. (16)

There is yet another reference to Your Worship when Lázaro, in the first chapter, forecasts the fulfillment of the blind man's "prophecy" — "If any man shal have happy chaunce with wine, it is thou" (21):

For his [the blind man's] sayings at that time proved afterwarde most true: Wherefore I have oftentimes sithence called to minde his wordes, whereby it appeared that he had a great gift in prophecying, and therefore it hath often repented one of my cruell dealing towards him, although his deserts were evill, seeing that his wordes of Prophecie proved so true, as hereafter your worship shall plainely understande. (21)

The second chapter has not a single reference to Your Worship, and neither have chapters 4, 5, and 6. In the third, however, the invocation to Your Worship reappears at the moment of transition from the section where Lázaro tells of his being deceived by the squire's outward appearance to the section where he describes his disillusionment upon grasping the reality of his poverty:

Your worship may well thinke that when I heard these wordes I was ready to fall downe dead, not so muche for hunger, as for playnely perceiving, that then fortune was altogether mine ennemie. Then began my sorrowes to appeare unto me againe, and I to lament my misfortune: then came there to my mind. (39)

Finally, three references to Your Worship occur in chapter 7, but with a new function: the immersion in the present moment. By acting anaphorically as a link to the prologue's metadiscourse (now recognized as a cataphora), these references close the tale's cycle and identify Your Worship as the superior and friend of San Salvador of Toledo's archpriest whose servants are Lázaro and his wife, the situation that had created the case that Your Worship wishes cleared up and from which followed the account of Lázaro's whole life (so as to give "ful knowledge of my person" [6]). Lázaro begins with an account of how he came to procure a royal appointment and adds: "I live in my office, and exercise it to Gods service and yours [your worship's]" (68). This appointment, that of town crier, puts Lázaro in contact with the archpriest who marries him to his servant (and concubine):

> In this meane time, master Archdeacon of saint *Salvador* your
> [worship's] friend and servaunt at commaundement, having knowledge
> of my person and habilitie, especially since I had cryed his wyne, went
> about to marry me with his mayd. And after that I had considered, that
> with having to doe with such a man as master Archdecon was, I cold
> not receive but honestie and goodnesse, I determined to doe it. (69)

Having finished the account of the matter and made clear how peace could be maintained in his household (that is, that no one bring up the matter in front of him), Lázaro sets his tale in time by referring to a historical event (and to Toledo, where he is writing) and invokes Your Worship for the last time:

> This was the same yeere that our victorious Emperour entred into this
> noble citie of Toledo, wher his court was kept with great geastes and
> triumphes, as your mastership hath heard: finally, it was then that I was
> in my prosperitie, and in my chiefest time of good adventure. (71)

The recurrent references to Your Worship (or to Your Mastership), then, have a structural function in Lázaro de Tormes's tale, as Lázaro Carreter (1969) has pointed out, although he interprets them as "reminding the reader of the epistolary character of the tale" (45). I consider them marker-connectors of narrative sequences and indicators of the internal addressee of Lázaro's autobiography. By interrupting the chronological arrangement of related events and by introducing the present time of the narration itself, they both create the temporal space of the tale and highlight the narrative act itself.

Beyond the mere anecdote (the satire of social groups by the characters who surround Lázaro and who become the objects of his critical evaluation as he considers the world) and beyond the carnivalesque profanation of the spiritual lexicon and quotes from sacred texts, we discover in *Lazarillo* a narrative conscience that becomes the central theme of the work. *Lazarillo*'s fiction is thus not only a narrative illusion carried out through a clever literary device; its cognitive impact reveals the problematics of such a device, thereby dismantling the autobiographical confession as a ritual discourse of the time and converting it into a novel. One thing seems certain: this literary device is more complex than a simple letter. Furthermore, the book's title and the epigraphs at the head of the text's seven chapters or *tractados* (written in the third person) objectivize Lázaro, illustrate the text's institutional functioning, and point to the existence of a nontemporal narrator or presenter outside the discursive space that generates Lázaro's tale. We saw earlier how this type of presentation is encountered in the autobiographical confessions of the time.

In addition to the Lázaro-Your Worship relationship, there are two others: Lázaro and the potential reader, and the narrator or presenter and the potential reader. Both relationships are explicit in the text. As one reads *Lazarillo*, one probably barely notices the mediating function of the title and epigraphs. For that reason, Américo Castro (1935) could state that in reading the *Lazarillo* "we are given the illusion that we are looking at life itself without any intermediary: here we have an individual inviting us, without more ado, to enter into his private life, to observe it from inside and from the point of view of his own experience" (138). Stressing the word "illusion" used by Castro, I find no fault in his emphasis on the text's subtle ambiguity. Given that the identity of the enigmatic Your Worship is not revealed until the end and that while reading we quickly forget the concreteness of the person appearing in the prologue's dedication, the text indeed generates an illusion of closeness and confidentiality between Lázaro and the reader. Claudio Guillén (1957) has accurately described this illusion of both closeness and distance with his interpretation of the expression "spoken letter": we "seem to be listening on the sly to Lázaro's confession to his protector's friend" (268). What I find unacceptable, however, within the communicative framework I have outlined, is Alonso Zamora Vicente's (1962) commentary on *Lazarillo*'s I and Your Worship: "Let us see on the first page. And we realize that we are meeting the anonymous author, directly, speaking to us in the first person in order to present himself: Your worship shal understande before all things, that my name is *Lazaro de Tormes*" (30).

If the illusion of closeness allows us to forget the personal and concrete character of the addressee of Lázaro's tale, and this to the point that we identify ourselves with Your Worship and consider ourselves appealed to by Lázaro, it is because we sense in the work an almost colloquial verbalizing reflected in appeals to Your Worship that use the verb recite ("whereof I will recite unto you [your worship]")—an aspect of the narration stressed by Claudio Guillén, as we have just seen. Lázaro's account cannot be considered a letter unless it be a spoken one, perhaps either because in our culture, as Kristeva (1970) noted, a book is "a transcription of the oral word" (147) or because of the oral nature of the confession, whether sacramental or juridical. The difference between the two is minimal, especially at the time of *Lazarillo*'s appearance, when the Council of Trent defined the sacrament of penance as a "trial" where penitents fault themselves as offenders and the minister pronounces sentence as judge.[10] Similarly, the Inquisition tribunal, made up of clergymen, had the power or *jurisdictio* to absolve from the church's penalties and censorship the offender who appeared before it during the period of *edicto de gracia* to make a spontaneous confession of purported crimes.[11]

These comments on the Lázaro-Your Worship relationship, on the opening of the text to a potential reader, and on the existence of titles and epigraphs in the third person (epigraphs thus neither transmitted by Lázaro nor addressed to Your Worship) do not at all detract from Américo Castro's (1935) intuitive observation that *Lazarillo*'s autobiographical fiction and anonymity are "two aspects of a same reality," the author's "genial decision" to have Lázaro himself relate his own wretched experiences. Jenaro Talens formulated more precisely this dimension of the first picaresque novel. Although I do not agree with him that the "alleged verisimilitude" brought about by the use of the first person is reinforced by the factual and fictional levels merging into one transmitter (Lázaro) and into one receiver (Your Worship), I concur with his conclusion that "Lazarillo's anonymity, setting aside the numerous prevailing extratextual interpretations, is made necessary by the very discourse of the text, thus becoming an integral part of the work's structure" (86-87).

This is why the prologue's "I" must be identical to the "I" enunciating the autobiographical account ("that al men may have ful knowledge of my person," writes Lázaro, indicating that the same subject enunciates the discourse in the prologue and in the tale). This device has not always been used in subsequent picaresque novels where the known author was also explicitly present in the text. In these works, the author surfaces by penning in the first person the prologue, the dedication, and the notices to the reader. The author's "I" is later suddenly in contrast with the narrator's "I," which appears at the very beginning of the account, appealing to a "you" segregated from the tale, to a "curious reader" (Guzmán de Alfarache), or to an unspecified "señor" (Pablos).

The rupture of what Philippe Lejeune (1975) has called "le pacte autobiographique" confirms that we are looking at a genre that was already institutionalized as literary and accepted by society. A new pact was thus sanctioned. The genre's textual laws are therefore transparent and have us overlook the umbilical cord that connects its origins to discursive practices sustained by a repressive ideology and that will continue to flourish throughout the seventeenth century, the picaresque novel's apogee in Spain. While these instances of the picaresque genre constitute a self-reference that allows them to be read *in se*, *Lazarillo*'s *ab alio* requires a reading that takes into consideration the intertextual and interdiscursive tensions between the work and the subverted discourse it has borrowed.

This is how Cervantes interpreted the work in a reading that seems to confirm the present one. In chapter 22 of the first *Don Quijote*, the representation of the communicative situation specific to confessional autobiographical discourse is yet more audacious than that of *Lazarillo* (*Quijote* contains an explicit allusion to the "Santa Hermandad"). Interestingly enough, the passage in question alludes explicitly to *Lazarillo* — and that is why I can speak here of Cervantes's reading, if not of his intertextual reading, since he brings together the two texts. By questioning the galley slaves one after the other, Don Quijote not only recreates the narrative device of Lázaro's account (questioned by Your Worship), but he also presents in the most grotesque manner the judicial procedures and examinations of his time. During their examination, each of those condemned to the galleys will respond, addressing his interrogator (Don Quijote) as "Your Worship," with the story of his life and an account of his present state. Ginés de Pasamonte, who cites *Lazarillo*, speaks of writing his life and publishing it, overshadowing Lázaro de Tormes's work and making explicit the twofold purpose of the confessional autobiography, just as Lázaro had revealed in his prologue.

Because *Lazarillo* is at the juncture (or crossroads) of both discourses, its acceptability could also be investigated as a complex sign. This problem, however, is not pertinent here. The words of the needy (Lázaro) as well as of the fool (Don Quijote) are the discourse of those on the fringe of society, legitimate only insofar as they remain a carnivalesque subversion that exposes society's ritual discursive practices as tools of a repressive ideology.

Chapter 3
Autobiography and Ritual Discourse:
The Autobiographical Confession before
the Inquisition

During the years of Franco's dictatorship, an anecdote circulated in Spain that brings to mind both the intellectual training and the working methods of the Spanish Civil Guard. The post commander of a city receives this telegram from the provincial authorities: "Impending seismic activity—epicenter in your town—take appropriate measures." Three days later—after having had his men work unremittingly, we suppose—the post commander answers his chief's communiqué, also by telegram: "Seismic activity quelled—Epicenter and his men arrested."

Today, my childhood memories of Spain allow me to understand this anecdote as day-to-day experience embellished by popular imagination: the power of the state machine to force individuals to confess or to admit to an identity and deeds with which they have no connection, and of having other individuals acknowledge the accuracy of this declaration of, if not their actual implication in, the fictitious deeds.

Let us suppose for a moment that, following the traditional practice of the sworn deposition, the *atestado*, Epicenter's declaration, had been recorded in writing. Having identified himself by that name, he would have briefly listed his origins, police record, role in the conspiracy, the motives that led him to participate in it—all narrated in the first person. How would readers react to such an autobiographical confession? Would they accept it as authentic?

The anecdote's addressee, its ideal auditor, must have a minimal knowledge of seismology to respond with the guffaw that emancipates the oppressed. Familiarity with oppression, too, is part of the informational presupposition upon which the anecdote rests. The story also assumes an immediate addressee of Epicenter's account likely (because of his candor) to accept it as truthful and to

44

transmit it to his superior by telegram. To the naive addressee of Epicenter's story, the conditions of the "autobiographical pact" described by Philippe Lejeune (1975) are strictly fulfilled: the receiver or reader identifies author, narrator, and character as one. (Lejeune recalls this viewpoint when he comes to appraise the "author's situation" and the "narrator's position" that characterize the autobiographical narrative.)

In 1554, an autobiographical confession more elaborate than that implicit in the Epicenter anecdote was published almost simultaneously in Burgos, Antwerp, and Alcalá. After a prologue in which an "I" explains what, why, for whom, and at whose request he is writing—attesting thereby to the oneness of the subject of enunciation and the narrative's central character—the account begins as follows: "Your worship shal understande before all things, that my name is *Lazaro de Tormes*, son of *Thome Gonsales* and *Antona Peres*" (7). The anonymity of this short book has made more than one critic consider it the genuine autobiography of a Toledo town crier apparently named Lázaro. Only with Foulché-Delbosc's uncovering of the folkloric character of certain elements (if not of entire sequences) in the narrative did literary criticism come to realize that the very name of the principal character derives from folklore, that the true author has hidden his name, and that this book is not an autobiography as such. Actually, the text's internal contradictions should have sufficed as unequivocal signs that a cultivated author was writing about an illiterate character, Lázaro, whose education is limited to the lessons of life given him by the blind man, and thus of the fictionality of this autobiography. The naive reader, however, does not linger on such subtleties.

The similarity between the anecdote from the period of Franco's dictatorship and the first picaresque narrative is not exhausted by the referential ambiguity of the "I" as the subject of enunciation of the autobiographical confession, implicit in the anecdote and explicit in *La vida de Lazarillo de Tormes y de sus fortunas y adversidades*: each tale echoes contemporary discursive practices and both are transmitted and received as tension relievers; hence their humorous quality and the unburdening laughter they arouse.

The search for a contemporary discourse likely to explain the functioning of the autobiographical fiction characteristic of the picaresque novel's narrative modality in its first historical manifestation, the *Lazarillo de Tormes*, led me to the uncovering of certain contemporary ritual discursive practices used by Lázaro de Tormes as narrative procedures in the account of his life. The peculiar modality of the echo of those autobiographical confessional practices in *Lazarillo*, as we saw in the preceding chapters, is an unmasking, by means of an agrammatical discursive calque or subversive reading, of its own functional norms—just as the anecdote from the Franco dictatorship years echoes the confession wrested by a Civil Guard determined that no purported offense go uninvestigated and unpunished.

Let us now see what *Lazarillo de Tormes* reveals, when approached from the hypothesis that it is written as a reading of the autobiographical confessional discourse of its day, disarticulating it in order to convert it into a novel. We saw earlier how *Lazarillo* discloses, beyond the anecdotal aspect of its story, a discursive conscience that becomes the work's central theme. This conscience allows *Lazarillo* not only to create a perfect narrative illusion based upon the deception that author, narrator, and character are one (anonymity being required by the type of discourse conveying such a story); in its cognitive impact, the effort to create a state of narrative awareness also reveals the fiction to be an artifice, a sham. While *Lazarillo* creates the impression or illusion of movement, it reveals its puppet strings and the external hand that governs them. This disclosure of its functional rules brings about a desecration of the discursive ritual of autobiographical confessions, which are thus revealed as tools of a repressive ideology — and this discovery is accomplished by means of an imitation (mimesis) that incriminates itself before the addressee who is able to perceive it as grotesque and paradoxical.

The first point of contact between *Lazarillo* and the autobiographical confessions addressed directly or indirectly to the Inquisition tribunal is the fact of its being written as an act of obedience to an order, as an act of submission of an "I" to an "Other": "And seeing that you have commanded me to write the matter at length" (6). This formula is a cliché in this type of writing, a cliché repeated in the extended title of Teresa de Avila's *Libro de su vida*, written "at the behest of her confessor, to whom it is sent and addressed." This declaration is restated in the prologue, this time in the first person.[1] In María Antonia de Jesús's autobiography, we can also read: "Escrito por la misma M[adre] María Antonia por repetidos mandatos de su confesor el P. Fr. Josph de Jesús María, dividido en partes y capítulos por el mismo Padre."[2] Doña María de Vela y Cueto also echoes this practice with the opening declaration of the first chapter of her *Autobiografía*: "Esto hago por haberme V.M. puesto obediencia expresa."[3] Luisa Carvajal y Mendoza writes in the chapter dedicated to the "First Years" in her *Autobiografía*: "Necesario será, hasta los doce años, tratar de niñerías, pues tan de veras manda V.M. que no deje nada de cuanto se me acuerda."[4] These works, from different times and circumstances, have one feature in common: autobiographical writing as an act of obedience to an order. It is not therefore the "epistolary style" suggested by Lázaro Carreter (1972), who compares the passages of *Lazarillo de Tormes* quoted earlier with the following sentence from a Latin epistle by Doctor Francisco López de Villalobos: "Expetis me generosissime pater status fortunae meae narrationem explicitam" (45).

In the case of the autobiographical confession submitted directly to the Inquisition tribunal, the sign of submission is patent in the interrogation conducted by the tribunal, to which the accused will respond orally or in writing, in the *moniciones* or in the *edicto de gracia*, which provoke the supposedly spontaneous confessions of those who seek a reconciliation. This context of communication that frames Lázaro's account of his life merits close attention, for it shows how that account reproduces a ritualized context of communication. There are nevertheless differences between the standard pattern and the use to which it is put in *Lazarillo*—differences that are precisely the indicators of Lazarillo's reading strategy.

The first thing we should observe is the intervention, in the official ritual discourse, of interlocutors characterized by specific and well-determined functions in the text: the tale's author-narrator-character identified by name and surname and ecclesiastical or monastic title versus the established authority (that is, the personal spiritual adviser, the Inquisitor, the confessor) interrogating that individual in the performance of its duty. In *Lazarillo*, on the contrary, otherwise prolific with spatial, temporal, and personal details (for instance, the archpriest of San Salvador of Toledo, Emperor Charles V, the French king, the battle of Guelves), a folkloric "I" appears: Lázaro de Tormes facing an unidentified Your Worship, who stays unknown both as a person and in the function as interrogator, appearing camouflaged in the *moderatio* and *captatio benevolentiae* topics. Only at the end is it indirectly revealed (and vaguely at that) that this enigmatic Your Worship, whom Lázaro addresses all too frequently as the account's addressee, is the friend and perhaps also the hierarchical superior of the archpriest whom Lázaro serves. Lázaro gives us this information while speaking of the archpriest in the seventh chapter: "In this meane time, master Archdeacon of saint *Salvador* your friend and servant at commaundement, having knowledge of my person and habilitie" (69). Besides, his enigmatic condition contrasts with the important structural function played, as we saw in the preceding chapter, by the repeated invocations to Your Worship, another agrammaticality.

A further abnormality or agrammaticality lies in the discursive echo performed by *Lazarillo*: the explicitness of the autobiographical confession's many other addressees, which is in opposition, if not contradictory to the confidentiality and submission transcribed in the communication circuit of I, Lázaro de Tormes, versus Your Worship (that is, narrator versus addressee) and which reduces the confession to a grotesque imitation. Indeed, it is difficult to reconcile the invocations to Your Worship in the prologue and in Lázaro's autobiographical confession with the declarations in the prologue. To Your Worship, Lázaro addresses such lines as: I beseeche your worship, receive with willing hart this poore token of my true affection . . . ; Your worship shal under stande before all things . . . ; I rejoyce to declare unto your worship these Childish toyes . . . ; But to retourne to my blynde master, and to shew his nature, I assure you [your worship] . . . ; You [your worship] must understand that there was never a man so wretched a niggarde . . . ; But now because your worship shal understand how farre his crafte did extende . . . ; As hereafter your worship shall plainely understande . . . ; I live in mine office, and exercise it to Gods service and yours [your worship's] . . . ; Master Archdeacon of saint *Salvador* your [worship's] friend and servaunt at commaundement . . . ; As your mastership hath heard. . . .

Compare such invocations to the following declarations in the prologue:

I am of opinion, that things so worthy of memory, peradventure never heard of before, ne seene, ought by all reason to come abroad to the sight of many. . . . Very fewe would take penne in hand to pleasure one man only, seing that they can not bring their workes to ende without great travell: And when they have ended their labor, they rightfully desire to be recompenced, and not with money, but only that men with curteous minds will read and allow their workes. . . . Wherefore nowe that all thinges passe after such a sort, I confessing my selfe to bee no holier than my neighbours, am content that such as finde any taste in this my grosse Stile and noveltie, may pleasure and delight themselves therwith: and they may perceive how a man liveth, after so many fortunes, daungers and adversities. (5-6)

It is true that in the autobiographical confessions dealt with so far the overt addressee is but a sort of mediator between the narrator and the confession's true addressee(s)—that is, in addition to the confessor or spiritual adviser, the Inquisition tribunal, and the general public for whose enlightenment the confession might serve as an example. But the identification of this (or these) addressee(s) is less explicit. In the case of soliloquies, only the text's organization (the title and epigraphs of its components) points to an addressee different from the "You" (God, Jesus Christ) addressed by the text's enunciating subject. The situation is the same with the autobiographical confession presented to the Inquisition tribunal and incorporated with introductory epigraphs into the proceedings' trials. Exemplary autobiographies are even more explicit. Thus Leonor de Córdoba writes the *Relación de su vida* around 1400 in order that

my deeds and the miracles shown me by the Holy Virgin Mary should be remembered [in order that] all beings in tribulation may be assured . . . , if only they commit themselves with all their hearts to Her, of the consolation and welcome she has extended to me.[5]

A similar declaration of purpose can be found in the "Proemio" to Martín de Ayala's (1503-66) autobiography.

So that no one lose the faith that should be held in [God's] great mercy, the benefits of which, we have not only understood and believed in, but almost touched and experienced in this worldly life.[6]

Teresa de Avila also writes her autobiography "so that God's mercy and my ingratitude might be manifest" and expressly authorizes its publication:

I write what has happened to me, as I have been told to, and should it not be suitable, he who receives it may tear it up, for he shall know better than I what is right. I beseech him, for the love of God, that what I have written of my wretched and sinful life be published. From this moment on, I extend this consent to all my confessors of whom he is one and to whom this is addressed. And should they so desire, that it be [published] during my lifetime.[7]

None of these declarations of purpose, however, comes close to the insistence found in *Lazarillo*'s prologue on unmasking the innermost motive of any human undertaking as "the desire for honor." Lázaro cites three examples to support his assertion that this desire is such a common denominator: the soldier risking his life, the preaching master Doctor (for all the latter's concern with the welfare of the soul), and the delight of a gentleman flattered by a scoundrel. "So likewise in Arte and learning," concludes Lázaro, who shortly before quoted Cicero's *Tusculanae* to demonstrate that "Honor doth mainteine art or cunning" (6).

Lázaro does not consider himself more righteous than others who write, and it will therefore not displease him that "such as finde any taste in this my grosse Style and noveltie, may pleasure and delight themselves therwith." But he hopes to do more than divulge to the world "things so worthy of memory": Lázaro hopes to find those readers who would "agree" with him or share his point of view—other readers would merely be entertained. Lázaro thinks that his confession should make those with inherited titles consider

what small praise is due unto them, seeing that Fortune hath dealt parcially with them: and how much commendation they deserve, which in despite of cruell fortune, with force and industrie, by rowing out of tempestuous seas, have arived to fortunate and happie havens. (6)

In short, Lázaro hopes that all derive some benefit from his confession and that, above all, his person be renowned. Lázaro's insistence on revealing addressees of the account other than Your Worship and on justifying this maneuver in the name of the Ciceronian principle that honor fosters art is problematical: the "happie haven" to which Lázaro arrives is not exactly exemplary; thus, through his autobiography, he becomes the "crier" of his own dishonor. This internal textual contradiction echoes the external one: the work is made public but the true author remains anonymous. This seems to be but a means of attracting attention to the calqued discourse that a kind of archaeological reading should be able to restore in its true context of communication.

In light of such considerations, the "*Lazarillo* diagram" proposed by Jenaro Talens (1975) is difficult to accept. His diagram merges the external and internal addressees of *Lazarillo* into a single receiver, Your Worship—the only explicit receiver, according to Talens—as a consequence of the unique transmitter, Lázaro, the fictitious author of the tale of his life. The rupture of this schema—which could be summarized as the deceptive appearances of the communication context typical of the autobiographical confessions of which *Lazarillo* is an echo—is that which explicitly turns the prologue into a denunciation, a denunciation that becomes *Lazarillo*'s authentic archaeological *reading* of such discursive practices. This echo is more than the simple recreation or reproduction of socially determined signs: it interprets their functioning by unmasking their true communication context and by placing these serially with similar contexts illustrated by the three examples brought forth by Lázaro.

A consideration of the basic operational laws of the calqued discourse in *Lazarillo*'s prologue thus discloses two categories of addressee of this autobiographical confession: (1) Your Worship and (2) many others. To these may be added what might otherwise be easily overlooked, the title of the book and the epigraphs that divide the account and introduce it in the third person and thus turn out to be neither Lázaro's own words nor an address intended only for Your Worship. In addition to the Lázaro-Your Worship relationship, in chapter 2 we saw two more explicit relationships in *Lazarillo*: Lázaro-virtual reader, and narrator or "presenter"-virtual reader. These relationships pertaining to book writing are not confined to autobiographies intended for publication; they also occur in soliloquies and even in acts or testimonials of inquisitorial trials where they manifest the dual purpose of their production. The institution of the Inquisition thus functions, as does the institution of book writing, as a sort of publicity platform that allows the subject to "register his life and his presence in time," as Adrienne Schizzano-Mandel (1980, 162-63) pointed out regarding Sor María de San Jerónimo's self-accusation before the Inquisition.

In a different context, Michel Foucault (1975) has also brought to our attention how clinical examination and the archival institution led to a Copernican revolution by the generalization of what was before the "privilege" of "being looked at, observed, reported on in detail, followed from day to day by an uninterrupted script" (193). Foucault's analysis forces a rethinking of the traditional understanding of the communication situation that frames *Lazarillo* (as well as its model, the autobiographical confession of that particular time, if not in general). This is why I have proposed, at the First International Congress on the Picaresque Novel (Madrid, 1976), the following schema as a response to the view of *Lazarillo* as a letter (Claudio Guillén, Fernando Lázaro Carreter, and Francisco Rico) and to Jenaro Talens's diagram (see schema 1).

The importance of my correction of *Lazarillo*'s context of communication as an echo of that of the autobiographical confession is based on the fact that the self-image projected by the enunciating subject will be elaborated according to both of the tale's addressees, creating tension in the account itself. This tension, which corresponds to the dual function typical of any language act in which the emitter addresses a receiver while knowing that he or she will be heard (or read) by others of a different nature, eventually creates a truly conflictual situation: the internal situation of the enunciation (that is, a situation of confidentiality in communication, as institutionalized in confessional practice) is in conflict with the external situation of uncontrollable reception (whether because of the judicial consequences stemming from an appearance before the inquisitorial court—an institution that has control over possessions and lives—or because of its circulation by the book-reading institution). The subject, who must respond adequately

Schema 1
Communication Context in *Lazarillo de Tormes*

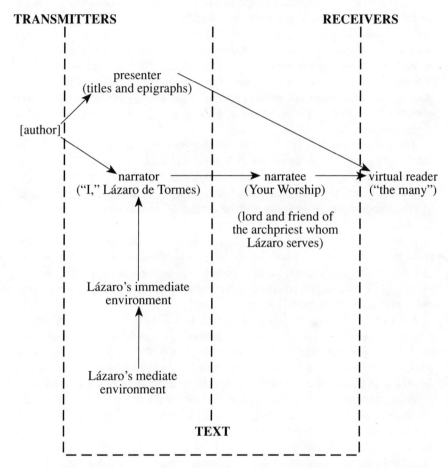

TRANSMITTERS   **RECEIVERS**

presenter
(titles and epigraphs)

[author]

narrator   narratee   virtual reader
("I," Lázaro de Tormes)   (Your Worship)   ("the many")

(lord and friend of
the archpriest whom
Lázaro serves)

Lázaro's immediate
environment

Lázaro's mediate
environment

TEXT

and simultaneously to the two conflicting situations, feels confronted with two contradictory norms of behavior, a circumstance that gives rise to the paradoxical situation that communication theory calls the double-bind.[8]

Between empirical text or true-life experience and autobiographical text lies not only the difference between the chaos of disparate events as they occur and the order and selection dictated by a writer capable of converting contingency into coherence; the very coherence of the autobiographical text organized into a discourse points to a design that, according to Benveniste (1966), is itself part of the definition of discourse: "Enunciation implying a speaker and a listener and the former's intention to influence the latter in some manner" (241).[9] This intention, to which is subordinated the selection and the ordering of narrative material, is doubly polarized in the corpus of the autobiographies studied here: on the one hand, it focuses on the many conflicting addressees outlined in the schema I proposed in 1976 as an exponent of *Lazarillo*'s communication context; on the other hand — and here the schema should be complemented — it focuses on Your Worship, who is not only the internal addressee (*destinataire*) of Lázaro's account, but also the one who dictated the order to write it, its addresser (*destinateur*), in the sense proposed in the earlier analysis of the practice of writing an autobiographical confession in obedience to a command. With this in mind I propose the amended schema 2 as an exponent of the autobiographical confession's context of communication at that time, as well as of *Lazarillo*'s reading of that discursive practice.

The enunciating subject's twofold polarization brings about, in the corpus of autobiographical texts that concern us here — and perhaps, *servatis servandis*, in every autobiographical text — the total disintegration of the "autobiographical pact's" illusion, that is, the oneness of author, narrator, and character, as well as of the subject of the enunciation and the subject of what is enunciated.

Such a oneness is first of all a *contradictio in terminis* of the "pact" and its elements as defined by Lejeune (1975). Lejeune indeed asserts in his second point that "the story of a personality" is the autobiography's "qualified subject"; yet in his fourth point Lejeune postulates a oneness of person and outlook as the typical "narrator's position" in an autobiography. His first assertion proposes evolution, his second destroys it.

Most of the autobiographies dealt with here are the result of a more or less sincere conversion that marks a rupture between the "old being" who executes the actions of the tale and the "new being" who narrates them as an act of contrite confession after conversion. *Lazarillo* offers eloquent contrasts in this sense, as we saw in the previous chapter. The first instance of nonidenticalness between narrator and character identifies the breach between the enunciation's subject and the subject of what is enunciated. But it is not only the difference in personal attitudes that separates narrator from character in every autobiography, and particularly in the confessional one; it is above all knowledge that separates the saved narrator (the one who relates his navigating, once arrived into "happie haven" — to use a metaphor from *Lazarillo*, Teresa of Avila, and other spiritual biographies) from the subject who lives the vicissitudes of the navigation with anguished uncertainty. Along with this awareness, power also separates the narrator as actant-subject of the narration, capable of fashioning himself into a demiurge organizing the story, from the actant-object, the protagonist of the story. This power is nevertheless limited in the corpus of the present study, for the distance separating the enunciating and narrating subject from the narration's object is replete with mediators who — some unconsciously, others more or less consciously — predispose and predetermine the communication act or presentation of the enunciated object to its multiple addressees.[10] This more or less in-

Schema 2
Actantial Table of Commanded Autobiography

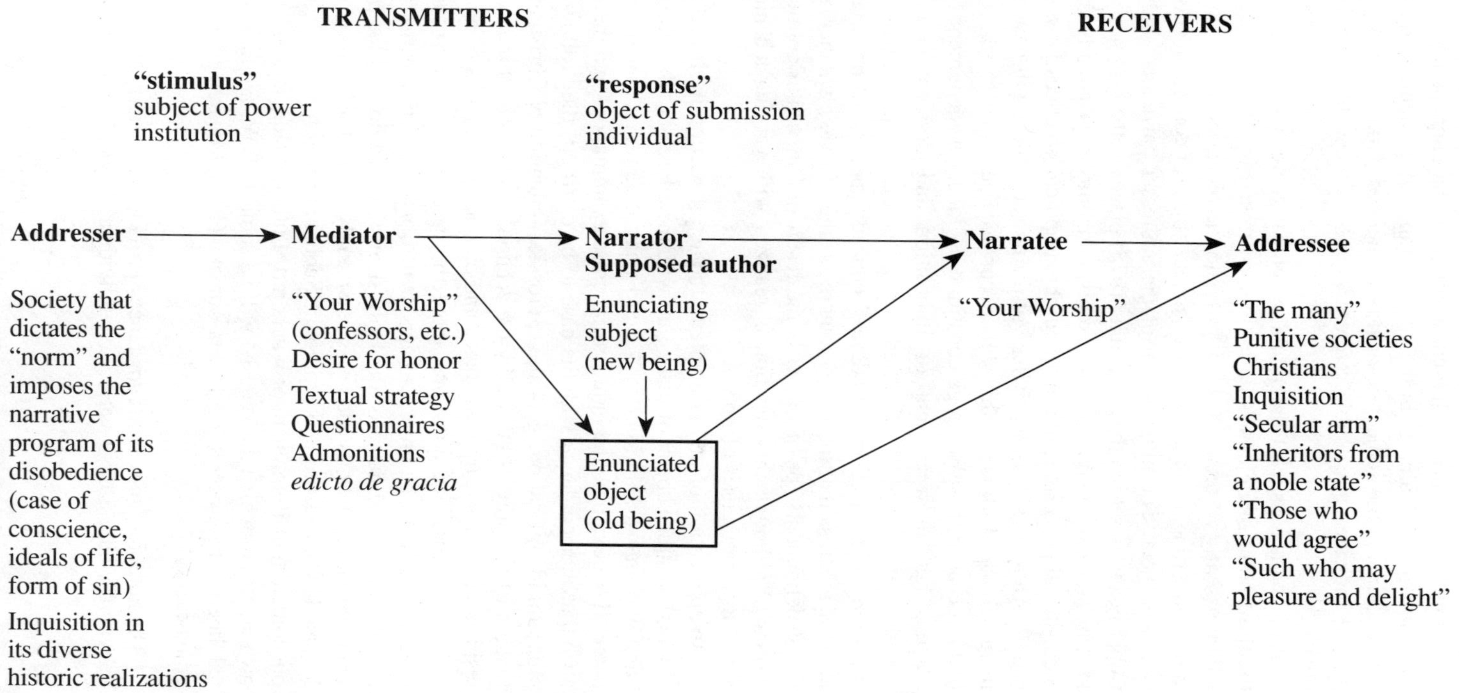

TRANSMITTERS

RECEIVERS

"stimulus"
subject of power institution

"response"
object of submission
individual

Addresser → Mediator → Narrator → Narratee → Addressee
Supposed author

Enunciating subject (new being)

Enunciated object (old being)

"Your Worship"

Mediator

"Your Worship" (confessors, etc.)
Desire for honor
Textual strategy
Questionnaires
Admonitions
edicto de gracia

Addresser

Society that dictates the "norm" and imposes the narrative program of its disobedience (case of conscience, ideals of life, form of sin)

Inquisition in its diverse historic realizations

Addressee

"The many"
Punitive societies
Christians
Inquisition
"Secular arm"
"Inheritors from a noble state"
"Those who would agree"
"Such who may pleasure and delight"

tervening manipulation of the enunciation by the enunciating instance destroys the claimed identicalness, in the autobiographical account, of the subject of the enunciation and the subject of what is enunciated. Grammatically, the use of the preterit indicates the double referent of the ''I'' and thus the aforementioned breach.[11]

As a characteristic of the autobiographical genre, the ''author's situation'' — the third point of Lejeune's definition, promoted by Jean Starobinski (1970) — will apparently be retained, for it refers to the object-account, which constitutes at the same time an object of desire and an object of communication of the enunciating subject. The introduction of the addresser participant indicates that the Copernican revolution that Foucault (1975) places at the origin of clinical examination and cataloguing by the archival institution is already at work in the inquisitorial process, if not in all autobiographical practices, as a castrating procedure. The longstanding privilege of the power-subject will now reach the more marginal social classes. This will occur, as Foucault stresses in *Surveiller et punir*, because these writings constitute no longer a monument for future generations but an instrument of imposition and domination of the subject: ''putting into writing'' has shifted from a ''heroicizing procedure'' to an ''objectification and subjection procedure.'' Foucault speaks of ''one man's chronicle'' in order to stress that the meticulous recording of lives, whether of the mentally ill, of delinquents, or of kings, is the result of ''a certain political function of writing,'' although this function is realized with varying techniques and subjected to various uses of power.

An application of this principle to the act of writing itself and to autobiography replaces the subject of that genre with the addresser who, through the mediation of Your Worship, dictates Lázaro's narrative program and even Epicenter's name. If we examine the inquisitorial cross-examinations and their ritual, we realize that in accordance with the case to be clarified, they follow a preordained program: identification, genealogy, cross-examination of Christian culture (verification of the prayers known by the accused, and so on), life story (birthplace, residential changes, travels, stages and chronology in cases of a change of state or of a conversion), questions about the case (inquiries into the reasons that brought about the summons to appear in front of the Inquisition tribunal), and admonitions in the name of the Holy Trinity. In addition to this procedural program, certain situations and cases persistently recur (for instance, the practice of Mosaic law, consisting in keeping the Sabbath or in refusing to tolerate pork; the phenomenon of illuminism or witchcraft; Lutheran ''deviations''), each with its own clichés to which the accused will be subjected. We are far from the individual liberty that, according to Starobinski (1970), characterizes the ''autobiographical style'':

> The autobiography's circumstances provide but a fairly large frame
> within which a large variety of individual ''styles'' may be used and

displayed. . . . Here, more than anywhere else, style will be a personal performance. . . . In an account where the narrator's theme is his own past, the markings of an individual style will be of special importance: to the narration's explicit self-reference, the style adds the implicit self-reference value of a singular mode of elocution. . . . The style's self-referential value refers then to the time of writing, to the actual "I."
. . . The "truth" of bygone days is only such to the conscience that, by embracing today their representation, cannot but impose on them its form, its style. All autobiography—even if it limits itself to a straightforward narration—is a self-interpretation. . . . As doubtful as the related facts may be, writing will at the very least produce an "authentic" image of the personality "holding the pen." (257-59).

The distance that separates the "autobiographical style" from the canalization of the narrative flow dictated by the addresser's program-pattern might lead us into thinking of our corpus as something other than a corpus of autobiographies. This, however, would be a simplistic solution to the problems, encountered in every autobiography, of stereotyped situations at the story level and of stereotyped narrative resources at the discourse level (including the bourgeois autobiographies of the eighteenth and nineteenth centuries upon which are founded the more widely circulated studies on autobiography as a genre). Michel Beaujour (1977) has insisted, in opposition to Starobinski's "style," on this "cultural tradition" paradoxically running through writings that give the illusion of the most absolute individuality by means of "ready-made categories": "categories of sins and merits, of vices and virtues, of tastes and distastes; the five senses; humours and temperaments; faculties; honourable men's psychology, including their passions and earnestness; elements taken from characterology or from psychoanalysis; astrology, race, environment, time" (10-11). These categories of the self-portrait are in part those of the autobiography, although they do not represent an exhaustive inventory. They operate, according to Beaujour, like "procedure variations, as collective and as precisely coded as they were before rhetorical inventiveness and memory," although such a production machine "is no more perceived by the writer than are grammatical rules by the majority of speakers, or the processes of persuasive rhetoric by those who unsuspectingly use them constantly" (11).

From a different perspective, Eugene Vance (1973) has brought to light the discursive displacement in Augustine's *Confessions* as the "account's language suddenly gives way to sacramental language" when the author confesses his sins to the world, for "by using words, one is not experiencing the expression of one's self, but rather the *loss* of one's self" (168) within Augustinian sign theory—a theory defined by Vance as a concatenation in which "the written word is but a sign of the spoken word; the spoken word, in turn, is a sign of the internal Verb that is incorporal and has been placed into our intellect by the Other" (170).

"To speak accurately is really to speak being inhabitated by the Other's voice," as we could conclude if we extend to our entire corpus what Vance calls "l'ontologie des *Confessions*." This Other is understood in the Freudian sense of the suprapersonal instance (superego) from which issue the moral as well as linguistic directives (that is, parental and, through them, social prohibitions) unconsciously internalized by all individuals since their earliest years. If we interpret the addresser in terms of psychoanalytic language, we necessarily observe in the texts of our corpus (as well as in any autobiography) more than the subjects' introspection and expression of themselves. The Other that permeates them and manifests through their "I" is the father's voice, not a "letter to the father," which in turn echoes, in an enervating manifestation of surveillance and imposition of behaviorial patters, the institution that has created the spoken ritual, the "I, sinner, do confess." The (active) pact is replaced by the (passive) ritual, and the (active) instinct is channeled by the sublimating (passive) submission of the id into ideals that replace the libido and with which every subject tends to identify.

It has been said that the Spanish mystic-ascetic tradition generates a profound psychological intelligence because of the introspective rigor it fosters in the individual. But as Paul Ricoeur (1969) observed, "To the short path of introspective psychology, one must substitute the longer and surer course of reflection on the dynamics of the great cultural symbols" (286). We should question the society that creates for itself the spectacle of a ritual fiesta and burdens the propitiatory victim with its sins in a sadomasochistic act differing from Abraham's sacrifice only in that as the death command comes not from a transcendental voice but from its own death urge. There is a need, then, for going beyond the individual "I" writing or pronouncing his autobiographical confession and to focus on the power superstructure that produces it. Rhetorical laws and mental mechanisms internalizing the parental (social) image operate not just within the autobiographical confession studied here; their influence undermines all autobiographical writing. Not only are all autobiographies indeed the products of the tension between their subjects and their multiple addressees, where the subjects are prompted by addressers who impose their death urge and the language with which to express it; but the frame in which autobiography finds its realization is the fiesta, the social spectacle in which symbols are crystallized and ideology manifested in repetitive, preestablished ceremonials. A life story is thus less a source of information about an individual subject's trajectory than a symptom of social behavior. As an "epidictic discourse," the autobiographical confession does not inform about the individual self. The speaking subject is here but the vicar of the true subject. Like the "This is my body" of the transubstantiating consecration, "I, sinner, do confess" is the voice of the Other marked with an "I" of referential ambiguity. Lázaro and Epicenter understood this and bring out this ambiguity with their mimetic denunciations of the repressive ritual ceremonials of two different periods of Spain's history.

Foucault (1975) observes that at the end of the eighteenth century, the "chronicle of one man," and its "being put into writing" ceases to be the privilege of the power-subject by changing into a new kind of imposition on and control of the individual, who is thus converted into an "outcome and object of power" and an "outcome and object of knowledge." Foucault also notes at this juncture the emergence of the human sciences: individual observation and archival documentation fostered the depiction of the singular and, in so doing, made possible the "individual's appearance (and not the species's) in the realm of learning." Foucault adds:

> The case is not, as in casuistry or jurisprudence, a set of circumstances modifying an act and liable to alter a rule's application. It is the individual that may be described, rated, measured, compared to others, and this in his very individuality; it is also the individual that must be trained or retrained, that must be evaluated, normalized, excluded, etc. (193)

Thus, according to Foucault, is born the discipline of the human sciences for which the singular difference, individuality, constitutes the object of study. Yet to consider this individuality as the new object of knowledge and power is necessarily to take into account the transhistorical reality that runs through the most diverse collective behaviors and transforms them into variations upon a theme: the power structures. Only in this way shall we understand that it is precisely in those spheres, as Foucault states, that "the modern course of coercion on body, gesture, performance originated."

Neither our modernity nor its institutions seem so distant from the historical reality (in time and space) reported by Lázaro de Tormes and Epicenter.

Chapter 4
Narration and Argumentation
in Autobiographical Discourse

The inclusion of autobiography in the narrative genre is not as evident as it may seem. By establishing two systems or "two different levels of utterance" ("history" and "discourse") that concurrently distribute the French verb tenses and grammatical persons, Emile Benveniste (1971) expressly classifies autobiography as discourse, along with "correspondence, memoirs, plays, didactic works, in short, all the genres in which someone addresses himself to someone, proclaims himself as the speaker, and organizes what he says in the category of a person" (209). Historical utterance, on the contrary, which was once defined as "narration of past events" and is presently confined to written language, is now defined as

> The mode of utterance that excludes every "autobiographical" linguistic form. The historian will never say *I* or *you* or *now*, because he will never make use of the formal apparatus of discourse, which resides primarily in the relationship of the persons *I: you*. Hence we shall find only the forms of the "third person" in a historical narrative strictly followed. (206-7)

For Benveniste, the historical utterance is characterized in opposition to the autobiographical by its use of the "simple past" or "past definite" (the French "passé simple," which Benveniste prefers to call by its Greek name, the "aorist"), which is always in the third person. The imperfect and the pluperfect are also historical tenses for Benveniste; the present, however, is excluded, with the exception of a present to which Benveniste refers as "atemporal," an instance of which would be the "present of definition."[1] It is this combination of tense and person that characterizes "history," whether this be the evocation of historical events themselves or the invention of a novelist. His statement in this regard is categorical:

> It can be stated as a fact that anyone who knows how to write and who undertakes the narration of past events spontaneously employs the aorist as the fundamental tense, whether he evokes these events as a historian or creates them as a novelist. (210)

The "autobiographical form par excellence" according to Benveniste, however, is "the perfect in the first person," for "the perfect creates a living connection between the past event and the present in which its evocation takes place" (210). Thus, if the historical utterance is characterized here as the objective presentation of events (real or invented) without intervention from the narrator—"As a matter of fact, there is then no longer even a narrator. . . . No one speaks here; the events seem to narrate themselves"[2]—then discourse, and with it autobiography, is characterized "by contrast" by its pragmatic situation, by the indispensable presence of speakers or transmitters who make use of word or pen in an attempt to influence in some way their interlocutor or audience. We have here the well-known definition of discourse formulated by Benveniste: "Any utterance assuming a speaker and a hearer, and in the speaker, the intention of influencing the other in some way" (209).

The distinction established by Benveniste between historical and discursive utterance has as its base the complementary distribution of tenses and persons in the French verb, a distribution that explicates via the establishment of two taxonomic morphosyntactic axes, in contrast to the traditional grammars that established the paradigms of French conjugation based exclusively on a morphological point of view. This distinction has been received by critics as universal, despite the failure of such a complementary distribution of tense and person to hold up in other languages. German and English use only the imperfect, both in written and in spoken language, because no other simple form of the past is available to them; Latin and Spanish employ the aorist (indefinite) in the first person, with the result that there is no temporal difference between narration in the third person and the first. The antonomastic example of the Latin aorist is Caesar's "Veni, vidi, vici"—and it would indeed be difficult in this sentence to establish a clear border between history and autobiography as Benveniste differentiates them. The epic preterit is known in all of these languages, in each person, singular and plural; but the distinction is irrelevant from the point of view of modern narrative theories and speech act theory. Regardless of whether the utterance has the same grammatical subject or another (second or third person), the enunciating subject of the utterance, explicit or not in the text, is still a subject, individual or collective, that speaks (or writes) in the first person, singular or plural (without the plural necessarily signifying multiplicity, given the use of the "majestic plural," the royal we). And there is no utterance without an enunciating subject who assumes it in an act of parole.[3] Thus, the difference between a discourse of "I" (or "we") about itself and a discourse about a second or third person (singular as well as plural) in which the speaker is equally "I" or "we" is a difference between objects, not between uttering subjects. There is no doubt, then, that we are always dealing with a (first) person who guarantees the uttering as an instance of utterance, constituting himself or herself as an uttering subject.[4] Hence I include in the autobiographical genre the autobiography written (or dictated, as in the case of Ignacio de Loyola) in third person, a modality held dear by the Jesuits and customarily explained as a gesture of humility.[5] I note it as a break with the traditional model of the instructive spiritual autobiography, a break that becomes in turn a model for generating new texts.

The preceding considerations are not to be taken as an attempt to return to an individualistic subjectivism that affirms the position of the uttering subject as the true organizing demiurge or creator of the autobiographical text, of biography, and of history in general. I speak of narrative discourse, regrouping its subgenres and characterizing it as uttered by an individual or collective subject that refers back to its past in order to explain its present, precisely in order to show that the autobiography functions in the double tension that frames all narration. As discourse, one must always understand autobiography as existing vis-à-vis a receiver/audience or at least vis-à-vis the explicit narratee to whom it is directed with the intention of "influencing it in some way." In its function as social convention, all discourse is inscribed in a social framework as well, with a logic that must be respected by all coherent narration, with norms that regulate the uses of the word (and genre), with the values recognized in acts, gestures, and words—in sum, with the entire repertory of imperatives of behavior (ethic as well as linguistic) and aspirations (individual and collective) that all individuals unconsciously internalize from infancy onward and that constitute the parental and social superego instance. There is also that double tension we saw earlier wherein the enunciating subjects of autobiography, in the selection and strategic ordering of their narratives, are more or less conscious of the heterogenous composition (on the cognitive as well as on the affective levels) of their audience. The anonymous author of *Lazarillo* demonstrates an extraordinary awareness of this reality. If, on the one hand, he imitates faithfully a preconstructed and repetitive model as discursive officiality or ritual, on the other, he fills it with folkloric anecdotes (which the character shows as untrue of the supposed vita). Furthermore, the effort expended in assuring coherence between the narrated events and the final resulting situation shows at the same time the fictionality and the verisimilitude of the account (see especially Gómez-Moriana 1980a). This verisimilitude is more indispensable for audience persuasion than is truth itself, as Plato well knew (hence his condemnation of well-organized discourse capable, through rhetorical antics, of persuading both judge and audience—a discourse whose persuasive effectiveness is decisively exemplified by Gorgias's *laudatio* of Helen and defense of Palamedes).

Thus there is in *Lazarillo* a working on language, on ritual discursive practices, and on other media, verbal or nonverbal, of interaction active in its context and which the text disarticulates. Here the way *Lazarillo* reads history and inscribes itself in it can be seen. Other texts operate on a lower level of consciousness, which does not mean, however, that they do not function according to the program already designed by traditional rhetoric in the selection of elements to be transmitted (*inventio*), their strategic ordering (*dispositio*) and their formulation in the tone most appropriate to the desired end (*elocutio*). An analysis from this perspective of the autobiography of Teresa de Avila would open the way to an understanding of more than the mere sophism of such apparent naiveté. This end, and the relevance of the means leading to it, is not the work of the individual who writes; it is a question of sociohistorical variables, moments that act as stimuli for that to which all the rhetorical devices used are but part of an answer. The history of the autobiography should be limited neither to the history of writing nor to its mere classification as model or rupture, as if each new wave were no more than the result of a rupture with the previous model. I would include those stimuli (sociohistorical variables) with which autobiographies dialogue (consciously or unconsciously) in their argumentative discourse. In discursive narration this refers to the response to a stimulus of functional (self-)representations that obey a series of axiological postulates, and not merely the horizon of purely generic or literary expectations. Not always explicit in the text, these postulates must be discovered by their implicit presence in the text in which, without saying it, the narrator responds to meet his or her own needs.

An example from everyday experience, itself a brief, functional autobiography, will illustrate this individual-social dialogue in which I inscribe the autobiographical narrative — the curriculum vitae. In a world framed by the division of labor, specialization has become an imperative. An applicant for a position will have to construct a curriculum vitae that responds to the specialty described in a want ad or professional listing. This will be the more or less conscious criterion that the subject-utterer will put into play when selecting which courses and professional activities to list. Other courses or activities might go unmentioned, certainly those inappropriate to or incompatible with the training required by the position. Furthermore, the same individual applying for two or more positions — not unusual in today's world — would probably prepare not one curriculum, but several, to respond to the specific requirements of each "external stimulus." Undoubtedly, the *curricula* will have much in common with each other, especially the formal aspect of their presentation; but they will differ in other aspects, especially in content, in the personality described in the historical unfolding, given that the applicant must respond in each case to a different function. In this dimension of functionality lies the truth of a *curriculum vitae*. Through functionality we may read the stimulus-response tension or, in other words, the subject-utterer/society framework in which the text is inscribed. It would be an error, then, to analyze curricula in the absence of the texts describing the positions, as if one were dealing with autonomous and autotelic texts. This practice of ignoring the context of textual production is a direct extrapolation from principles of immanentist structuralism, including individualist psychology, for all the depth that one might find in such (psycho)analysis. The latter will always be partial, since it will analyze the id without taking into account the superego. Furthermore, by analyzing the id one imagines oneself to be analyzing the subjective individuality of the author—and this signals the return to the traditional biography mentioned earlier.

To alleviate this lack in the curriculum vitae—in the autobiography if not in all historiography—I propose that we investigate that other text that exists within the "actual" text, the one that is explicitly absent but present in the implicit dialogue that it generates. It is simply a matter of analyzing the text with all the understandings and suppositions, as well as all the informational assumptions, with which it holds dialogue. A curriculum vitae, an autobiography, will be presented to us as an incomplete syllogism, an enthymeme whose major premise (the supposition) will be the description of the vacant position. In the case of an autobiography that is destined for publication and thus more widely diffused, this supposition would be the horizon shared by the uttering subject and his multilayered (that is, spatially and temporally as well as cognitively and axiologically layered) audience. The text of the curriculum—the autobiography—would be but the minor premise, and in its quality we should analyze the actualized verbal part. The context is considered here as an integral part of that whole, larger and more complex than the sum of the phonemes, morphemes, or lexemes that the subject-utterer emits or transcribes in the act of communication. The conclusion, explicit or implicit, will enable us to judge the accuracy of the selection of the rhetorical means deployed by the subject-utterer.

If my hypothesis is accepted, we will agree that a curriculum vitae, an autobiography, is but an argument that responds to the stimulus of a specific variable, and that one will have to inquire into the social horizon of expectations in which is inscribed the curriculum (autobiography).[6] Clearly, this is not new: I am merely taking a backward step in order to link present narrative and discursive theories with the Sophist models and classical oratory developed by Rome in its juridical function (defense of the accused) and political role (manipulation of the Senate and people). This functionality changes when the Jesuits, for instance, appropriate it for their theological arguments or for sacred oratory, or when the modern world appropriates it for commercial purposes to influence mass consumption, tastes, and ideas. It is through the study of these functionalities and modes of argumentation that the history of the autobiographical models and their changes can be established, for in them matter and form (or content and style) are individually and socially united. The landmarks of the history of autobiography, as testimonies not only of an individual but of an epoch, thus turn out to be the landmarks of collective history. Here we may find the reason behind the simultaneous predominance at a certain historical period of the spiritual, the soldier, and (as a counterpoint) the picaresque autobiography. In a subsequent age, we witness the secularization and change of feudal mentality into bourgeois mentality, where the latter produces a new autobiographical style, a new type of adventure and merit that coincide with the disappearance of the picaresque, at least in its progenitive tone, perhaps because that tone becomes the currently dominant style.

Returning to the curriculum, this time with a concrete text, we see that the use of the curriculum as an example presaged the study of the Cervantes text about to be presented. Among the hundreds of curricula soliciting positions in the Indies (authentic autobiographies at times, many of which are preserved in Seville's *Archivo General de Indias*), we find that presented by Cervantes.[7] We know of Cervantes's petition through his biographers' references as well as from its negative result. Perhaps thanks to this denial we now have texts like *Don Quijote* and the *Novelas ejemplares*. What is certain, however, is that this document shows us, contrary to the often-affirmed statement, that Cervantes's father had done everything within his power to raise the ransom for his captive son in Algeria after having spent his diminished fortune to rescue Miguel's brother Rodrigo de Cervantes, also captive in Algeria. Although curious names and facts appear in the adduced testimonies, it is less the facts of Cervantes's life that attract my attention than the silences and lacunae of the writer—lacunae where I believe one can discern an interesting criterion of selection that follows the strategy that Cervantes considered most propitious for obtaining the solicited position.

As Ignacio de Loyola through Rivadeneira have done before him, Cervantes presents himself through a relator, Dr. Nuñez, who offers an entire curriculum that emphasizes Cervantes's services to "His Majesty," especially as a soldier who lost an arm at Lepanto, who had fought earlier in Italy, Goleta, and Tunisia, and who suffered long captivity in Algeria. The self-presentation is accompanied by a document from the Duke of Sesa, and the response prepared by Cervantes's father in 1578 is incorporated in this curriculum with a new rubric dated May 29, 1590, in Madrid. Its presentation, however, somewhat postdates it, since it begins with the declaration that he "has served for the past 22 years; in the naval battle there, he lost a hand when he was shot with an arquebuse." If twenty-two years have elapsed since the battle of Lepanto (October 7, 1571), it would be 1593. When he wrote this curriculum, Cervantes had for some time known success in the theater with works such as *La destrucción de Numancia*, *Los tratos de Argel*, and *La batalla naval*; he had brought about a whole series of changes in the *comedia*, if his own testimony in another curriculum vitae, that of letters and not of arms is to be believed;[8] he published *La Galatea* in 1585; he contracted marriage with Catalina de Salazar y Palacios. None of this appears in this curriculum, just as the other makes no mention of his life as a soldier. But whereas his literary curriculum deals only with the publication of his unstaged theatrical works and thus covers only the activity relevant to that specific area, the solicitation for a position in the Indies should logically entail a more complete curriculum. Or would one not serve his majesties in sixteenth-and seventeenth-century Spain by authoring comedies, novels, or poetry? The response seems to be negative. At the very least, Cervantes must not have considered his writing of fiction a relevant qualification for obtaining a position in the Indies.

Chapter 5
Evocation as a Literary Procedure in *Don Quijote*

Under the pretext, by no means original at that time, of parodying books of chivalry, *Don Quijote* emerges as a true *Literaturroman*.[1] This dimension of Cervantes's novel surfaces not only at the level of the story, as it relates the antics of a fool whose pathological distortions of his readings lead him to confuse fiction with reality, but also at the level of narration, which strictly speaking consists of a discursive and fictitious historical interplay between author, reader, and text.[2] In this manner, it can account both for its own production in the novel itself as well as for its reception: indeed, the first part of the novel, the *Don Quijote* of 1605, as well as Avellaneda's imitation of 1614 become reading-books in the *Don Quijote* of 1615 and the subject of discussion between the novel's characters. In one such discussion Don Quijote and Sancho consider themselves objectively dealt with by Cervantes but denounce the lack of objectivity in Avellaneda's treatment.[3] A semiotic play is at hand here: while his (distorted) interpretation of novels of chivalry delineates Don Quijote's program (and Cervantes's narration) in the second part of the novel, the dukes' and other characters' reading of the first part will allow them to enact that program and, more particularly, the promise made to Sancho to raise him to the rank of governor of an island. Literature is thus a prophecy that becomes historical reality once it is embodied by the various characters of the fable who know how to interpret it, or once it is materialized in the events that these characters recognize as the accomplishment of what was announced and therefore awaited.[4]

What is at hand here is far removed both from the mechanical reproduction of a traditional institutionalized model, which implies adhesion to that model and to its value system, and from the parodical deformation of the chivalresque epic.

65

"Parody of chivalresque novels," "a chivalresque novel nevertheless, the last and, perhaps, the best of all" — such typical assessments hardly exhaust the complex reality of *Don Quijote,* given the array of stimuli merging in it and the various means by which Cervantes appropriates these stimuli and enters into a dialogue with them. To understand *Don Quijote* as a semiosis, it is necessary to inquire into the whys and wherefores of the redistributed elements in the textual space or, to use Bakhtin's term, the *dialogical space.*

If every text is a mosaic in which are organized disparate elements borrowed from the cultural legacy of a social group or community, then only by grasping both the function of the text's elements within the text itself and their function in other texts from which they proceed, can one gain — through a sort of cross-reference — a better understanding of what Julia Kristeva (1968) calls *productivity of meaning.* As we saw earlier, the components of a text carry a mark or semantic load by having been previously integrated in other signifying systems or texts during the course of their cultural past or present, or what Mikhaïl Bakhtin calls the *chronotopos* of sign organization. However novel the function assigned to borrowed elements, the sanction by use weighing upon these elements persists and therefore cannot be disregarded. These elements thus act on the reader not only through what the author has them say, but also through what they themselves convey and perhaps, as is the case of subversion, through the dialectical conflict or opposition between a sign's two dimensions.

In this intertwining, we must note both the elements or borrowings that are explicitly integrated in the new text and the allusions that are likely to bring to the reader's mind — without any explicit explanation — the stories, ideas, myths, or realities of daily life. The allusion or implied motif is not usually recorded as one of the story's functional elements; it breaks instead the syntagmatic string, inducing the reader to switch from short-term memory — the memory used to follow the thread of the story — to long-term memory — that used to identify what is referred to by allusion (Teun A. van Dijk, 1980). The element with the power of recall that we ascribe to allusion thus functions in the text as an anaphoric element, though not in the transphrasal but in the transtextual sense: it refers to a cultural patrimony shared by the author and the reader. This presupposes that the information necessary to reading the text exists in its writing or production. An authentic dialogue is thus established between the text's organizing transmitter and its addressee, that is, the receiver likely to recognize its evocative allusions.

Because it presupposes more information than it delivers, every statement is in reality incomplete in everyday as well as in literary communication. Explicit information in a statement is but a key that opens up an entire context and world of which it is part; such information is but a fragment of a larger and more complex unit of representations and memories that it can conjure before the receiver. I am not referring only to pronouns, deictics, or anaphoric elements deciphered in an intratextual context; even if their reference to past or future information is assumed, these elements usually refer to a statement in the text itself and thus reinforce the texture of the literary work—or of verbal communication, which also consists of texts and not merely of independent utterances.[5] Neither am I referring to the context of communication, to the *hic et nunc* of the utterance where the speakers' presence reveals the pronouns' referents because of the concrete intersubjectivity of the "I" and "you" in the act of communication, particularly oral communication. I am referring more specifically to the rhetorical figure that Fontanier describes in his *Figures du discours* as "allusion." The allusion consists of bringing to mind the connection between something that is said and something that remains unmentioned. This allusive dynamic I shall call *evocation*. Paul Zumthor (1976), inspired by Julia Kristeva's "Grammes lecturaux," groups "citation" and "réminiscence" under modalities of "variation," which is defined in a narrower sense than the *variatio* of rhetoric: "a procedure which consists of introducing in the text, either—literally—parts of a pre-existing text, or—allusively—formal markings considered as characteristics of a specific group of other texts" (323).

Referring to the French *grands rhétoriqueurs*, Zumthor mentions other intertextual forms, all of which are characterized in the text by the tension between mention and diction, between a *continuum mémoriel* (the living cultural tradition maintained in texts) and the text itself (a concrete performance with the more or less considerable transformation that diction always operates on mention). Together with variation, we have duplication and *conjonction des discours*: whereas duplication generates polyisotopic texts by means of the opposition between *lettre* and figuration, the complex phenomenon of *conjonction des discours* results from a "symbiotic combination, in the text, of two (or sometimes more) distinct codes, whose chosen elements may be decoded as well in one as in the other" (330).

All of these forms of allusion can be found to some extent in *Don Quijote*. Their manipulation by Cervantes is what I have called evocation as a literary procedure. Before we enter into a more detailed analysis, we should first examine the transition from the poetic discursive code to the veiled reminder of inquisitorial discourse in the narration of the scrutiny of Don Quijote's library that closes the first cycle of adventures and that some critics call the proto-*Quijote* or Urtext.[6] The first of the three cycles that constitute the whole of Cervantes's *Don Quijote* can be considered a novella that serves (by way of *amplificatio*) as the basis for Cervantes's later creation of a first corpus, the *Don Quijote* of 1605, and of a second one, the *Don Quijote* of 1615, in response to Avellaneda's *Quijote*. The text as a whole can also be considered to have been conceived as such from the very beginning. At any rate, there is no doubt that the first six chapters of *Don Quijote* form an entity that begins with the description of the hidalgo from La Mancha and his obsession with chivalry books and that closes—after his having put his readings into practice—with the eradication of the cause of his madness, the hidalgo's library. The logic of the narrative is impeccable: that the characters who intervene in the mise-en-scène of the library's destruction—the village priest, the governess, and the niece — all know the source of Don Quijote's antics is thus a breach neither of that logical thread nor of the reader's range of expectations.[7] Attentive readers will first be puzzled as they become aware of something to which little attention has been paid: the appropriation of lexical elements pertaining to other discourses, discursive displacements that create the polyisotopy described earlier. These displacements are barely perceptible in a first reading, for the various discourses produced by the narrator and the characters belong to what Michel Foucault (1969, 270) calls *espaces corrélatifs*. This might well explain literary criticism's oversight of such discursive displacements.[8] Because it was taken for granted that Cervantes's voice is echoed in those of the priest and the barber, literary criticism has indeed concerned itself more with the identification of the works in the library and with the priest's and barber's evaluation of their literary merit, thereby hoping to uncover Cervantes's own literary opinions. That Cervantes is cited as the author of *La Galatea* and that the text includes an appraisal of his life and art has only elicited praise for Cervantes's ingenious "self-criticism."

Let us, however, examine the vocabulary deployed in those literary evaluations: books are described as "sources of evil, injurious, excommunicated, damned" and (in the narrator's own words) as "innocents." Don Quijote's niece thinks that none should be pardoned and that all had best be burned, while the priest would rather examine them, "for it might happen some to be found, which in no sort deserved to be chastised with fire" (1:56). A dialogue follows in which verbal phrases like "forgive," "condemn to the stake," "have mercy," "make use of justice," "be worthy of pardon," and "spare someone's life for now" predominate. An instance of the superimposition of both discourses, the literary and the inquisitorial, can be found in the appraisal of the four books of *Amadís de Gaula*. At the priest's behest, the barber turns the books over to him "one by one" so that he might "read the titles at the least of everie book" and "peruse their arguments" (1:56-57):

> The first that Master Nicholas put into his hands, was that of *Amadis of Gaule*; which the Curate perusing a while, This comes not to me first of all others, without some mysterie: for as I have heard tolde, this is the first booke of Knighthood that ever was printed in Spaine, and all the others have had their beginning and origninall from this; and therefore me thinkes that we must condemne him to the fire, without all remission, as the Dogmatizer and head of so badde a sect. Not so, fie, quoth the Barber, for I have heard that it is the very best contrived booke of all those of that kinde, and therefore he is to be pardoned as the onely complete one of his profession. That is true, replied the Curate, and for that reason we doe give him his life for this time Let us see that other which lies next unto him. (1:57)

Stephen Gilman (1970) notes in the so-called literary criticism of Cervantes (which he prefers to consider instead of his sources — that is, López Pinciano and other Aristotelians so frequently mentioned by scholars — in order to grasp Cervantes's critical thoughts objectively) "the shocking use of inquisitorial terminology in expressing his literary judgments." Gilman compares the scrutiny commented upon here with the "second micro-scrutiny" of chapter 32 (regarding one of the few books Juan Palomeque keeps in his inn to be read at harvest time). He also compares it with the discussion on literary theory through which the canon (a "new alter ego, more cultivated than that of the priest and the barber") expresses the opinions Cervantes holds after the "evolution" brought about by his "creative activity" and the "satisfaction" he feels "upon seeing his novel completed, full-grown and very much alive." Gilman finds "unthinkable" the possibility that "the scrutiny could be a direct and superficial parody of the Holy Office." Although he admits that "the priest and the barber proceed rather summarily and carelessly at times," Gilman nevertheless maintains that "the opinions they express are those of Cervantes," and he goes so far as to add, "On this subject, it would be very risky to disagree with the critics of *Don Quijote*. We cannot therefore, absolve *Don Quijote*'s 'stepfather' from his responsibility as the creator of this implacable literary tribunal" (6). In order to mute Cervantes's "responsibility" (for want of absolving him), Gilman points out that the "violence of the critical language" is not a phenomenon specific to the Spanish Golden Age because it still exists today, and that in the case of Cervantes, it might be a linguistic echo of the polemic against Góngora and his followers. Nevertheless, according to Gilman, "it is clear that if Cervantes borrowed the Inquisition's figures of speech, he did so not for their violence but rather as a parable in order to show us his own critical stand" (8).

I cite Gilman as an extreme example of the difficulties mentioned earlier encountered by literary criticism. Although he understands the inquisitorial practices and recognizes the relationship between these practices and the chapter under consideration, Gilman can free himself neither from the traditional identification of Cervantes with his characters, nor from the no less traditional practice of trying to uphold Cervantes's opinion at all costs.[9]

In spite of how "unthinkable" some critics may find the inquisitorial connections, in addition to the aforementioned discursive displacements we also find in the text a series of allusions that are parts of a picture or icon that evokes the inquisitorial scene, above all to a public familiar with it: the governess appears with a bowl and sprinkler of holy water; the stake is mentioned twice; the enclosure where it is usually erected, the "corral," seven times; "fire," eight times; "smoke," once; "ashes," once; the verb "to burn" in various forms, nine times; the verb "to set ablaze," once; and the verb "to blaze," once. The same characters exchange the deliberative function of the ecclesiastic tribunal for the executive function of the "secular arm" — a technical term mentioned in the text. The twofold mise-en-scène (of the inquisitorial tribunal and of the auto-da-fé or execution of the sentence) almost immediately brings to mind the two activities of the Holy Office: the scrutiny of private libraries and bookstores, and the trial of persons. This occurs within a doubly metonymical symbiosis (the book in lieu of the character, the book in lieu of the author) that ends with a second evocation, inasmuch as the condemned books are personified.

A few examples: *Amadís de Gaula*, as we have seen, is called a "dogmatizer and head of so badde a sect"; after its fate is discussed, it is decided that "we doe give him his life for this time." Of the *Sergas de Espandián* ("Amadis of Gaules lawfully begotten sonne"), the priest says that "his fathers goodness shall nothing availe him," and with these words, "good Esplandián" is thrown into the courtyard "to expect with all patience the fire which he was threatened to abide." *Don Olivante de Laura* will also end up in the courtyard for being "foolish and arrogant"; the *Caballero Platir* shall keep the others company "without any replie"; the characters of *Espejo de caballerías* are condemned to perpetual banishment; and *Don Belianis* is accorded an "overseas term" (*terminus ultramarinus*, that is to say, a postponement) that should allow him to "purge his excessive choler." As with the others that have escaped burning at the stake, "as they are corrected, so will we use mercy or justice towards them." The same fate awaits Cervantes's *La Galatea*: it is kept prisoner (*recluso*) while the second part announced by the author is awaited, and "perhaps his amendment may obtaine him a generall remission." The author of *Tirant lo Blanc* is sent to the galleys because of his excellence—a lesser sentence in any case than that of many books thrown so heedlessly into the fire "without further search or regard" that the narrator adds in conclusion, "If the Curate had seene them, they should not have past under so rigorous a sentence" (1:64).

These discursive displacements—from literary criticism to inquisitorial discourse, from deliberative to executive discourse, and from censorial (of books) to judicial discourse about individuals—merge so perfectly in the text that the transition from one to the other is almost imperceptible. The sentencing of the *Amadís de Gaula* was an example of the displacement from literary criticism to inquisitorial discourse. Let us now examine an example of the transition from deliberative to executive and from censorial to judicial discourse:

> This that followes is *Florismarte of Hircania*, quoth the Barber. Is Lord Florismarte there? Then replied the Curate, Then by mine honesty hee shall briefly make his arrest in the yard, in despite of his wonderfull birth and famous adventures; for the drouth and harshnesse of his stile deserves no greater favor. To the yard with him, and this other (Good Masters). With a very good will, Sir, quoth old Mumpsimus; and straightway did execute his commaundement with no small gladnesse. (1:58)

The visiting and subsequent expurgating of bookstores and private libraries (above all upon the death of their owner and before the heirs were authorized to appropriate and distribute their contents) begins as an inquisitorial practice in

1558. Not only the "heretical, dubious, and scandalous" books forbidden by the famous Index but also any book printed abroad (without state or ecclesiastical censorship and therefore not subject to royal decrees and duties) could be confiscated or burnt publicly during these visits.[10] These practices of the Holy Office evoked by *Don Quijote* were surely well known to its readers. For today's reader, unfamiliar with these inquisitorial practices, the evocative power of those hints or allusions will be null or almost so. Such is the inherently ephemeral nature of parody. As Zumthor (1976) tells us, "The more manifest and stable is the tradition (the better known and acknowledged as 'natural' are its characteristic tropes), the more effective is the parody. Hence the recurrence of play on words with a tendency to distort religious discourses at a time when the Church, though shaken, has lost none of its mythical power" (324-25).

Conversely, an evocation that proves excessively remote and irrelevant to the present day will be ineffectual and will make all the more difficult the interpretation of the text apart from the sphere of its creation. The more removed a text from the cultural arena of its production, the more difficult it will be to spot the trace of the discursive and ideological practices recalled by its components. This is why I have emphasized the need to understand the text as a sort of crossroads, as an echo of one or more previous discourses on the basis of which a new one is generated and where transformational rules intervene to govern the new performance. Along with the confluence in every text of elements taken from preceding texts (the diachronic dimension) and the reelaboration or redistribution of these elements in the new text (the synchronic dimension), we must also try to uncover the new purpose that underlies that redistribution (the teleological dimension) and the unit's organization in accordance with a strategy befitting that purpose (the pragmatic dimension of textual production). Only by taking into account these dimensions will we understand the signifying dynamics of a literary work.

To fulfill this broad program, we must also attempt to reconstruct what W. Schmid (1973) calls *die zitierte Welt*, the quoted universe. Complementing the "universes" identified by Harald Weinrich (1971), the described universe or *besprochene Welt* and the narrated one or *erzählte Welt*, Schmid describes the quoted (or evoked?) universe as "the universe recalled by the discourse of the novel's characters." Referring to the *Textaufbau* of Dostoyevski's narrative production, Schmid stresses that every character in a novel represents an interpretative and ideological stance likely to confirm, complement, or contradict other ideological stances in the novel that form part of *die dargestellte Welt*, the whole represented universe (27). Moreover, if fictional actors (aside from characters) turn out to represent various narrative voices (particularly the narrator or narrators who perform in styles that range from interior monologue to third-person narration with the distancing of indirect free speech, passing through the autonomous character's discourse, direct speech, and so on), then the framework of the novel may be considered "plurivocal" or polyphonic. In the novel a confrontation thus occurs between various enunciative instances, undermining the monological vision that would have everything originate from the author. This plurivocal framework, moreover, has the advantage of being able to conjugate several relationships between fictitious universe and external discursive reality.

Wladimir Krysinski (1975) points out that from Cervantes to Broch and Arno Schmidt, including Dostoyevski, Joyce, and Musil, the novel is defined as a *volonté de totalité*, with the result that "the novel's significance merges with the image of reality as a whole." If such is the case, then the semiosis of reading (the text's recreation, which complements a first semiosis, or the "novelist's organization of signification," so Krysinski tells us) is but "a decoding of the novel's signs that the reader must put into relation with a reference" (70). This is why Krysinski speaks of a "lock on reference" and a "quest for reference" by the author and the reader of every novel. No global signification exists in the novel, only "particular sign configurations forever creating meaning by locking in on reference" (71).[11] There is in other words just the reading of a reading: the reading of the novel is at the same time the reading of reality and the reading of the genre's peculiar system or program; that is, the novelist's double transcoding (or "compiling," to use Krysinski's computer terminology). "First the novelist interprets reality, then he interprets the system, a sort of absolute novel, or he produces the novelistic genre as a program" (73).

This reading, which links the writing of the novel with the writing of religion (see Grivel et al. 1979), is manifested in Cervantes's text through a manifold narrative conscience in which all *Don Quijote* "actors" take a stand vis-à-vis the external world and the literary genre of the novel in which they operate. As a function of this stand, each echoes various discursive practices pertaining to respective correlative spheres by way of the discursive displacements mentioned earlier. *Don Quijote* thus evokes the complex reality of its era through a contradictory or complementary framework in which converge the most varied discursive types, some justifiable within fiction (in accordance with various "regions of the imagination" described by Martínez Bonati [1977]) and some less justifiable owing to the ritualistic character of their use in the *chronotopos* from which Cervantes drew them. The less justifiable types form a "usurped discourse," to use Edmond Cros's expression about Quevedo's Buscón, whose function in *Don Quijote* has apparently been insufficiently studied.

To remedy this lacuna, we should first examine the convergence in *Don Quijote* of various legitimized and contemporary discourses, focusing also on their use or abuse by the novel's actors. Having established the discourses' boundaries or "selection restrictions," an examination of their possible displacements should include other regions (the discursive areas adjoining each of the "regions of the imagination") and thus demonstrate that the distinction between regions is less ontological than conventional. If this hypothesis is confirmed, then the issue in the fiction/reality dichotomy (often equated with the dichotomy of literary/ scientific, historical, economic discourses) is not that of the presence or absence of an objective predicate—as if the referent of the second group were unbiased reality and that of the first, free creative imagination. Discourses feed on one another, and every discourse must distance itself from its object in order to transcend the latter's presence and reach its representation.[12] Every discourse is therefore an organized arrangement not of realities but of concepts and, as such, is always of a symbolic character and of a contractual value. The distance between scientific and literary discourse becomes a historical and cultural variable, a convention, in other words, that varies according to place and epoch.

Once the issue has been stated in this manner, it becomes important to highlight the communicative value, the effect, of a particular type of discourse on a particular type of reader. No less important is establishing the pertinence of a given discourse in accordance with the norm laid down by the "circumstance ritual" which constitutes, along with the "object taboo" and the "speaker [subject]'s privileged right," according to Michel Foucault (1971), the first external control imposed by society on the use of any discourse. This external control composed of three elements in perpetual mutation is *l'interdit*, the prohibited. Foucault describes this first group of restrictions imposed by every society on the use of discourse as follows:

> We know very well that we are not allowed to say everything, that we
> may not speak of everything in every circumstance, that everyone,
> finally, cannot say everything. Object taboo, circumstance ritual,
> speaker's privileged right: here are the three types of prohibitions that
> intermix, reinforce or compensate for one another, forming a complex
> grid that is continually modified. (11)

On the basis of these three components of society's first instrument of external control over discursive practices, and of those practices' conventions and changing value, I tried in an earlier chapter to determine some of the criteria of acceptability, or grammaticality, of a given work's discursive practices in order to grasp what I have called the "subversion of ritual discourse." By different means, but also with the understanding that the contractual character of circumstances allows for a certain type of discourse, Félix Martínez Bonati (1977) has shown the relationship in Cervantes's work between the character's spatial change and the passage from one "stylistic convention" to another, from one "region of the imagination" to another. According to Martínez Bonati, this "display and contrast between the regions of the imagination" already appears in *La Galatea* and persists in *Persiles*, passing through *Don Quijote* and the *Novelas ejemplares* whose whole, he tells us, "glows magnificently when observed through the transparent variety of the spectrum of the imagination." His hypothesis is framed as follows:

> Generally, *Don Quijote* presents its characters on their way, going from
> one adventure to the next (and from one conversation to another),
> changing places over and over again. There are, of course, certain kinds
> of places that appear more than once: Quijote's homestead, the "camino

real,'' the inn, the woodland, the hidalgos and señores' residences. The
mere change of position—from one spot to another in the ''camino
real,'' for example—does not imply in general a more significant
change, a relocation of the imaginary ambience. But I believe that the
moves from one type of place to another correspond, more frequently
than merely exceptionally, to an alteration of the stylistic convention. In
such moments we can sense that not only are we passing from one point
to another in Don Quijote and Sancho's itinerary, but we are also
moving to a different sphere of literary fantasy. (44)

It seems unnecessary to insist on the difference between the changes described
by Martínez Bonati and the space transfer functions (function 15 in Propp's inventory, 10 in Greimas's), the departure from the family sphere (11 in Propp, 7 in
Greimas) and the return to it (20 in Propp, 14 in Greimas). These functions aim
at a condensation of the tale into episodic units on the basis of which Propp will
interpret the tale's syntagmatic units as stable semantic segments. From this
closed inventory and these ordered sequences, Propp will be able to draw out
constants despite the numerous manifestations of each of these constants in the
popular Russian short story corpus he examines in his *Morphology*. The spatial
changes or ''atmosphere'' noted by Martínez Bonati refer to the laws of the text
or type of discourse in use and to the complicity pact between author and reader
that allows a type of discourse to be acceptable according to circumstance. In
other words, whereas Propp's functions refer to the unfolding of the plot, the correspondence between spatial and stylistic change noted by Martínez Bonati refers
to the narrative art of the tale in accordance with its own norms of verisimilitude.

Quijote's intrigue progresses within the frame of three departures from the
family sphere and three returns to it, in a thrice circular structure. But the unfolding of the plot interests us here less than the convergence of various discourses promoted and emphasized by the spatial setting—something similar to
the well-known *composición de lugar* that precedes every meditation in Ignacio
de Loyola's *Exercises*.[13] This convergence has allowed Martínez Bonati (and myself, as a follower) to break free from the simplifying outline imposed like a
straitjacket on *Don Quijote* by traditional literary critics who would reduce the
novel to a conflict between Don Quijote's fantastical idealizations and the realistic vision of the world presented first by the narrator and then by Sancho and
other characters.

Martínez Bonati (1977) describes how Cervantes avails himself of various
means in order to pass from one imaginary region to the other: he occasionally
marks this transition by a series of thematic (or ''tonal'') anticipations, by violent
contrasts, or by the ''superimposition'' or ''collision'' of several stylistic conventions ''within which opposite archetypes are blended or linked (at times dis-
cordantly).'' The examples Martínez Bonati proposes (and others could be
added; his purpose was not to exhaust the subject in the framework of his article)
show the adaptation by and integration into *Don Quijote* of the entire literary rep-

ertory of Cervantes's time: the epic, the popular epic, the courtly, the chivalresque, the historical, the Moorish, the tragic, the sentimental, the pastoral, the
Byzantine, and the picaresque novel, comedy, and so forth. As we follow Don
Quijote and Sancho in their journey through the imaginary replicas of Spanish
highways and byways, we ourselves are "passing through our literary fantasy's
interior regions: through our close vision of daily and domestic experience, we
may reach the idealization of comedy, romance, chivalry; pastoral utopia; picaresque comedy; baroque hyperbole; courtly intrigue and Byzantine peripeteia—in
short, a system of aesthetic conventions with common and opposite characteristics, perhaps binarily so" (51).

One should note, however, as Martínez Bonati (1977) briefly does, that the
aesthetic regions in *Don Quijote* "seem to have a weak spot in their structure,
something like an area where stylistic violence betrays itself," or what he calls
elsewhere the "form's transcendental excess" (48). From this consideration,
Martínez Bonati infers that Cervantes's ironic style consists of turning the constituent forms of literary imagination into objective components. He thus calls
Cervantes's work a *crítica de la razón poética* (albeit a tacit one), for it exposes,
as we have seen, the "conditions and limits of imaginative experience." It is true
that *Don Quijote* is not merely a parody of chivalry books and pastoral romances
in the style of baroque realism, as critics have often maintained. *Don Quijote*
evinces an ironic break with all literary representations or, as Martínez Bonati
puts it, "an estrangement of literature itself from its constituent form." By converting the literary forms of his time into an actual theme, Cervantes makes of
literature an objective phenomenon whose system of poetics can be parodied.
Don Quijote, then, is a "satire of literature itself as a whole" (42), although this
does not exclude Cervantes's own creative input. "Irony turned on itself in a literary production does not thwart the display of the creation's expressiveness and
vitality" (52).

If we rephrase Martínez Bonati's conclusions, we could say that Cervantes, by
revealing in *Don Quijote* all of the subjacent laws of literary (only literary?) discourse, performs a kind of archeology of its systems of signification. Narrative
conscience would thus go much further than would the rhetorical awareness of
persuasive tactics or textual strategies (pragmatics) in including—together with
the writer's savoir faire, his competence—a metarhetorical, metapragmatic, and
epistemological intelligence. Not only is Cervantes a reader who interprets signs
according to a particular code and becomes a writer or performing reader (that is,
a reader who interprets by means of a new semiosis taken from the very same
code); he is also a watchful witness to and active denouncer of the semiotic process that he reveals and unmasks.

If what I have called a writer-reader favors the paradigm over the syntagma,
the code over the performance, the ritual over the act, then Cervantes's activity—
this archeology that brings him to a metasemiotic intelligence and to its
display—is more than that of a ceremonial communication where preoriented

signs are materialized. It calls attention to the communication process itself and to its laws. I would venture to say that by means of this archeology, Cervantes produces an authentic subversion of ritual discourse. But this proposal needs clarification. As I have pointed out earlier, *Lazarillo de Tormes* subverts the autobiographical confessional discourse of its day, the official discourse of an individual before the institution of the Inquisition, by revealing the functional laws of that discourse, and the result was the emergence of the picaresque novel as a fictional autobiographical confession.

By relativizing the conditions that validate various literary discourses (as well as other ritual discourses of that time that belong to correlative zones but are appropriated by and integrated into fiction), *Don Quijote* not only objectivizes those discourses and sets itself at an ironical distance, as Martínez Bonati has shown, but it also has these discourses operate contrary to their original mark. By revealing the laws underlying ritual discourse and by showing them to be masks, *Don Quijote* strips them of their ritualism, profanes them, and, finally, disarticulates them. Stripped of their initial innocence, they betray themselves as instruments of a repressive ideology. In other words, Cervantes's narrative conscience is not only directed against "*l'empire rhétorique*" (Perelman 1977) in its aesthetic dimensions; Cervantes's criticism of "poetic reason" targets also the imputative dimension of ritual discourse understood here in the sense proposed by Harald Weinrich (1979): "language within language that comprises the integrated paradigms of the imperative and performative and encompasses all enunciations likely to change the moral, social or political circumstances of a person." In this enlarged paradigm, Weinrich includes not only Austin's performative but also other socially accepted codes that turn speech into an implicating act: honor, legal, political, scientific, magical, and etiquette codes. Thus defined, imputative speech acts include "the diachronically variable but synchronically stable set of all verbal acts allowed by the language code or by one of its sub-codes, i.e., comprising all the expressions that are at the same time actions and bind the speaker in the same way as the acts he may perform" (345).

It would seem superfluous to insist on the contractual character of such codes or on the need for a precise situation that insures the relevance of their use, as defined in the theory of language. I insist, however, on the diachronic dimension pointed out by Weinrich. If, as Martínez Bonati showed us earlier, spatial variations govern the various modes of poetic discourse, then the historical moment is decisive in determining the barely perceptible barrier between play and ritual, disguise and attribute. This dimension, part and parcel of *chronotopos*, also plays a decisive role in *Don Quijote*, which is indeed replete with anachronisms recognized as such even then, as is demonstrated by the break in the "reciprocal perspectives" of various actors in certain episodes. These anachronisms extend to the field of Don Quijote's language and arms, as well as to his suit of armor, to the emblematic, axiologic, and socioeconomic fields.

Such anachronisms must not be confused with epic distance. The epic erects its world in a mythical past that has no common ground with the narrator's and the audience's common daily experience. Heroes and their scale of values are removed to an inaccessible time and place. Severed from the present by an epic distance that legend cannot overstep, the hero is by nature inimitable. The chivalresque novel partakes of these characteristics of the epic. Bakhtin (1978) defines its *chronotopos* as "the world of the fantastic in an age of adventure" (300). In such a world, Bakhtin points out, heroes of the chivalresque novel feel at home because although they are not in their country, they are quite as fantastic as that universe: "Fantastic are [the hero's] origins, the circumstances of his birth, his youth and his adolescence; his physique is wondrous, and so forth. He is flesh of the flesh, bone of the bone of this world of marvels, its most shining representative" (300).

None of this is to be found in *Don Quijote*. On the contrary, *Don Quijote* corresponds precisely to that type of change that Bakhtin describes as the passage from the epic to the modern novel: "To represent an event at the same temporal and axiologic level where one and one's contemporaries are positioned (thus based upon personal experience and imagination) implies a radical revolution, the passage from the epic world to the novelistic one" (450).

It is not only in the *composición de lugar*—illustrated by those highroads traveled no longer by errant knights but by merchants—that *Don Quijote* betrays the stylistic violence noted by Martínez Bonati. It is above all the temporal conscience that continually betrays the anachronism of the hero's epic project. Even Monika Walter (1977), who sees in *Don Quijote* the project of a new realistic epic capable of a new *Weltaneignung*, insists at the same time on the changing functions of the hero and his values, on his "trials" and adventures. Thus emerges a new type of *Heldentat*, of heroism, that Monika Walter describes in this manner:

It is a question of a personal way of facing reality, of grasping it, of actively intervening in it. In this manner, the epic adventure is doubly dis-articulated: as a true or false representation of reality and as an authentic or chimerical area of human endeavour. (639)

The end result of this project, as Walter indicates some pages later, will be that "the everyday life of Spain penetrates the epic through a romanced fable that has nothing to do with daily existence" (654). In vivid contrast to the everyday, the *Alltag*, the twofold dream of a fantastic past (*phantastische Vergangenheit*) found only in chivalry books and other fiction and of a no less fantastic future ("eine ebenso phantastische Zukunft") then had to be actualized.

A new type of "grotesque contrast," this time with a temporal dimension, is introduced here: anachronism. All of the novel's actors (and not only Don Quijote) join in a polyphony where their voices carry spatial (diatopic), temporal (diachronic), and social (diastratic) marks as indelible signs of their dissimilarity. Only Don Quijote, in his madness, in his "homosémantisme" (Foucault 1966,

63), sees some resemblance between the various worlds. Hence his confusion. It would be simplistic to effect a complementary distribution of time, space, and social status and thereby to categorize narrowly each actor in the novel; such a temptation, which literary criticism has not always been able to resist, would overlook the complex reality and the contradictions of the world recalled by *Don Quijote*. *Don Quijote* evokes a transitional period where elements of different worlds coexist; it reflects the chaos specific to ages of epistemological rupture. It would therefore be most inappropriate to try to eliminate or gloss over its contradictions in the name of a unifying criterion that purports to define the novel's structure.

In her Marxist interpretation of *Don Quijote*, Monika Walter rightly emphasized the not necessarily peaceful coexistence of different socioeconomic systems and their contradictory components. The tension that Cervantes creates between the ''imitated'' genre(s) and the mode of imitation (discursive subversion) creates a novelistic space in the present in which strains of the traditional past still survive:

> In the tension between the image and the modality of representation lies the artistic treatment of a fundamental contradiction in the feudal society of that time. It is apparent indeed that in this society there are abilities, experiences and ways of thinking which, in reality, do not correspond to the new productive currents and political factors, but rather to political and ideological traditions inherited from the past and vested now with new meanings. (650)

The only way to structure the complex body of converging stimuli in *Don Quijote* without resolving these objective contradictions into a false harmony would be to incorporate them inexorably into a whole made up of oppositions, as in the ''structures of feeling'' that Terry Eagleton (1976, 25) defines as ''a set of received ways of perceiving and responding to reality.''

Dialectal opposition articulates the different images and gives unity to the text. An example: to Don Quijote's fantasies, which are fed by chivalresque novels and produce magical mental images, the governess and the niece in accordance with their Catholic faith will oppose church rituals when the time comes to destroy those novels. In this manner, magicians and demons, balms and holy water are placed on the same level. The priest, with a Licentiat's learned smile (to use the words of the narrator of that given moment), picks on the ''simplicity of the goode olde woman'' and proposes more efficient solutions than those of ritual practices whose effectiveness the Council of Trent has just valued almost on a par with that of the sacraments, while recommending at the same time other, more efficient means in the struggle against Reformation. In *Don Quijote*, actors and spatial and temporal categories (some present, others recalled) collide, as do their corresponding discursive practices. An example lies in the gracious manner (the actual title of the chapter) in which the chivalresque rites of investiture degenerate. The legal text that regulates this ceremony in Alfonso X's *Las Siete Partidas* is explicit about what constitutes the subject's "irregularities":

> Who once acquired the knighthood through derision should never become a knight. And that could be by three manners: firstly, when the person who granted it did not have the authority to do so; secondly, when the person who received it was not the proper one for it, for one of the said reasons [referring to the exclusion mentioned earlier of the madman and the poor man from knighthood]; thirdly, when the proper person received it deliberately through derision. . . . [After explaining the reasons for this restriction—that is, that knighthood may not be acquired through derision—the *Partida* insists once more on the invalidity of knighthood acquired in jest.] Consequently, it was established by the old law that those who wanted to deride as noble a cause as knighthood would be derided by it, so that they would never have it. (Chapter 21, law 12 of the Segunda Partida)

In light of this text, a reading of the first three chapters of *Don Quijote* reveals two things: (1) the entire narrative program of those chapters corresponds *in negativo* to the prescription of law; (2) not only does Don Quijote not receive the order of knighthood at the hands (and mouth) of the innkeeper, but he also becomes ineligible to receive it later (unless he were in fact already ineligible because of his madness and poverty) for having accepted it once in jest. To begin with, the hidalgo from La Mancha squanders his meager estate in order to buy novels of chivalry with which—at the expense of hunting and the administration of the little that is left him of his estate—he spends nights from dusk to dawn and days from dawn to dusk, until he eventually takes leave of his senses. Book reading is thus in the first chapter both the mediator of Don Quijote's desire (to become a knight) and the root cause of the financial and mental states that keep him from realizing that desire. His haste in carrying out his unreasonable dream will take him from his home with no legitimate means other than his ancient arms and outdated attire, with the result that he is smitten with "a terrible thought": "He remembred that he was not yet dub'd Knight, and therefore by the lawes of Knighthood neyther could nor ought to combat with any Knight." So with "his follies prevayling more then any other reason," he decides "to cause himselfe to be Knighted by the first he met" (1:29). The ambiguous "first" can refer here either to "the first knight" or to "the first individual" he meets.

When he arrives at the first inn, a clash between two worlds, two languages, and two attires takes place, and Don Quijote's raiment and language will be perceived as outdated by the maids of the inn, as can be gathered by their reaction. Don Quijote is neither perturbed by the laughter he provokes in those whom he encounters nor is he wont to imagine what might be needed to transform the inn into a castle. The one thing that disconcerts him is "that he was not yet dubbed Knight, for as much as he was fully perswaded, that he could not lawfully enterprise or follow any adventure, untill he received the order of Knighthood'' (1:35).

The third chapter is the ceremony in which an unfit subject is knighted by a minister without the authority to do so who reads from ''a booke . . . wherein he was wont to write down the accounts of the straw and Barley, which he delivered from time to time, to such Carriers as lodged in his Inne . . . reading in his Manual (as it seemed some devout Orison) . . . (always murmuring something betweene the teeth as if he prayed)'' (1:42, 47). To make a laughing stock of the ancient ceremony would be only amusing entertainment were it not that, in the course of its mise-en-scène, it evokes another ceremony of great concern to the theologians of Trent: the administration of sacraments and the conditions pertaining to it (the substance, the language, the minister, and the subject), as well as their effects *ex opere operato*.[14] I am not referring here to the parallel between the requirements for becoming a knight-errant and those established by the council for becoming a priest and a bishop; Cervantes stresses this parallel by giving knighthood the same title as the corresponding sacrament: orders (mentioned five times) and wretched order (once). This parallel simply corresponds to the common origin of both of these initiatory and exclusive rites, where the number of eligible candidates and ministers licensed to ordain new ones is limited, in accordance with established procedures.[15] I am referring specifically to the emphasis of the text on the ceremony's anachronism and the conditions in which it takes place: it is so stripped of all ritual significance by the innkeeper, the maids, the mule drivers, and the narrator that it borders on the grotesque. A comparison frequently made in literary criticism of the text of *Las Partidas* with the third chapter of *Don Quijote* shows that Cervantes's insistence on the ceremony's anachronism conveys no special meaning. If, however, we take into account the numerous allusions in *Don Quijote* to the canons and norms dictated by the Council of Trent and then compare both texts, the anachronisms seem like an insult.[16]

The theme was too touchy and too serious at a time when Spain considered the Counter-Reformation a national cause and the Council of Trent and its Counter-Reformist decrees as the protective shield of the state's unity. Furthermore, one reason *Don Quijote* remains relevant to this day is that we are perhaps not as far removed as we would like to believe from the segregation apparent in *Las Partidas* and the canons of the Council of Trent. This relevance is confirmed, for instance, by the fact that it is with terms from the sacrament of baptism that Austin illustrates his speech act theory, and that it is with terms such as ''prohibition'' and ''l'interdit'' that Michel Foucault in his *Ordre du discours* describes the means of exclusion by which societies restrict the use of discourse and specify the subject qualified to speak, the sanctioned object, and the ''ritual of circumstance'' that legitimizes specific discursive practices. These means bear an uncanny resemblance to knighthood rituals, to the church's sacramental rituals, and to Austin's performative rituals. Above all, they coincide with the set of codes and subcodes of language grouped by Harald Weinrich under the concept of "imputative language" (including, along with the performative, honor, legal, political, and scientific languages) and placed on a par with etiquette and magic codes. These languages implicate the speaker, it is true, but their access is controlled.

> Bringing them into play must be regulated, certain rules must be followed by individuals who use them so as to not make them freely accessible to everyone. Hence the increased scarcity of speakers; no one will enter in this discursive order without complying with the requirements or without being qualified from the outset. (Foucault 1971, 38-39)

The temporal dimension not only betrays anachronism but reveals another indication of ritual subversion in Cervantes's text: haste, precisely the opposite of the ritual act. Don Quijote is in such a hurry to be dubbed a knight that he closes his eyes to the "minister's" qualifications and to the circumstances of place, language, and gesture. The innkeeper is in a hurry to dismiss his guest after Don Quijote twice came to blows with the mule drivers who "desecrated" his arms by using them to clear the trough in order to water their beasts. To avoid further incidents, the innkeeper decides to "abbreviate, and give him the unfortunate order of Knighthood forthwith, before some other disaster befell" (1:41). The same haste characterizes the examination of Don Quijote's library, which explains why so many books were thrown into the fire "without search or regard." Contrary to what occurs during the investiture ceremony, however, haste in this last case corresponds to the ritual norms of the Holy Office's regular visitors as they examine and expurgate libraries.[17]

Let us return to our analysis of chapter 6 of *Don Quijote*, the narration of the scrutiny of Don Quijote's library, to see just how remote we are from an inquisitorial Cervantes and from the immoderate literary criticism attributed to him. On the one hand, the grotesque situation and the mingling of discursive planes now seem to indicate an ironic distance; on the other, the excessively accurate copy of the visit's ritual norms mingling in the text with their violation now seems to unmask an appropriated discourse. I believe that we can only interpret as a subversive calque this mise-en-scène (with the help of unqualified actors, metonymically camouflaged objects, and circumstances bordering on the grotesque) of a prevailing ritual practice. The production's violent performative language is altogether ineffective because we are dealing with fiction; but perhaps precisely for this reason it has become a language that incriminates its users. Far from expressing unconscious wishes transposed into dreams, it expresses, I believe, unconscious fears transposed into nightmares. The canon's long discourse (chapters 47 and 48 of the first part) must be similarly interpreted. This discourse is the basis of Riley's (1962) codification of what he considers to be Cervantes's theory of the novel (although it also embraces other genres), which proposes that comedy be censured before being represented. It is in light of this proposal that we must also interpret the discussion that follows up to chapter 50, where Don Quijote speaks of censuring books before their publication and expresses at the same time his feelings about public opinion:

> That were a jest indeed, quoth Don-Quixote, that bookes which are printed with the Kings licence, and approbation of those to whom their examination was committed, and that are read with universall delight and acceptance; and celebrated by great and little, rich, and poore, learned and ignorant, Plebeans and Gentlemen, and finally by all kinde of persons of what state or condition soever, should be so lying and fabulous; specially seeing they have such probabilitie of truth; seeing they describe unto us the Father, Mother, Countrey, Kinsfolke, Age, Towne, and Acts of such a Knight, or Knights, and that so exactly, point by point, and day by day: Hold your peace, and never speake againe such a blasphemie, and beleeve me, for I doe sincerely counsaile you what you, as a discreet man, ought to do herein; and if not, reade them but once, and you shall see what delight you shall receive thereby. (2:260)

In addition to the epistemological displacement brought about by Don Quijote's putting on the same plane "truth," "pleasure,"[18] and public opinion, we also have here an allusion to censorship and to the imprimatur that is not exactly in accordance with the canon's suggestion. Why then should Cervantes's own judgment be identified with that of the canon instead of that of Don Quijote? I believe that neither opinion implicates the narrator, let alone the author. The same thing occurs when two or more narrators relate an event, as in the case, for example, of Don Quijote's first sally (part 1, chapter 2). Must we accept the style of the imaginary narrator of *Quijote* or the everyday language that is its counterpart? Perhaps neither: the author maintains an equal distance between both and leaves the readers—the vectors, in this case—to judge for themselves.[19]

In the adventure with the galley slaves (part 1, chapter 22), reference is made to the Santa Hermandad's judicial practices and usual arguments—again from Don Quijote himself. Sancho, upon espying a group of chained men led by agents of the king's justice, armed and on horseback, cries out: "This is a chaine of Gally-slaves, people forced by the King to goe to the Gallies. How? people forced? demanded Don-Quixote, is it possible that the King will force any body?" (1:195-96).

The ensuing dialogue between Don Quijote and the convicts takes on the character of the most grotesque judicial cross-examination. Félix Martínez Bonati (1977) considers it a precise example of the "global contrast between various spheres of the imagination," given the enormous distance that separates the world of chivalry recalled in *Quijote*'s preceding chapter from the world suddenly introduced in this chapter, "the world of the picaresque, the satire of man's miserable condition transposed by Cervantes's making light of it, to the humorous level of comedy'' (47). We saw earlier that this is a reproduction of that era's (if not of all eras') judicial interrogations, which brings to mind the confessional autobiographical discourse that subverts *Lazarillo*, a work to which *Don Quijote* expressly alludes here. From this allusion I have inferred an intertextual reading of *Lazarillo* by Cervantes that would confirm my own. We undoubtedly have here, as in other examples we have seen, a combination of role appropriations with disproportionate objects and circumstances, spatial, temporal, or other. This operation transforms *Don Quijote* into a carnivalesque misalliance that profanes and subverts ritual discourses. Whereas the canon dictates literary theories, Sancho Panza will dictate theological ones, quoting the canons of the Council of Trent in conditions and circumstances as irrelevant and unsuitable as those prevailing when he quotes from his collection of proverbs. Whereas the village priest vests himself with the "canonic mission" of inquisitor and calls the governess the "secular arm." Don Quijote becomes a knight and administers justice, thanks to an innkeeper's cunning.

Although the transparency of this interplay is greater in the *Quijote* of 1615, it faithfully follows the scheme of broken conventions already taking root in the proto-*Quijote* chapters, particularly in chapter 5 where Don Quijote, in his delirium, personifies and confuses the characters of Valdovinos's romance, thereby recalling the *Entremés de los romances*, his remote model (see Menéndez Pidal 1920). None of the characters behave according to their adopted role. Don Quijote proclaims himself the liberator of the oppressed while at times accomplishing the opposite, as in the liberation of Andrés in chapters 4 (illusion) and 31 (disillusion) of part 1. Speaking with Sancho about the galley slaves, Don Quijote has this to say about his function:

> I say not so, answered Sancho, but that it is people which are
> condemned for their offences to serve the King in the Gallies perforce.
> In resolution, replied Don-Quixote, (howsoever it be) this folke,
> although they be conducted, goe perforce, and not, willingly. That's so,
> quoth Sancho. Then if that be so, here fals in justly the execution of my
> function, to wit, the dissolving of violences and outrages, and the
> succouring of the afflicted and needefull. (1:196)

"Dissolving violences," however, was not exactly the reason behind his demand of an act of faith by the Toledo merchants going to buy silks in Murcia (chapter 4, part 1). On the contrary, when they "were so neare as they might heare and see him, he lifted up his voice":

> Let all the world stand and passe no further, if all the world will not
> confesse, that there is not in all the world a more beautifull damzell
> then the Empresse of the Mancha, the peerelesse Dulcinea of Toboso.
> (1:48)

The resemblance of this text to Miguel Cid's verses and to the Marian oath by which Sevilla champions the dogma of Immaculate Conception seems to me evident, as well as the contamination of Dulcinea's excellence in Don Quijote's words by Marian theological terminology (in sermons, verses, and so on).

Although multiple examples exist, I will not elaborate further on other allusions to discourses and to the correlative zones they might evoke. I have insisted above all on the displacements of religious discourse because these are most evident in *Don Quijote* as well as in *Lazarillo* and other works. My concern is not to explore the reasons for this phenomenon (the literature of a converted dissident? the influence on Cervantes of Erasmus or the Reformation?). Perhaps the only plausible explanation is that advanced by Paul Zumthor (1976): whenever the church is powerful, the appropriation of religious discourses becomes more frequent. Zumthor refers to the era of the great French rhetoric masters. The same phenomenon occurs in France during the 1600s, as Jacques Truchet (1979) observed:

> One might prefer to restrict oneself to a more general consideration of collective mentalities. One could then say that the repeated presence of the religious discourse under various guises in every part of seventeenth-century literature is the sign of an ambiguous culture placing side-by-side its own contestation and its own confirmation. Mundane discourse and Christian discourse intervene like the world of God and the world of man: a convergence generating scandal and edification, and perceived as being brought on, depending on the case, by the devil or by divine grace. (38)

Truchet then suggests that "forms of religious discourse that can, in the seventeenth century, produce comic" include "writings, predications, apologetics, hagiography, liturgy, even theology" (30).

That both Cervantes and the author of *Lazarillo* focus their criticism on the religious discourse of repression as a practice of (*Don Quijote*) or submission to (*Lazarillo*) this discourse might highlight the particular situation created in Spain by the Inquisition in those "difficult years" (Tellechea Idígoras 1968) of the sixteenth and seventeenth centuries. But this criticism might also be the voice of those who suffer *persecuciones por justicia* with the ambiguity conveyed by this phrase when it is spoken by outcasts. Unless our interpretation is of the work's entire structure, we do not come across the ambiguous use of the gospel in *Don Quijote* that we find in *Lazarillo* and, before that, in *Celestina*. But *Don Quijote* can be considered a reading-writing production that engulfs it in its totality, more than does the *Entremés de los romances* scheme, transforming it into a book of books. Cervantes's book would be a burlesque reproduction of Christianity's attitude toward the Bible: it puts its texts (the Gospels, the Apostles' Acts, the Epistles, the Apocalypse) on the same level as those of Mosaic law and the prophetics—the former being in the figure of Jesus the fulfillment and the plenitude of the latter—according to the saying *Vetus testamentum in novo patet, novum in vetere latet*. Something of the sort occurs in *Don Quijote*, whose program is traced by chivalry novels; however, it is above all the first *Don Quijote*'s completion in the second *Don Quijote* that, at the end, justifies the protagonist's prophetic mission.

Chapter 6
Discourse Pragmatics and Reciprocity of Perspectives:
The Promises of Juan Haldudo
(*Don Quijote* I, 4) and of Don Juan

Perhaps their working on language and on the imaginary defines the specificity of literary practices, their social dimension (and social role) as well as the confluence of different discursive formations in the literary text. It does not follow, however, that the literary text organizes itself in a purely mechanistic way. On the contrary, it is located in dialogical interaction with a concrete sociohistorical conjuncture, is mediated by various ideological instances, and participates in the contradictory network of the discursive formations of its surroundings. Thus a contextual boundary must be established that might allow an understanding of the "grand dialogue" in which takes place, according to Ducrot, the *petit dialogue* of the characters or actors of the dramatic space (and, one might add, of the novelistic space).[1] The promises of Juan Haldudo in *Don Quijote* and of Don Juan in Tirso de Molina's *Burlador* function within such a boundary, a greater whole that comprises the struggle between two diametrically opposed systems of interpretation and of representation of reality that coexisted in the Spain that produced and consumed these two works. The matter at hand, then, is one of discursive archeology. Between a reality and its interpretative representation, a series of mediators is interposed that (pre)determines and (con)figurates perception and the articulation (by means of language) of this perception; there is also a collective imaginary that varies not only according to place and epoch, but also according to the nature of different antagonistic groups that societies integrate and hierarchically organize. In this collective imaginary (which interprets the world, attributes values to things, regulates acts and human attitudes, and stratifies diverse social components) every individual and group necessarily, albeit for the most part unconsciously, participates. Because individuals interiorize during childhood and in the acquisition of language itself a series of epistemological cate-gories, values, and social roles that are hierarchically organized within the social or-der, they come to identify themselves with a group more or less outlined beforehand within such an order. The coherence of thought and acts is therefore governed less by some reality than by the "order of the discourse" (Michel Foucault) responsible for the regulation of word (and gesture) about (supposed) reality.

By destroying the illusion that language is objective and by uncovering the mechanisms that regulate it (its grammar, its own laws of functioning), modern thought opens the way to a new illusion: the autonomy of language and thus the autotelic character of the language work of art. This rupture with the mimesis of the real corresponds to the clash postulated by Machiavelli of political (or eco-nomic) techné with ethicoreligious imperatives. But the economic and ideologi-cal dependence of both the artist and the politician should one day reveal those old links renewed. The unmasking of this illusion created by so-called modernity (and developed by the intellectual and ethical projects of the Enlightenment) lies in the analysis not of language as a stable system of signs but of discourse as a (socially) regulated use of language. It is through its discourses that a society most clearly evinces (usually unawares) the aspirations as well as the censorship and taboos that it imposes on itself. It is thus the analysis of these discourses that can best uncover a society's ideals, contradictions, and inner tensions.

Analyzing *Don Quijote* will bring to light some of the implications of these theories. Rather than subscribe to the traditional reading of Cervantes's work as reflecting the struggle between realism and idealism, we should regard it as an interdiscursive crossroads; that is to say, as the mise-en-scène by Cervantes of a repertory of regulated and accepted modes of speaking (of discourses, in other words), in varying degrees of anachronicity and contemporaneity, of the social milieus represented in the novel. These discourses are occasionally contrasted with one another when they are made to describe the same object or to relate the same story. For example, soon after the description in chapter 1 of the social, physical, economic, and psychological conditions of the gentleman of La Man-cha, his wild plan, and the means by which he proposes to accomplish it, a triple conflictual discourse concerning the moment and manner of Don Quijote's first departure from home is offered to us in the second chapter of the first part. Here is the first:

> Accordingly, without informing anyone of his intention and without
> letting anyone see him, he set out one morning before daybreak on one
> of those very hot days in July. Donning all his armor, mounting
> Rocinante, adjusting his ill-contrived helmet, bracing his shield on his
> arm, and taking up his lance, he sallied forth by the back gate of his
> stable yard into the open countryside. (1:30)

This description by the narrator is soon contrasted with the discourse imagined by Don Quijote who, in order to narrate what he calls merely "my first sally so early in the morning," has the "learned chronicler" who "will record these feats" spew forth a genuine baroque piece:

> No sooner had the rubicund Apollo spread over the face of the broad and spacious earth the gilded filaments of his beauteous locks, and no sooner had the little singing birds of painted plumage greeted with their sweet and mellifluous harmony the coming of the Dawn, who, leaving the soft couch of her jealous spouse, now showed herself to mortals at all the doors and balconies of the horizon that bounds La Mancha—no sooner had this happened than the famous knight, Don Quixote de La Mancha, forsaking his own downy bed and mounting his famous steed, Rocinante, fared forth and began riding over the ancient and famous Campo de Montiel. (1:31)

The narrator's remark—"And this was the truth, for he was indeed riding over that stretch of plain"—has something in common with the opening of Robert Musil's novel *The Man without Qualities*. Musil too, after a (pseudo)scientific description of a "fine August day in the year 1913" that depicts the action of the isotheres and isotherms and the influence of the altitudes and latitudes, describes this same day in everyday language. Two discourses thus confront one another on the same object. Musil's narrating subject, who is the speaker of both discourses, inserts a judgment on them by introducing the second as follows: "In short, to use an expression that describes the facts pretty satisfactorily, even though it is somewhat old-fashioned."[2]

This judgment, which apparently affects only the second of the two discourses, in fact places them in grotesque contrast. In this confrontation, which can parody or even subvert both discourses, literature carries out its most important operation (assuming diverse forms since ancient times) on the socially regulated uses of language. Breaking through the barriers that isolate discursive formations according to different fields of knowledge, literature submits its discourses to an examination, weighs and contrasts them, and offers a plural vision of the society that generates and maintains them. Within literature, the novel (but also theater) is probably the privileged locus for trying out components of a society's discursive system. In this manner Musil theorizes and experiments in his novel, indicating that he is aware of a crisis in which he himself is plunged, as Walter Moser (1985) pointed out. Without theorizing on the matter, Cervantes unfolded three centuries earlier (as would Velázquez in pictorial art and Lope, Tirso, or Calderón in the theater) a whole series of procedures in interdiscursive experimentation.

Another example: after Don Quijote has been dubbed knight in a "gracious manner," as the third chapter relates, he has in the fourth chapter two encounters in which he endeavors to act according to the rules of knight-errantry that he believes he incarnates: one with a rich peasant who was whipping his servant, Andrés; another with some merchants from Toledo who are "on their way to purchase silk at Murcia.'' In both encounters we are confronted with dialogues that bring into play two conflicting conceptions of the world: that of the already decadent feudal society and that of the nascent bourgeoisie. The feudal conception of the world finds its expression in Don Quijote, who practices justice by means of challenges and on the basis of personal respect and his oath given (in the case of Juan Haldudo), or who requires an act of blind faith in Dulcinea (precisely from the merchants). The bourgeois conception of the world finds its expression in the economic calculations of Juan Haldudo and in the merchants' insistence on empirical knowledge ("We do not know who this beauteous lady is of whom you speak. Show her to us"). In answer to this request, so logical to the merchants, Don Quijote proclaims his (opposite) axiology—the equally logical consequence of his conception of faith and of virtue: "The important thing is for you, without seeing her, to believe, confess, affirm, swear, and defend that truth" (1:45).

Both adventures end unhappily: the merchants knock Don Quijote from his horse and leave him beaten; Juan Haldudo deceives him with promises and oaths. Don Quijote will be advised of the promises' emptiness when in chapter 31 of the first part he meets Andrés again: the reader, however, has been informed immediately.

Perhaps the best commentary on the discursive opposition of the feudal and the bourgeois worlds lies in the description of the historical and revolutionary role that Marx and Engels attribute to the bourgeoisie in their *Communist Manifesto:*

> The bourgeoisie, historically, has played a most revolutionary part.
>
> The bourgeoisie, wherever it has got the upper hand, has put an end to all feudal, patriarchal, idyllic relations. It has pitilessly torn asunder the mostly feudal ties that bound man to his "natural superiors," and has left remaining no other nexus between man and man than naked self-interest, than callous "cash payment." It has drowned the most heavenly ecstasies of religious fervor, of chivalrous enthusiasm, of philistine sentimentalism, in the icy water of egotistical calculation. It has resolved personal worth into exchange value, and in place of the numberless indefensible chartered freedoms, has set up that single, unconscionable freedom—Free Trade. In one word, for exploitation, veiled by religious and political illusions, it has substituted naked, shameless, direct, brutal exploitation.
>
> The bourgeoisie has stripped of its halo every occupation hitherto honored and looked up to with reverent awe. (1954, 18-19)[3]

What Marx and Engels describe as the result of a long historical process, Cervantes integrated into *Don Quijote* by means of a narrative fiction that evokes living social actors in the mind of its potential readers, not only of his time (and who thus share the conflictual ideals and contradictory values of Cervantes's society) but of different epochs. The historical process described in the *Communist Manifesto* in the past tense has not yet been consummated: residual elements of the feudal order intermingle with the bourgeois order and erode its contour while contaminating its discourses—one reason, no doubt, why *Don Quijote* remains relevant to our time. In Cervantes's novel, we encounter constant interdiscursive contaminations, along with the contradictory discourses of two coexisting social systems. Don Quijote moves, for example, from challenging the peasant, whom he calls a "discourteous knight" and whom he invites to take up the lance, and making various chivalric threats, to reasons of economic nature, to the settling of accounts. Although it is true that Don Quijote errs when he multiplies Andrés's nine months of work by the seven reals per month that he is "entitled to in return for his services," he accepts the discussion in economic terms (even though such preoccupations are far removed from his usual concerns or his mentality) before adopting the tone of a judge passing sentence.[4] One of the merchants from Toledo, imitating in a burlesque of the language of his interpellator in defense of empirical knowledge, lets loose a tirade in a chivalric tone:

> Sir Knight, responded the merchant, I beg your Grace, in the name of all the princes here present, in order that we may not have upon our consciences the burden of confessing a thing which we have never seen nor heard, and one, moreover, so prejudicial to the empresses and queens of Alcarria and Estremadura, that your Grace will show us some portrait of this lady, even though it be no larger than a grain of wheat, for by the thread one comes to the ball of yarn; and with this we shall remain satisfied and assured, and your Grace will likewise be content and satisfied. (1:46)

Interdiscursive contaminations, which prevent a sociolect from remaining (or being studied) isolated from the larger frame of discursive practices of the society in which it is integrated, are not confined to literary artifice: we find them also in everyday praxis and in the most diverse fields of knowledge. Analyzing the web of a society's discourses is even more difficult when this society is enmeshed in a historical crisis. Because in our particular case such an analysis is best able to detect and diagnose such a crisis, it is as important to study conscious discursive usurpations (as in the case of Juan Haldudo, of the merchants, and, as we will soon see, of Don Juan) as to study unconscious contaminations in the subject's verbal slips.

Concerning Tirso de Molina's *Burlador*, I will focus my analysis on the functioning in the play of two repetitive syntagmas: the "Prometo" (I promise), later elaborated to "Juro cumplir mi promesa—mi *palabra*" (I swear to fulfill my promise—my word), in which Don Juan verbalizes the mockeries of his four victims, and the "Muy largo me lo fiais" (You will entrust it to me for a long time) that—with few significant variations—is repeated seven times throughout the text as Don Juan's answer to the admonitions of the valet, victims, chorus, and statue. *Muy largo me lo fiais* is even the title of some editions of variants of Tirso's text and clearly corresponds to Lope de Vega's *La fianza satisfecha*, even though the theological thesis dramatized by Lope is the opposite of that drama-tized by Tirso, since Leónido is saved in Lope de Vega's work thanks to his faith in the redemptive "satisfaction" of Christ. Don Juan's punishment in Tirso's drama consists of the negation of this "señorío sobre el tiempo" (domination over time) that this syntagma proclaims. When Don Juan asks for a confessor once he recognizes the imminence of his death, the statue of the Commander responds: "No hay lugar; ya acuerdas tarde" (There is no more time; you arrive too late), a sentence that the chorus underlines with the general warning: "No hay plazo que no llegue, ni deuda que no se pague" (There is neither a term that does not expire nor a debt that is not to be repaid).

The promises and oaths made by the farmer Juan Haldudo to his servant Andrés in the presence of Don Quijote and those made by Don Juan to his victims both lack an "ideological community." The convictions of such an ideological community, linked by the acceptance of the procedure and by the intention of participating in the linguistic action, constitute according to Austin (1962) the triple condition for those speech acts that in a "performative" manner carry out what they enunciate. It is this lack of ideological community — or of "reciprocity of perspectives," as the sociologists call it — that allows for Juan Haldudo's and Don Juan's deceit and derisive mockery. Both texts therefore manifest in their language the symptoms of the crisis that represents the social frame of this derision — the struggle between diametrically opposed social systems in intersys-temic collision in baroque Spain. In that period there coexisted, as we saw earlier, elements pertaining to a not very remote past (elements already anachro-nistic) with elements pointing to a not very distant future (elements not yet en-tirely accepted by the hegemonic discursive system). The contradictions involved are not confined to the clash between Don Quijote's outdated garb and demeanor and the boundary of expectations of other characters, but two worldviews so ir-reconcilable that any genuine dialogue between their protagonists becomes im-possible. Not that speech has lost its efficiency for Don Juan and Juan Haldudo: it is this efficiency of seduction by speech that shows (as a result and a symptom) the depth of the crisis, of the epistemological rupture taking place. In the social duality, therefore, must be situated (and explained) the origin of the continual quid pro quo that characterizes the conflictual dialogues as much in *Don Quijote* as in *El Burlador de Sevilla y Convidado de Piedra*: the interlocutors do not share the same epistemological and axiological boundary; there are no conventions. The signs thus function in a double code in the *petit dialogue* of both texts. Only the reader (in the case of Cervantes's novel) or the spectator (in the case of Tirso's drama) resolves, as a vector on the vertex of both codes, the homonym that gives rise to the equivocal in the *grand dialogue* of the reading or of the play per-formed. The basis of this *grand dialogue* is this communicative competence lack-ing in the characters but presupposed in the audience or the reader as a condition of the progressive recognition (anagnorisis) of the duality on which both texts work.

Evidently, both Juan Haldudo and Don Juan recognize the duplicity of the signifieds in the signifiers used in their oaths and promises. This knowledge endows them with an almost demonic power to persuade others to believe in the word, a rhetorical power that makes of them modern men, while their victims—those of Don Juan's deceit, nobles as well as villains, and Don Quijote himself vis-à-vis Juan Haldudo—show that they still live in an earlier ideological stage of good faith. (This good faith, it might be noted in passing, is what politicians and advertising agents exploit even today—hence the continuing relevance of this verbal seduction in Don Quijote and the *Burlador*, which is conditioned by a sociohistorical conjuncture that in many respects coincides with ours).

In her analysis of Molière's *Don Juan*, Shoshana Felman (1983) compares Austin's theoretical seduction with Don Juan's rhetorical seduction. By thus bringing together myth and theory, she is able to elucidate the donjuanesque myth by means of the Austin-Benveniste controversy and the theoretical polemic itself by means of the myth. Situating herself at the intersection of these disciplines, she proposes a triple reading of a literary, a linguistic, and a philosophical text that should allow her "to articulate not so much what is *said* or could be said but what is happening, taking effect, producing acts, what is being done or could be done between speaking bodies, between languages, between knowledge and pleasure" (8–9). We have here an entire program whose realization is reduced to a recuperation of Austin's original distinction (later rejected by Austin himself) between constative language and performative language, already carried out by Benveniste, and to a few somewhat iconoclastic deconstructionist sketches that make a tabula rasa of Austin, Benveniste, Nietzsche, Freud, Lacan, and Marx. It is interesting to note that Felman falls into the same trap that she professes to uncover in Don Juan: she defines rhetorical seduction as the use of the performative by means of which seducers maintain themselves in the order of the act and in the register of the enjoyment of the language (the latter being self-referential for Felman). Their victims interpret such language as if it were constative, thereby bringing it to the order of meaning and to the register of knowledge. She concludes: "The trap of seduction thus consists in producing a *referential* illusion through an utterance that is by its very nature self-referential." At the same time she ponders the truth or falsity of the seducer's words (thereby also bringing them within the order of meaning and the register of knowledge) in order to show without a shadow of doubt that "the seducer, strictly speaking, does not lie" (31). The more serious defect in Felman's approach is that, concerned as it is with the self-referentiality of performative language, it fails to take into account the diachronic dimension, that is to say the historical moment, which after all is a decisive element in the tenuous line that separates the ritual from the game and from deceit. This diachronic dimension, I believe, is the basis of the rupture that we witness in these *dialogues de sourds* of the reciprocity of perspectives that I have already pointed out as being a condition indispensable to the ideological community postulated by Austin for the functioning of performative speech acts.

Let us apply from Felman's work, notwithstanding these objections, the notions of action-language and of seduction in Don Juan as "rhetorical seduction" to Tirso's drama in its historical moment. Then, following Harald Weinrich in what he calls "imputative language," I will insist on the conventional character of the codes and subcodes of action-language.

Weinrich (1979) also tried to recuperate Austin's performatives, integrating them in a paradigm, imputative language, that incorporates other forms of social interaction by linguistic communication. Weinrich takes the term imputative language from juridical discourse, where it designates the responsibility assigned by custom to certain acts. He uses this term to establish a complete paradigm that would include the defective one of the imperative (where the first person singular is lacking) and of the performative (which functions only in the first person and in the present). This paradigm of the imputative thus integrates all socially accepted codes (such as the code of honor, the legal code, the political code, and so forth), which make speech an act that implicates.

As a synchronically stable but diachronically variable convention, action-language functions only within the narrow limits of the ritual determined by the social community, and it does so in the time interval in which this community assigns such an effect to the realization of the verbal act. In periods of transition, of rupture, we witness its abuse on the part of those who recognize the efficiency of such a language and appropriate it for themselves as a discursive mask. It is therefore the coexistence of two social orders and ideologies in the society in which Juan Haldudo and Don Juan act that allows for their deceitfulness and, more specifically, for Don Juan's rhetorical seduction.

Don Juan is the actor par excellence because of the double theatricality characteristic of the dramas that put him into action. It is less the changes of his personality (disguised in the cloaks of others) than the usurpation of a language that is socially marked and efficient in his social environment. Disguised through this discursive usurpation, or discursive mask, Don Juan can talk to his victims in a language that is theirs but no longer his own. This action-language undergoes a mise-en-scène, as it also does in *Don Quijote*, except that here it is carried out within another scene — the dramatic space in which the deceiver and the deceived act — with the result that one could speak here of a "theater within the theater." In Tirso's work we also find a series of gestures that accompanies speech and is also codified by usage: the extending and shaking of the hand, for instance, is repeated throughout Don Juan's deceitfulness and again by the statue of the Commander who punishes this deceitfulness. Müller-Bochat (1973, 332) sees here "die Einheit — oder sagen wir besser: die konsequente Komposition — des *Burlador de Sevilla*" ("the unity — or better yet: the consequent composition — of *Burlador of Seville*"), based on the already-classical studies of Casalduero (1958) and Aubrun (1957) on the structure of drama. Archimede Marni (1952) interprets this correspondence between the final punishment and the anaphoric repetition throughout the play of its constitutive motifs (the hands, the symbolism of fire, and so on) to be a use on Tirso's part, at the moment of shaping the punishment for Don Juan's deceitfulness, of the Dantesque principle of the *contrapasso*. Marni thereby tries to solve the two problems that, according to him, create the statue's attitude: the false "Don't be afraid" that Don Gonzalo utters while asking for Don Juan's hand and the "There is no time, you are too late" with which he responds to Don Juan's request for a confessor before dying. Marni, who highlighted so many details common to Don Juan's acts of deceit and his final punishment, does not seem to consider how Don Juan is deceived precisely by the instrument of his deceit, by the deceit of Don Gonzalo's challenge. Marni also fails to consider how — if there is *contrapasso*, and I believe there is — this had to be applied above all to the (ab)use on the part of Don Juan of the "time of trial" conceded to a human being. Don Juan squanders this time, presumptuously considering it enough to accommodate his antics for the time being. His rigorous punishment consists of his unexpected confrontation with death, the end of the time of trial, and the sudden advance toward fortunate or unfortunate eternity in the conception of existence underlying both Tirso's drama and Spanish baroque in general. We thus find ourselves before the second verbal element: the "Muy largo me lo fiais" with which Don Juan responds when valet and victims warn him that there is a judging God and death.

Critics have focused less on the temporal unfolding of dramatic action in Tirso's work, in spite of the parallels established between Thisbe, the deceiver of men herself deceived by Don Juan, and Don Juan, the deceiver in speech deceived by the "true speech," and between the moments that repeatedly characterize amorous actions (three such moments, according to Casalduero: deceit, possession, and escape); and in spite of having identified the integration in *Burlador* of two traditional motifs, the punished libertine and the invitation of the skull, which undergo a mise-en-scène as do also the themes of human and divine justice.

Time constitutes the conceptual and discursive axis of *Burlador* in the double dimension of (economic) language and of continuous and inevitable use (spending, waste). The verb "fiar" (to trust, to confide) encompasses the double meaning of giving in trust and of trust placed in another person. United with lexemes of duration — "muy largo" (very long), "tan largo" (so long), "que largo" (how long), "si tan largo me lo fiais" (if you will entrust it to me for so long) — and their opposites — "breve te ha de parecer" (it will seem so brief to you), "siendo tan breve el cobrarse" (the time to repay being so brief), "fiar" carries with it the idea of "plazo" in its etymological sense of *placitum* (time accorded for something, always limited by deadline). All these elements of economic discourse that contaminate the theological discourse of the time are not confined to *Burlador*. We find them in the canons of the Council of Trent that define the theology of human salvation and we find them earlier still in Ignacio Loyola's *libro de los exercicios* and letters. Don Quijote himself is unable, for all his relentless idealism, to extricate himself completely from the irreversible advance of economic (bourgeois) mentality (and language), as we saw; neither can this advance be avoided by the chroniclers of the discovery and conquest of the Americas, for all their emphasis on evangelization, as we are going to see. Language discloses here a repressed (collective) unconscious that leaves its trace in the text. The notion of time thus takes on an economic meaning that also permeates the action and language of Tirso's drama.

In addition to *oikonomía*, Greek antiquity for the most part uses two words to designate time: *chrónos* (time that flows regularly, like a blind force) and *kairós* (a time interval especially appropriate for something, possible during this time and not before or after it). The *kairós* were marked on calendars, as is done today at the beginning and end of important periods in public life, in finance, and so forth. This concept of time-propitious-for-something appears also in the Bible with the meaning of "time of grace." According to an old allegory, of which prophetic books are the echo, God cuts out limited periods of time at certain moments in the history of salvation. These periods distinguish themselves from the normal course of time by being a "time of salvation." The Greek Septuagint here uses the word *kairós*. A well-known example of *kairós* is the prophecy of the "seventy weeks of salvation" in Daniel 9:24:

> Seventy weeks are decreed
> for your people and your holy city,
> for putting an end to transgression,
> for placing the seals on sin,
> for expiating crime,
> for introducing everlasting integrity,
> for setting the seal on vision and on prophecy,
> for anointing the Holy of Holies.

The Gospel of John also talks about a pool to which, in "determined moments," an angel descends and agitates the water. Those who entered the pool at this moment were cured of whatever ailments they had (John 5:4). And Saint Paul calls Jesus "shortened Kairós," emphasizing what is considered the brevity of "the time of salvation." On this brevity he bases his recommendation of celibacy for the apostle (1 Corinthians, 7:29-35). The parable of the talents likewise reduces the "time of trading" accorded to each person; at the end of this time they should give an account of who received five, two, or only one talent. The "time of salvation" always requires an answer from individuals and not infrequently puts their trust or faith to the test. That is the case, for example, in the sacrifice of Abraham. If such a response were not required, the justification of human being would be an automatic effect of certain legal ceremonies. It is this legalism, which characterizes the Pharisaic doctrine, that Jesus attempts to reform. But Christianity quickly becomes Roman, and the legal character of the relationship between individual and God reappears based on the Roman conception of religion that Cicero defines as "iustitia apud deos." A synthesis between Christianity and Stoicism therefore appears early. The "time of salvation" is thus converted into a "time of trial," and religion as a gift of God is converted into the religion of human productivity. From this point on, Patristics and synods vacillated between the emphasis on divine justice or on divine mercy. Saint Augustine finds himself facing both tendencies and struggles as well against Manicheans and Pelagians, developing in his refutation of both factions his doctrine of grace. It is thus that medieval soteriological theology arises: human salvation is an effect of supernatural grace and, at the same time, of the individual answering to this grace. This answering is free.

It is the scholastic synthesis in which Thomas Aquinas—and, most of all, later Thomism—will insist in the "unique truth." Because of this, the knowledge by means of the natural light, "rational knowledge," again approaches the supernatural, revealed. The natural (Aristotelian) ethic is therefore recognized as the source of meritorious acts achieved under the action of the supernatural grace. Thus were established the doctrinal and moral bases still in force in the Catholic church. Opposing these—from different points of view—are Machiavelli and Luther, who both have antecedents in French nominalism, the most successful medieval attempt to separate the competences (the human and the divine) and therefore the two truths: one acquired by the light of human reason and one revealed by God. For Machiavelli it is a question of liberating human action in the political domain from the opinions of religion and morality in order to convert politics into a genuine "techné"; Luther favors the divorce of faith from reason; salvation is the work of divine grace, and individuals will receive it by only having faith-hope in it. Luther therefore postulated a return to the ancient biblical conception of religion as a gift that would again interpret existence as a "time of grace and salvation" rather than a "time of trial." The Counter-Reformation of Trent, animated to a large extent by Spanish (neo)scholasticism in its struggle against Luther's doctrine and in its determination to return to the medieval synthesis, leads to a revitalization of the religion of productivity, of the growth and accumulation of "merits" ("riches").

The rapid growth of capitalism at this juncture causes the microeconomy of small investment to give way to the macroeconomy of total investment, and, in another order of things, the chivalric adventure to the financial adventure (see Nerlich 1977). It is not surprising that in such circumstances we also witness the formation of an ideology nourished mainly by the consideration of the brevity of life, thereby inciting the enjoyment of the moment. This explains the flourishing, for example, of the sonnet expressing the theme of "carpe diem" and of the Epicurean hedonism that characterizes Don Juan as well as his victims.[5] But this emphasis on the appreciation of the moment also leads to a conception of time economy that calls for the careful administration of time (precisely because of its brevity) in order to accumulate the most possible riches, not material, transitory riches, but merits for the greatest enjoyment of the eternal (enduring) life. It is this twofold ideology that contaminates theological discourse and thought in the period in which a return to the spirit of medieval religiosity is attempted. From this ideology — and participating in all its contradictions and tensions — arises Tirso's drama, *El Burlador de Sevilla y Convidado de piedra*, which crystallizes with tragic force the myth of Don Juan.

In the practice of the Exercicios, Ignacio de Loyola proposed, even before Trent, a program of salvation and accumulation of merits for the whole of eternity. His program arises from an imaginary anticipation of death that should move the readers or listeners to invest in this whole every minute of their earthly lives: Don Juan, on the contrary, represents on stage, by means of word and gesture, the contrary attitude, the negative of the Ignatian program that the canons of Trent sanction.[6] For this reason Don Juan, as Kierkegaard says, is a man without a history. Ignacio de Loyola and Don Juan participate nevertheless in the same pathos. They participate also in this contradiction that Marx denounces in the capitalist economy: to earn, it is necessary to spend. It is this wearing away minute by minute through Don Juan's action-language that the *Burlador*'s public is invited to follow.

Let us return to the role of literature within this broad plural and conflictual frame that is the discursive system of any society. Let us attempt to comprehend in this frame, in this concrete and discursive social conjuncture that is baroque Spain, what *Don Quijote* and the *Burlador* represent as dialogical spaces. Tirso seems simply to echo the objective contradictions that show us the critical analysis of the verbal uses of his time, but Cervantes seems to situate himself in a process of becoming conscious of such contradictions, in the interior of this system to which his own work belongs. Thus Cervantes's (ab)use of the discourses of his society is marked by an ironic critical distance. The author's point of view seems, consequently, to situate itself outside of the ideological, gnoseological, and axiological space that supports such discourses. Tirso's use, on the contrary, represents this conflictual world accompanied by a monologic solution: the exemplary punishment of Don Juan in accordance with the theology of the Counter-Reformation and dramatically elaborated, moreover, according to the Dantesque medieval principle of the *contrapasso*. Even though this "divine" punishment reveals the incapacity of (temporal) human justice to resolve this "magna quaestio" (Augustine) of the abuse of language that constitutes the lie (the false promise), the solution of the drama only reproduces a stereotype. In contrast to this solution, Molière transforms Tirso's (supernatural) tragedy into a (human) comedy by converting this punishment into a farce. Molière thus reaches a new step in this progressive discursive consciousness that seems to mark the working of literature on the discursive components of a given society. Cervantes intervenes by means of the same operation in the chivalric epos (and thereby in the feudal mentality), establishing the ironic distance that transforms it into a novel.

Chapter 7
The Antimodernization of Spain

The term antimodernization may call to mind the currently fashionable maneuver whereby to the poorly defined concept of "modernity" is opposed a concept that derives from it—"postmodernity," which is as poorly defined as the framework from which it originates. One does not always credit Spanish (a language where "isms" abound) with being able to distinguish between the terms of this contemporary debate and those forged by the historiography of Hispanic literatures, which has accustomed us to opposing an aesthetic movement known as modernism to what has been called the Generation of 1898, an ideological movement (as if aesthetics and ideology could ignore one another or were mutually exclusive). Thus today we frequently hear (or read in the daily press or in less ephemeral writings) about postmodernism without quite knowing what it actually stands for. Indeed, while in Spanish it still connotes a movement (the avant-garde?) subsequent to modernism, it is also occasionally used to designate ideological adherence (as emphasized by the morpheme "ism") to the postmodern vision—and this with a more or less clear awareness of what Lyotard (1979) calls the "postmodern condition." One also resorts to this term to refer to the movement in the plastic arts (architecture in particular) that reestablishes a dialogue with local tradition by means of parody or pastiche, and that by so doing fancies that it has overcome the excessive uniformity and internationalism of modern architecture. This term also refers to a current moment in literary or cultural criticism—the various strands of postmodernism—that coincides with the overcoming of structuralism, or to a politicoreligious attitude that considers itself bereft of the "errors of the moderns"; that is, the errors condemned by the first Vatican Council and, earlier still, by the "collectio errorum modernorum," the notorious *Sylla-*

bus of 1864 in which Pius IX recapitulated his condemnations from 1846 onward and which was taken up again in our own century by Pius X, who called them "errores modernistarum.")

The ambiguity and the inevitable conceptual instability of current uses of the adjectives "modern" and "postmodern" (along with their various nominalizations), although particularly complicated in Spanish, are in fact neither unheard of in nor confined to the Hispanic world. Ever since Baudelaire put it into circulation, the term modernity connotes both the emergence of modern poetry and a new vision of the world that conditions this emergence, at the same time reinforcing itself by means of it (it does after all feed upon this poetry). Hugo Friedrich (1976) has brought this notion to the fore in his work on Baudelaire's poetry and criticism:

> This is indeed one of Baudelaire's personal problems: to say how poetry is still possible in a world of trade and technique. His poetry shows the possibilities and his prose theoretically elaborates them. This maneuver leads to the greatest possible distance from the banality of reality to a zone of mystery but in such a manner that all of the elements of modernity are included therein and are endowed with a sort of poetic vibration. This is the starting point of modern poetry and of its both corrosive and magical substance. (40-41)

Friedrich underlines the conflictual duality implied by this perception of the world: in addition to the advantages afforded by the electricity and steam that progress puts at our disposal, modern humanity perceives the ugliness of the large metropolis as well as the loss, in the name of technical progress, of the natural and the idyllic. This conflict will give rise, through Baudelaire, to the new aesthetics: "All that is wretched, decadent, bad, nocturnal, artificial, all this is also an element of excitement which can perhaps be perceived by the means of poetry" (50).

The triumph of modernity has been considered a Pyrrhic victory: the awareness of the malaise and the critique that was supposed to have led to its overcoming were in fact already inscribed in its project.[1] In this sense, the modernity/postmodernity opposition is dialectical. This is not the case, however, with regard to the conceptual pair modernism/antimodernism in the sense given to it by the Syllabus of Pius IX, the "Pascendi" encyclical and the "Lamentabili" decree of Pius X, or the "antimodernist oath" — an abjuration ritual prescribed in 1910 by Pius X and practiced until relatively recently in certain Catholic university ceremonies. Such a sermon on the part of the teaching faculty was, for instance, part of the ceremonies of the beginning of the academic year in certain Spanish universities. These ceremonies occasionally turned into genuine exorcisms against the "errors of modernism" personified by the prosopopeia of a language that attributed to them a terroristic action of destroying the foundations of the "Christian West" — that is, of the supernatural (divine) origin of the Cath-

olic tradition and, along with it, of all authority, including that of the state, legitimized by that tradition. In lieu of a modernization (which, if not hoped for,
was at least proclaimed in other contexts and was at the very least experienced as
inevitable), there was established the ritual of an antimodernization or perhaps of
a sustained demodernization of Spain. Against the threats of this lurking enemy
appeals were made to deploy every means of defense—including the most violent ones.

The terms antimodernization and demodernization, in the sense implied by
such practices, have wider implications than do such German terms as *Entmythologisierung* (demythologization) or *Entnazifizierung* (denazification). At hand
here is not a rational cognitive operation whose task is to unmask an ideology and
a more or less irrational belief in order to purify a culture of the weight of the
residual elements of its already bygone past; neither is the matter in anti- or demodernization one of *Umbau* as a hermeneutic method of critical analysis (which
Derrida termed "deconstruction" in his translation of Husserl). Among the
mechanisms deployed in the demodernization of Spain, is that of purging, the
destruction of the other in the name of constructive criticism. We need only recall
(to mention but one example) the purging of the teaching faculty ordered by
Franco as the civil war was unfolding, which announced what the (uncivil) period following the war was to be all about. These operations, however, are oriented more toward a resistance to the new than toward future development by
means of a liberation from obsolete elements. At stake, then, in the practices aim-
ing for the anti- or demodernization of Spain is an antiprocess: the (positive) action to which is opposed a (negative) reaction.

Antimodernization, as sketched above, evinces a double dynamic: the irreconcilable opposition between antagonistic movements that nevertheless define
one another, since one springs from the other just as an answer springs from that
which prompts it. The interrelation of modernization and anti- or demodernization is also to be found, for instance, between the Reformation and the Counter-
Reformation—another somewhat Spanish movement the name of which is not far
removed, in its morphology as signifier (and perhaps—who knows?—as signified), from the term we are now considering. Indeed, the Counter-Reformation
was undoubtedly one of the first antimodernization movements of Spain and the
origin of all such movements that were to follow.

This antibody that is the demodernization of Spain, in addition to belonging to
a process that defines itself by opposition to another process of a contrary sign
(which is why I have allowed myself this analogy between their dynamics and the
action attributed by medical discourse to antibodies), has something else in common with the Counter-Reformation. In both cases, the reference process according to which their dynamics or reaction is defined turns out also to be a rupture
process (an attempt to overcome or to go beyond something known in both cases
as "tradition," whether Roman Catholic, Spanish, or Western) whereby the
Counter-Reformation and antimodernization can define themselves as the rees-

tablishing of order and normalization that follow from a crisis (it should be noted that in their own discourse, not only in mine, can be found the lexical elements of medical discourse). Their dynamics are specifically aimed against this crisis that endangers the (ideological) elements that form the basis of such an order and norm—that is, the traditional doctrinal authority of Rome, the *doxa* questioned as much by the Protestant Reform as by the "errors of modernity."

It can readily be seen that the anti- or demodernization of Spain is not merely one among many movements among the various "isms" of the twentieth century; it is rather a constant of the political, religious, and dominant cultural history of Spain. Its most ancient (and most recent) denominations have been the Crusade: against the "infidels" at the end of the Middle Ages, against "idolatry and human sacrifices" in the Americas, against Luther and "his accomplices" of Seville or Valladolid at the threshold of the Reformation, against the Turks at Lepanto, against Jews, "false converts," "illuminists," "witches," "heretics," and purported other "deviants" across the centuries, against liberalism and the "errors of the moderns" in the past century and even in the present one, against "communism", against "international Judaism," and against the (no less international) "Freemasonry" in Franco's era. The means at its disposal have ranged from social reprobation to armed intervention, passing through the Inquisition and military courts—in Franco's Spain also known as "courts of public order" (*tribunales de orden público*). Its activity extends to all realms of public and private life, and its primary (though not exclusive) objective is to stifle so-called offenses of opinion and any movement of change that fails to respect the unchanging character of "truth."[2]

Any study of the procedures used by the dominant culture to insure the demodernization of Spain will thus first have to turn to a symptomatic reading of the texts of this "crisis" that, because it endangers ideological props, determines the dynamics of the conflict and thus of its "anti." And any analysis of the texts produced or received during one of these periods of rupture or repression will have to consider those texts as a sort of enthymeme, an incomplete syllogism, to the extent that the texts at hand inscribe themselves in a large and interrelated sociocultural and ideological framework. These texts will thus have to be placed in a large intertextual and interdiscursive context in which come into play stimuli of varied origins and responses marked by social practices in varying degrees of consolidation. The context is an integrating part of a whole that is greater than a mere aggregate of phonemes, morphemes, lexemes, syntagmas, and micro- and macrostructures, which constitute only the quantifiable verbal materiality of text. To this neopositivism, which reduces the supposed scientific study of texts to linguistic material (the quantifiable aspect of the signifier), will have to be opposed a study of expression in its totality that omits none of the implicit or explicit elements that come into play during communication. In all acts of communication, the text's explicit information (that is, the actualized verbal part) functions as a triggering mechanism capable of evoking or mobilizing for the reader or listener the entire world of which it is a fragment, the world of representation that constitutes the shared horizon (the implicit part of communication) of transmitter and receiver.

This symptomatic reading of a text and the inclusion of the text in this intertextual and interdiscursive network is best illustrated by the following example, which also brings to the fore a sociocultural constant that has left its imprint on the dominant theory and praxis of Spain for some five hundred years and whose twentieth-century expression is found in the Generation of 1898, in Eugenio d'Ors, in Francoism, in the neothomism of Opus Dei, and in other integrist movements. In his introduction to *Falange y Literatura*, José-Carlos Mainer (1971), when describing what he calls "pre-Falangist attitudes," alludes to Eugenio d'Ors, the "intellectual arbiter" of the Catalan Noucentism and author of a 1905 doctoral thesis in law entitled *Genealogía ideal del imperialismo (Teoría del Estado-héroe)* (An ideal genealogy of imperialism: Theory of the hero-state) and directed by Gumersindo de Azcárate. Following Enric Jardi, the biographer of Xenius, Mainer recalls the time in the midst of the Spanish civil war when d'Ors leaves Paris to join the nationalists and, arriving in Pamplona, holds "vigil" over the "Falange's arms of knighthood" in Saint Andrew's Church. Mainer, who finds in Ors the "traits of a born organizer," also notes his "obsession for lavish rituals" and an "untameable inclination for symbols." He then credits Ors with having concocted the idea of the Institute of Spain (founded on January 6, 1938, as the "Senate of national culture") and of the "Protocol Commission in the commemorations of the Fatherland" (put into effect in accordance with the decree of February 18, 1938). Mainer writes:

> The prestige of d'Ors, as the nation's official in charge of Fine Arts and
> as professor of the science of culture, lasted a long time, and the
> Falange's university group paid him homage with the doctoral thesis that
> José Luis L. Aranguren devoted to his work. (23)

The following commentary by Jardi on the Institute of Spain is almost lost in footnote 14 of Mainer's text:

> The members of the Institute had to answer the following oath
> affirmatively: "Do you swear before God and your Guardian Angel to
> serve Spain perpetually and loyally under the rule and norm of its living
> tradition; in its Catholicity as embodied by the Sovereign Pontiff of
> Rome; in its continuity as represented by the Caudillo, the savior of our
> nation?" (23)

Because the performative language acts first require a social consensus that makes them symptoms of a collective mentality, and because of the continuity of such an oath, this text is not an isolated detail whose analysis should be confined to an anthology of anecdotes on the life of Eugenio d'Ors or on the history of the Institute of Spain. When I speak here of continuity, I am not referring to the "continuity as represented by the Caudillo" proposed by the oath, or to the inherent terminology of continuity of this discourse whose syntagmas "living tradition" and "Catholicity as embodied by the Sovereign Pontiff of Rome" evidently reveal a continuity oriented toward the past just as the syntagmas "perpetually and loyally" and "rule and norm" project this continuity into the future. Independently of the content of such an oath formula, the oath itself is already, as praxis, a residual element of the premodernity deeply significant in Spanish tradition. Not only in terms of the symbolic value and efficiency that it continues to enjoy, but also in terms of its constant use since the prehistory of the modern Spanish state, the oath constitutes a continued mark of Spanish hegemonic culture. It appears in the legend of the *Cid* and in *Las Partidas*, as well as in the *Fueros* and in *Don Quijote*. It is an essential part of the code of honor and law. It constitutes the subject matter of Don Juan's deceit as well as that of the prelude to any challenge. Oaths and abjurations were ritualized by the practices of the Inquisition, which condemned false oaths and perjury. The antimodernist oath ordered by Pius X was practiced until very recent times in university ceremonies. The Institute of Spain established its oath in the midst of the civil war just as other groups and institutions established theirs. There were oaths to the flag in the army, in Catholic Action, in the Falange, and in the *Requetés* or *Cruzados*. Both at city hall and the cathedral of Seville oaths were taken to defend the Immaculate Conception of Mary ("to the last drop of blood") centuries before Immaculate Conception had been declared an article of faith. In Franco's era fidelity was sworn to the *principios del movimiento*, which were declared "imperishable" by the Spanish courts. Finally, today fidelity is sworn to the new constitution.

I considered in the preceding chapter the contextual boundary and the historical conditions that allowed for the "functioning" of Juan Haldudo's oaths and Don Juan's promises. These verbal acts function in both *Don Quijote* and *El Burlador de Sevilla* within a whole far more complex than the organization of those works' lexical and grammatical components: the struggle between diametrically opposed systems of interpreting the world that coexisted in the Spain that produced and consumed these works, just as (at least to a degree) they are consumed by the reader of today. It is from the perspective of a reader of the twentieth century that I again turn to the texts of Cervantes and Tirso de Molina.

The figure of Don Quijote as a prototype of the wandering knight constitutes a point of reference as much for the Generation of 1898 as for d'Ors and the Falange (—recall d'Ors's vigil over the "arms of knighthood of Falange"). Before Cervantes's novel, however, the wandering knight (*a lo divino*) served as a model for the autobiography dictated by Ignacio de Loyola, an advocate of the Counter-Reformation, to his biographer, Father Rivadeneira. We thus once again find ourselves before a constant of the (hegemonic) Hispanic collective imagination that symbolizes its secular struggle against the modernization of Spain, if not (considering its "will to Empire") against the modernization of the entire world.

Because it is within the framework of a social order's sacralization that demonic profanation of that order becomes possible, Kierkegaard regarded Don Juan and Faust as products of the Middle Ages. This framework constitutes the aesthetic foundations of rebellion characteristic of both characters as well as the cathartic effect of their exemplary punishment. One cannot disregard Don Juan's generally acknowledged medieval origin and Tirso de Molina's (or whoever it was who wrote *El Burlador de Sevilla y Convidado de Piedra*) fusing of two medieval legends into a single text. The double title of the drama betrays its origins: *the Deceiver*, the tale of punished cunning; and *the Guest*, the tale of inviting a dead. The medieval feature as well as the modernity of the central figure and his language—theological theme and solution aside—make *Don Juan* a drama of Counter-Reform Spain.

The functioning of two syntagmas that are repeated in the elaboration of the drama (and that go beyond the juxtaposition of two medieval legends) supports this claim: (1) the response (of an economical order) "You are giving me long-term credit" (*muy largo me lo fiais*) with which Don Juan answers the reminders of death on the part of his valet, his victims, the statue, and the chorus; and (2) the "I promise" (*prometo*), emphasized by "I swear to keep my word" (*juro cumplir mi promesa/mi palabra*), by means of which Don Juan succeeds in his deceit (see chapter 6)..

Don Juan is "the actor par excellence" because of the double theatricality of the dramas that compel him to action. It is less the changes of his personality disguised in the cloaks of others that allow him to trap "those women who are waiting" than it is the usurpation of a language that is socially marked and efficient in his social environment. This discursive usurpation makes it possible for Don Juan to talk to his victims in their language, not his. A discursive mask, then, allows Don Juan, in his oaths and promises, to disguise speech by means of speech. The counterpoint of this discursive mask is constituted (as if it were a reality against which the mask reveals itself as false) by promises in negative, the serious threats uttered by his valet, his victims, the statue, the chorus, in a vertiginous crescendo that, thanks to supernatural intervention, will lead Don Juan to his demise and to silence. This makes it possible to affirm that Tirso's drama only reproduces, like an echo, the problematical verbal uses of its time. It will be through Molière, by means of irony, that Don Juan's final punishment will make of Tirso's supernatural tragedy a human comedy, thereby testifying to the increasing social and discursive awareness that seems to constitute the historical role of literature.

Unlike Tirso, Cervantes seems to participate in the growing awareness of the crisis. In this sense, Cervantes coincides with Molière. By his use of irony, Cervantes manages to transform the chivalry epic into the novel, at the same time turning the highest values of feudalism into the grotesque. Since *Don Quijote* is a series of interdiscursive confrontations in which irony operates on both opposing worlds (and not on the feudal world alone), then what we have here is a critical distance, an ironization of two opposed worlds—the feudal and the bourgeois—and the deconstruction of the opposition itself. This distancing, at any rate, removes the text from the purely mechanical reproduction space of those discourses that are represented. Cervantes's work thus inscribes itself in the process of modernization that is later destroyed by the parameters that condition a reading that demodernizes the text during its historical reception. The aforementioned commentaries on *Don Quijote* as well as other reuses of the text or of quixotic ideals have contributed, consciously or not, to the demodernization of Cervantes's work.

During my detour through the oath as a constant of the hegemonic Spanish collective imagination in its struggle for the anti- or demodernization of Spain, and taking advantage of the margin authorized by the ambiguity of the title that named, without defining, the subject of my proposition, the concept of antimodernization has gradually taken the form of a reaction against a modernity beyond the "modernity" of Baudelaire. Indeed, this process, while always reaching new areas of application throughout the centuries, inscribes itself to a certain extent in a dynamics of liberation of the humankind: faced with myths in general (*Entmythologisierung*); faced with the ideology of feudalism (bourgeois emancipation); faced with the limits of politics traditionally prescribed by religion (the political technique serving but the "state reason," proposed by Machiavelli); faced with the limits imposed by religious beliefs on science, ethics, and art (the secularization proclaimed by the Enlightenment); faced with the limits imposed by nature on human activity (technological development); faced with the constraints of mimesis and the representation of the real (the autoreferentiality of art, of the novel, and of modern poetry); faced with any reference to the real (epistemological rupture and the founding of the *Wertfreiheit* that characterizes the modern market economy based on conventional *exchange value* and not on (real?) use value).

My goal is not to defend modernity. Neither would I under any circumstances advocate the continuous and unlimited progress of the humanity that rejects its past and present in the name of the future, or the alienation of human being by technical mastery over a hostile nature, for there is nothing more hostile than the denaturalized milieu we have inherited from so-called technical progress. My aim here is neither a defense of the project of the Enlightenment that ignores its aporia, nor a critique in the manner of postmodernist nostalgia that does little else but clamor (in an almost delirious neoconservatism) for a return to a new Middle Ages. A critique along these lines would only legitimize the anti- or demodernization that I have traced through a period of several centuries of Spanish history, as if it were a movement that anticipated (prophetically, as usual) the rest of the world. My aim has been only to sketch some prologomena to a literary historiography of twentieth-century Spain by emphasizing a methodology, discourse analysis, as well as a horizon that extends beyond the restrictions of an isolated historical moment (here, the twentieth century) — an extended horizon that allows an understanding of the dynamics of historical continuities that Paul Ricoeur (1969) has called "the long path . . . of reflection on the dynamics of cultural symbols" (286).

Chapter 8
Narration and Argumentation in the Chronicles of the New World

In Spanish historiography the year 1492 is doubly symbolic, for it coincides not only with the crowning of a long process of national unification, but also with the beginning of Spain's territorial expansion on a global scale. National unification was consummated with the armed conquest of the last Islamic bastion in Iberian lands, the kingdom of Granada, and the expulsion by decree of the Jews. The territorial expansion that would lead to the annexation of the earldoms of Rosellón and Cerdaña (1493), the occupation of the kingdom of Naples (1503), the conquests of Melilla (1497) and Orán (1509), and other incursions in Africa, and that would later result in the religious wars in Europe with the subjugation of the Netherlands, began with Christopher Columbus and his taking possession of the West Indies in the name of the sovereigns of Castile and Aragón on October 12, 1492.

In this same year, the first Castilian or Spanish grammar was printed in Salamanca. Antonio de Nebrija dedicated it to Queen Isabella with words that manifested a national conscience and an early interpretation of the past and future of Spain—matters that language, as "companion of the empire," would serve. In the Dedication, Nebrija indicated that "the scattered members and pieces of Spain, which were spread about, were consolidated and joined in a body and unity of the kingdom" ("los miembros e pedaços de España, que estauan por muchas partes derramados, se reduxeron e aiuntaron en un cuerpo e unidad de reino"). For Nebrija, this process, which was above all the work of "divine goodness and providence," coincided with the formation and development of the Castilian language and would "reach the monarchy and peace that we enjoy." It was also the outcome of the "industry, work, and diligence" of the Crown. Nebrija concludes:

> So that after purging the Christian religion, for which we are friends of God, or reconciled with Him; after the enemies of our faith have been vanquished through war and force of arms, from which our own received so much harm and feared even greater; after the justice and execution of the laws that unite us and allow us to live equally in this great company that we call the kingdom and republic of Castile; there is nothing left but the flowering of the arts of peace. Among the first ones is that which language teaches us.[1]

In *The Prince*, Machiavelli offers a historical interpretation similar to Nebrija's, although his extra emphasis on the political dimension unmasks Ferdinand of Aragón's use of religion, which turned him into a "new prince":

> Nothing brings a prince more prestige than the accomplishment of great deeds and giving uncommon examples of himself. In our time there is King Ferdinand of Aragón, the present king of Spain. The latter can practically be called a new prince for from being a weak king he has become, through fame and glory, the first king of the Christians; and if you consider his actions, you will find all of them to be great and some extraordinary. In the beginning of his reign he laid siege to Granada: and that undertaking was the foundation of his State. . . . Besides this, in order to be able to undertake even greater campaigns, always making use of religion, he turned toward a pious cruelty, expelling and eliminating the *marranos* from his Kingdom. There could not be a more pitiless or more uncommon example than the latter. Under the same mantle of religion he attacked Africa; he carried out the Italian Campaign; he recently attacked France; and in this manner he has always performed and carried out great projects which have always kept his subjects in a state of suspense and admiration and intent on their outcome. And these moves of his have followed so closely one upon another and in such a way that he has never allowed people time and opportunity in between those moves to be able to quietly counter them. (119-20)

In order to understand this convergence of the linguistic, religious, and political dimensions on the symbolic date of 1492, we must go back to the moment when Spain was born as a modern state and to the process of gestation of this nation-state around the last centuries of the so-called Reconquest. Only in this way can we understand the dynamic impetus that propelled the young Spanish state to the American adventure as a historical enterprise realized under the sign of a "religious mission" entrusted to it by the pope as the "Vicar of Christ [of God] on earth."

The birthdate of the Spanish nation-state can be fixed as October 18, 1469, another symbolic though less exploited date in Spanish historiography. Its place of birth is Valladolid, where on that date the two great Christian kingdoms of Castile and Aragón were united through the marriage of Isabella I of Castile and Fernando V of Aragón. This was during the last stages of the Middle Ages, a period that witnessed the rise of many national European blocks as monarchies emancipating themselves from the Roman pontiff and the Christian emperor.[2] It would be a mistake to explain the rise of the Spanish nation-state within this framework alone. Though situated in the same historical period, the Spanish nation-state emerges under the opposite ideological sign. To better understand the mission and the significance that this new state attributed to itself, it is important to analyze the founding act, the marriage arranged between Isabella of Castile and Ferdinand of Aragón, as well as the immediately ensuing struggle against the Arabic kingdom of Granada.

The moment immediately prior to the constitution and consolidation of the Spanish state, the situation to which that marriage responds, is the same situation from which the new state will emerge as a project conceived of as a historical mission. Once the Arabs established themselves on the Iberian Peninsula, this territory was fragmented into small kingdoms, some Christian, others Islamic. Agitated by a continuing struggle for territorial expansion, they established their alliances according to the strategic convenience of the moment rather than through religious beliefs. In Toledo, we witness a major cultural undertaking in which the three great religions that coexisted on the Iberian Peninsula during the Middle Ages — Judaism, Christianity, and Islam — closely collaborated. Yet in spite of this collaboration, the Christian kingdoms developed a consciousness of a common religious mission against the infidels that called for the expulsion of the Moslems from Iberian lands after Pope Innocent III launched this notion by declaring the wars that Alfonso VIII, king of Castile, was preparing against the Arabs a "Christian cause," and by according him a Crusade bull. In that enterprise, Castile was joined by the kingdoms of Navarra, León, and Aragón as well as the other kingdoms of Christian Europe, which sent troops in a common undertaking that would be crowned by a victory at Las Navas de Tolosa in 1212. The lucrative spoils of this enterprise reinforced the notion of a holy war and instigated a series of military alliances and marriages that contributed to the gradual unification of the Christian kingdoms. In this manner, the multitude of Christian kingdoms (Galicia, Asturias, León, Navarra, Castile, Aragón, Catalonia, and Portugal) slowly began to contract until two Christian states emerged to dominate the entire Iberian Peninsula: Castile and Aragón, whose union in 1469 led to the victory over Granada, and Portugal. The union of Castile and Aragón thus marked the end of the long historical process initiated by the pope's declaration of the Castilian conquest as a "Christian cause" and "crusade."[3]

The idea of Reconquest thus constituted the bonding element of the various Christian kingdoms of the Iberian Peninsula in a dynamic process that would lead to this union of Castile (which had fused under its crown the old kingdoms of Galicia, Asturias, León, and Castile) and Aragón (which had united Navarra, Aragón, and Catalonia). The idea of Reconquest also generated the political and religious ideal that converted into chieftains (*caudillos*) of the "crusade against the infidels" those very kings who had earlier called themselves emperors in order to encompass under their crowns Christians, Jews, and Moslems. Their ideal became the establishment of "purity of faith" in their territories, and their expansionist drive became ideologically confused with the expansion of Christianity at the very time when Christianity was witnessing a decline in Europe.

During the first centuries of the period designated in general terms by Spanish historiography as the Reconquest, Jews, Christians, and Moslems lived side by side in each of the kingdoms established on Iberian lands, and temples were erected for the three faiths. Yet as soon as the idea of a crusade against the infidels solidified, the Moslems and Jews living in "Christian territory" had no alternative but to convert to Christianity or to flee. Under such circumstances, false conversions proliferated. In response the Catholic kings created in 1478 the inquisitional tribunals, whose difficult task consisted of watching over "the religious and social unity" of the new state. This new politicoreligious institution further influenced the domestic politics of those kings, who considered themselves guarantors of their subjects' purity of faith. Freed from the inner enemies of the faith through the vigilance of these tribunals, it is hardly surprising that the kings should then seek the expansion of that faith in literal compliance with the "religious mission" assigned to them by the pope, the "Vicar of Christ on earth." Proof of the interest shown by Rome in the total elimination of the Moslem presence in the Spanish territories is a series of Crusade bulls that preceded and inspired the conquest of Granada. On November 13, 1479, ten years after national unification, Pope Sixtus IV promulgated the first of these bulls—a gesture repeated with the concession of new privileges and new indulgences in 1482, 1485, 1487, 1489, and 1491. Chroniclers relate that when news of the capitulation of the kingdom of Granada to the Catholic kings reached Rome, bells tolled and the "Christian triumph" was celebrated with religious and secular feasts lasting several days.

Immediately after the conquest of Granada military expeditions were organized to attack the north of Africa, where between 1497 and 1512 the Spaniards conquered fortified towns such as Melilla, Alcazaquivir, Orán, Tripoli, and others. Military bases thus established permitted both the defense of Spanish possessions in southern Italy and their expansion, thereby assuring Spanish control over the Mediterranean (*Mare nostrum*)—all of this under the pretext of the Turkish threat to Christianity. It seems as if *homo hispanus* had so identified with the chivalric ideal of the crusade that, having achieved an interior purity of faith, he sought to impose it on the entire world (see Bataillon 1937, especially 55-65). When the Protestant Reformation surfaced, Charles V fought it with the same zeal with which his predecessors had fought the Moslems in and outside of

Spain. The same policies continued under Philip II, who managed to ruin the Spanish economy with his religious wars in Europe and his expedition against the Turks, which ended with a victory in Lepanto in 1571. The struggle of the Spanish infantry in the Netherlands and the "Invincible Armada" sent against England were also military expeditions undertaken in the name of a frustrated politicoreligious expansion of the great Catholic power with which the Habsbourgs wanted to oppose the Protestant Reformation.

But in the conquest and colonization of the New World the ideological identification of Spain's expansionism with the evangelical expansionism of the Catholic church is most clearly manifest. Just over six months after Columbus stepped into the New World, the Spaniards were granted a bull (*inter coetera*) by the Spanish pope, Alexander VI, for the purpose of propagating Christianity in the "discovered" territories. It was a kind of *missio canonica* that charged the Spanish kings with preaching the gospel and converting the so-called Indians to the Catholic faith. The extent to which the Catholic kings literally interpreted the "religious mission" assigned to them by Rome can be seen in the title designating their role in this "Christian cause": royal apostolic vicarage (*Regio Vicariato Apostólico*). If one considers the church's development and expansion in the New World by the early seventeenth century, one also sees how assiduously the Catholic kings followed their charge. A little over a century of missionary work led to the establishment of five metropolitan seats, with twenty-nine subordinate episcopates; the number of missionaries that accompanied conquistadors, settlers, adventurers, and gold-seekers in the New World had reached many thousands, and the number of churches, convents, and cathedrals erected was considerable.[4]

More significant here than the well-known abuses committed in the name of this "religious mission" are the divisions of opinion and property claims in the West Indies based on this mission. Thus for Father Bartolomé de Las Casas and for Pedro Mártir de Anglería, the native people were subjected to slavery in the name of God and the gospel, and what the Spaniards brought them was not God's law but greed, envy, and anger. In Columbus's account (which is reminiscent of Ovid's Golden Age in *Metamorphoses*), they lived in a purely natural state.[5] For other authors such as Francisco López de Gómara, the chronicler of Cortés, the colonization of America signified the epic of "the redemption of the most primitive people on earth" ("la redención de los pueblos más primitivos de la tierra") who until then had lived with "cannibalism, poligamy, polytheism, not free of cruel human sacrifices" ("canibalismo, poligamia, politeismo no libre de cruentos sacrificios humanos"). With biblical allusions, López de Gómara's *Historia general de las Indias* describes the conquest of America as "the liberation of the Indians from the slavery of Egypt" ("la liberación de los indios de la esclavitud de Egipto") and likens it to the "conquering of the vineyard of the Lord" ("conquista de la vid del Señor") and to the "conquest of the promised land" ("toma de posesión de la tierra prometida") by the "chosen people of God" ("pueblo elegido de Dios"). In a description of the military strategy of the conquistadors, Martin Fernández Enciso (1519) uses the biblical passage of the conquest of Jericho literally, thus underscoring the "divine election" ("elección divina") of the Spanish people:

And then Joshua commanded those [officers] of the first city, which was Jericho, to take possession of the land which the Lord God had given them to possess.

[E después envio Josué a requerir a los de la primera ciudad, que era Jericó, que le dejasen e diesen aquella tierra, pues era suya porque se la había dado Dios.]

Indeed, before they were engaged in battle, the native people were read a *requerimiento* (requisition or injunction), a theological treatise that evoked "the history of Man's health," from the creation of the world and original sin to redemption through Christ and the founding of the church as the depository of such redemption and of the authority of Christ. The pope, as vicar of Christ and as head of that church, had entrusted those lands to the king and queen of Castile so that in their name and authority might be exacted the inhabitants' acceptance of baptism and their acknowledgment of the Spaniards' authority over them. A well-known anecdote attributes to the people of the Sinú region (present day Colombia) the following reaction upon hearing the *requerimiento*:

Those Indians agreed that there was only one God, but as to the claim that the Pope was the master of the universe, and that he had granted those lands to the Kings of Castile, they said that the Pope must have been drunk when he did so, for he was giving what did not belong to him. And that the King who asked for and accepted such favor must be crazy, for he asked for what belonged to others.

[Estaban de acuerdo aquellos indios en que no havía sino un Dios; pero en lo que decía que el Papa era señor del Universo y que él habia fecho merced de aquellas tierras a los reyes de Castilla, dixeron que el Papa debiera estar borracho cuando lo fizo, pues daba lo que no era suyo. Y que el rey que pedía y que tomaba tal merced debía ser algún loco, pues pedía lo que era de otros.][6]

The disputed vision of the conquest as reflected both in the controversy instigated by the texts of Bartolomé de Las Casas at the University of Salamanca regarding the *títulos de dominio* (titles of domain) legitimizing the presence of the Spaniards in the New World, and in the controversy between Las Casas and Sepúlveda over the nature of the "Indian," reflects a mentality based on common premises: the existence of a religious mission in the New World, be it well or poorly carried out by the Spaniards, and a description of its inhabitants (whether idealized as *bon sauvage* or condemned as barbaric) that insists on their differences vis-à-vis the Spanish. These positions therefore differ not in their basic assumptions but only in the purported selection of the narrated facts in accordance with an interpretation of a conquest whose legitimacy is questioned by none—not even by those who stress its disastrous effects. An analysis limited to the study of the narrative contents of this textual corpus can only contribute to the dualist, Manichaean position that has dominated for centuries the historiography of the Spanish presence in America.[7]

A change of mentality in Spain has both produced and consumed these texts. By focusing on the lexical and morphosyntactical organization of the narrative and on the text's pragmatics rather than on that which is narrated, discursive analysis allows us to go beyond the explicit information selected by the text to the implicit that the same text conceals more or less intentionally. Let us take as an example the first vision of the "Indian" as described by Columbus in his *Diario* (Diary). This text, whose original has been lost, has been transmitted to us in the compilation of Bartolomé de Las Casas.[8] The entry dated Thursday, October 11, 1492, in which the happenings of October 12 are also related, ends in the following manner:

> The words that follow are the formal words of the Admiral, in the book of his first voyage and discovery of these Indies. "I [says he], to gain great friendship, for I realized that they were people who could be surrendered and converted to our Sacred Faith better with love than by force, gave some of them colored caps and some glass beads which they put around their necks, and other things of little value which gave them much pleasure and they ended up being ours to an amazing extent. Thereafter, they came swimming to the boats of the ships where we were and they brought us parrots and balls of cotton thread and spears and many other things and exchanged them for other things which we gave them such as little glass beads and bells. Finally, they took everything we offered and gave of what they had willingly. But I thought that they were poor people who lacked so much; they were all as naked as their mothers made them, even the women, although I only saw a very young one and all I saw were all lads for I did not see any older than thirty. They were well made, with very beautiful bodies and very beautiful faces; their hair was short and almost as thick as the bristles in a horse's tail; their hair comes down to their eyebrows, except for a few strands in the back, which are long, and which they never cut; some of them painted themselves blackish and they are of the color of canaries, neither black nor white, and some of them paint themselves white and some red, and some in whatever they find, and some paint their faces, and some their whole body, and some only their eyes, and some only their nose. They don't bear arms, nor do they know them, for I showed them swords and they grabbed them by the blade, and cut themselves out of ignorance. They have no iron; their spears are like poles without metal points, some with a fish tooth on the end, and others with other things. They all are in general of good stature and size, and of good expression; well built; I saw some with signs of

wounds on their bodies, and I asked them with gestures what they were, and they showed me how these people came from other nearby islands who wanted to take them, and they defended themselves; and I thought, and think, that here they come from firm land to take them captive. They should make good servants, and of a good nature, as I see that they quickly answer all that is said to them, and I believe that easily they could become Christians, as it seems they did not belong to any sect. I, God willing, will bring back to Your Highness from here at the time of my departure, six so that they learn to speak. I saw no animals of any kind on this island, except parrots." All these are the words of the Admiral (*Diario*, 1:95-96)[9]

Before the quoted passage, Las Casas compiles the day's events in the usual form, that is, as an account told in the epic preterit with quotations in indirect style:

At two hours past midnight, land was sighted. . . . They worked the sails . . . , waiting until daylight on Friday, when they arrived at an islet of the Lucayos, which was called in the Indian language Guanahaní. Then they saw naked people, and the Admiral left for land in the armed boat, with Martín Alonso Pinzón and Vicente Anes, his brother, who was captain of the Niña. The Admiral took out the royal flag. . . . Once on land they saw very green trees and much water and many kinds of fruit. The Admiral called to the two captains and the others to come onto land, and to Rodrigo Descovedo, clerkrecorder of the armada, and to Rodrigo Sánchez de Segovia, and told them to administer to him by faith and testimony, as he would take before them all, and as he in fact took, possession of the island for the King and Queen, his monarchs. . . . Then many people of the island gathered there. (*Diario*, 1:95-96)[10]

In his *Historia de las Indias* [History of the New World], Bartolomé de Las Casas proceeds in an almost identical manner as far as direct quotes of the admiral are concerned. At the end he also adds the quasi-liturgical formula "All these are the words of the Admiral." But in addition to the quote in direct style, an argumentative interpretation picks up in an indirect style the same quoted sentences. This sheds light on Las Casas's intention to show that the inhabitants of that island were those "beings" that Pliny, Pomponius Mela, Strabo, Virgil, Isidor of Seville, Boethius, and other authors call "most holy and most happy" ("santísimos y felicísimos"). Here is the summary that precedes the quotation in direct style:

The Admiral, seeing them so good and simple, and that as much as they could were liberally hospitable, and as such were so pacific, gave them many glass beads and bells, and some colored caps and other things, with which they felt contented and enriched. (1:204)[11]

Countering the accusations of aggression, Las Casas insists on the pacifism of these people who do not feel ashamed of their nakedness: "It seemed that the state of innocence had not been lost or had been restored" ("parecía no haberse perdido o haberse restituido el estado de inocencia"). Unlike Sepúlveda who, on the basis of Aristotle's texts, considered the "Indians" inferior beings "without a soul" whose servitude to the Spaniards was thus justified, Las Casas emphasizes their human qualities. In fact, his text seems to seek to prove that they are endowed with the three faculties—memory, understanding, and will—that distinguish human from beast in Aristotelian-Thomist scholasticism. He also highlights their favorable disposition to becoming Christians, for they "did not belong to any sect." This last consideration is crucial because it raises the possibility of evangelizing native peoples rather than destroying them as infidels. For Las Casas, the Spanish presence was legitimized by the evangelizing mission conferred upon the Spaniards by Rome. Sepúlveda, on the contrary, seemed not to have fully understood that if those people were not human beings, they were not appropriate subjects for baptism. The property titles over the new lands, which were based on the Spaniards' evangelizing mission, thus would be destroyed in favor of a greater liberty in subjugating and enslaving its people.

Las Casas ultimately uses the October 11 *Diario* entry as an authoritative argument: he identifies it, by defining the pragmatics of its enunciation, as Columbus's report to the king and queen of Spain. This important fact regarding the internal receiver of Columbus's report is brought out in the text itself: "I, God willing, will bring back to Your Highness from here at the time of my departure, six so that they learn to speak." Contrary to what happens in the *Diario*'s presentation formula, however, which insists that it reproduce the "formal words of the Admiral," the presentation of Columbus's text in the *Historia de las Indias* reads as follows:

Who [the Admiral], in this book of his first voyage, written for the Catholic Kings, says as follows . . .

[El cual (el Almirante), en el libro desta su primera navegación, que escribió para los Reyes Católicos, dice de aquesta manera . . .

The circumstances of its enunciation turns the cited text into a reliable document on which Las Casas can base his affirmations about the natural condition of the natives before their corruption at the hands of the Spaniards. But the communicative circuit from which this text emerges also allows us to deduce that its enunciations constitute a symptom of the collective mentality then dominant in Spain. Because any argumentation is organized in function of its addressee, it is more the expression of the receiver's mentality than that of its author. Therefore, my conclusion refers more to the Spanish collective mentality than to Christopher Columbus as an individual—or to his nation.

In his *Historia del almirante*, Hernando Colón freely resorts to these texts. Chapter 23, "How the Admiral Stepped on Land and Took Possession of It in the Name of the Catholic Kings" ("Cómo el Almirante salió a tierra y tomó posesión de aquélla en nombre de los Reyes Católicos"), gives us the following account about the condition of the "Indians":

> This feast and gaiety was attended by many Indians, and when the Admiral saw that they were peaceful and tranquil people, and of great simplicity, he gave them some red caps and things of little value which were more highly regarded by them than if they had been high-priced stones.

> [Asistieron a esta fiesta y alegría muchos indios, y viendo el Almirante que eran gente mansa, tranquila y de gran sencillez, les dió algunos bonetes rojos y cosas de poco valor, que fueron más estimadas por ellos que si fueran piedras de mucho precio. (112)]

The transformation of the fixed syntagma "precious stones" ("piedras preciosas"), an apparent condensation of use-value, into "high-priced stones" ("piedras de mucho precio"), a condensation of exchange value, evinces a shift in the reading of the text: the idyllic scene—the *locus amoenus* that dominates the act of taking possession of the utopian island—is now converted into a market scene of exchangeable goods. An analysis of the text on the basis of its contamination by economic discourse confirms the reading of his father's diary suggested here by Hernando Colón.

Let us begin by focusing on the morphosyntactic organization of the narrative sequences in the words so insistently attributed to the admiral by Bartolomé de Las Casas. The alternation of the verb tenses corresponding to what Harald Weinrich calls the "narrated world" with those corresponding to the "commented world" shows us in the text's first sequence a predominance of verbs of action in the preterit—in the first person singular (Columbus) and the third person plural (the people of the island). In the second sequence verbs in the imperfect or in the present predominate. Finally, in a third sequence we find modalizations such as "I believe" ("creo") or "should be" ("deben ser") as well as verbs in the conditional or future tenses.

The first sequence, where verbs of action in the preterit predominate, comprises a series of final clauses, some explicit ("in order to gain their friendship"), others implicit in copulative conjunctions that unite action with intended result ("I gave . . . they ended up being ours to an amazing extent"). The verbs corresponding to these final sentences alternate between "to give" ("dar") and "to do" ("hacer") or equivalent verbs. The structure of the sentences in this first sequence corresponds precisely to the contractual formulas codified in Roman law. They also correspond to our present division of commerce, depending on whether it deals with the exchange of goods, the exchange of services, or a mixed exchange:

I give in order that you give (*do ut des*).
I give in order that you do (*do ut facias*).
I do in order that you do (*facio ut facias*).
I do in order that you give (*facio ut des*).

In addition, the adjectives that modify the objects of that continuous exchange limit themselves to a comparison of what is given to what is received: "I, to gain great friendship, . . . gave some of them colored caps and some glass beads . . . and other things of little value . . . [They] brought us parrots and balls of cotton thread and spears and many other things and exchanged them for other things which we would give them such as little glass beads and bells."

All of these comparisons lead to a double conclusion: the first, implicit in the comparison itself by virtue of the disproportion between the given and the received, is that of a profitable exchange; the second, which is somewhat insistently explicit in the text, is that the final result of this commercial exchange consists of the possession of those people ("they ended up being ours to an amazing extent"). In addition, there is established an equivalence between friendship, self-surrender, and conversion ("to gain great friendship, for I realized that they were people who could be surrendered and converted to our Sacred Faith better with love than by force").

The transition to the second sequence, which deals with the "nature and customs of those people" (to use the title given by Hernando Colón to chapter 24 of his *Historia del almirante*, which refers specifically to the second sequence of Columbus's *Diario* discussed here), is effected by a summary of the previous sequence ("Finally, they took everything we offered and gave of what they had willingly"). The descriptive section is followed by the frequent use of a rhetorical device common in discourse on the Golden Age: the litotes ("They were all naked . . . I did not see any older than thirty. . . . They don't bear arms, nor do they know them. . . . They have no iron"). Finally, remarks mingled with prior observations befitting a European Renaissance man end this sequence. The observers remark on physical beauty ("They were well made, with very beautiful bodies and very beautiful faces. . . . They all are in general of good stature and size, and of good expression; well built") and hairstyle and the colors with which the people adorn themselves, but they also express surprise and astonishment at the sight of female nudity. In this last sequence an initial paragraph detaches itself, although it seemed at first to constitute both (1) the conclusion of the two preceding sequences and (2) the logicosyntactic element that gave the whole its textual coherence. At any rate, we find here the functional explanation of the preceding observations concerning the behavior and traits of the "Indian": "They must be good servants and of a good disposition, for I see that they soon say everything that I told them, and I believe that they would easily become Christians, for it seemed to me that they did not belong to any sect."

I have previously tried to show the impact that a discourse specific to bourgeois economic mentality can have on the discourse of official ideology, including the (neo)scholastic one that informs the political and religious thought of
imperial Spain precisely at a time when there is an attempt to restore the already
obsolete medieval mentality. Don Quijote himself, despite his resilient idealism,
cannot escape the contamination of his chivalric discourse by the increasingly
hegemonic (even if not yet officially recognized) discourse of economic calcula-
tion. Is it possible that in the American adventure lay none of that quixoticism
that the Generation of 1898 tried to read into it when it completed its economic
"reappraisal"? Perhaps this diagnosis was simply a result of the coincidence of
the moment of their meditations after the independence of America (considered a
colonial disaster) with the third centenary of the publication of *Don Quijote*. The
beginnings of an answer to this question may be found in a few documents that
deal with the conquest of Granada and the colonization of America and that, like
Columbus in his attempt to idealize the "enterprise," cannot entirely conceal the
increasingly obvious presence of an economic discourse that corrodes the missionary discourse of those politicians concerned with the health of the soul.

The following two documents indicate that we are dealing here with a constant. The first, dated March 1485, refers to the struggle that Ferdinand and Isabella were preparing against the kingdom of Granada; the second, dated Sep-
tember 1632, refers to the evangelization of America. The first document is the
reply sent by Ferdinand V of Aragón to Pope Innocent VIII through his ambassa-
dors in Rome, Antonio Graddino and Francisco Rojas, to the pope's desire to re-
tain for the apostolic seat a third of the money obtained through the Crusade bull
that he had just decreed in favor of the struggle against the kingdom of Granada
(his argument: *facio ut des, do ut des*). After the king's declaration that in this
fight he sought neither power nor wealth, the document continues:

> But the desire we have to serve God and the zeal toward his holy
> Catholic faith, makes us postpone all interests and makes us forget the
> continuous toils and dangers that accrue to us for this cause. And while
> in a position of being able to safeguard not only our own treasures, but
> of having many more from the Moors, who would voluntarily grant
> them to us for the sake of peace, we reject [the treasures] that are
> offered to us and we spill our own, hoping only for the advance of the
> holy Catholic faith and for the elimination of the peril which
> Christianity has here at its doors if these infidels from the kingdom of
> Granada are not extirpated and thrown out of Spain. (Góñiz Gaztambide
> 1958, 672)[12]

The second document was written by a commission named by King Philip IV
in order to make a strong case to the apostolic nunciate in Madrid for the right of
the Spanish Crown to maintain certain privileges (*regalías*) that Rome sought to
abolish. It mentions the services rendered by the Spanish Crown to the apostolic

seat in the defense and propagation of the faith. Rome was expected to honor its commitments by maintaining such privileges (*do ut facias, facio ut facias*). Point 38 of the document prepared by the commission states:

> This Crown spends its treasures and uses all of its powers in defense of the faith, and has propagated our holy religion through so many kingdoms and faraway provinces, bringing the Spanish nation other new worlds to the obedience of the Apostolic Seat. ("Parecer de la Junta sobre abusos en Roma y Nunciatura," in Aldea 1961, 143-354)[13]

It is in reality a historical constant that has lasted Spain until recently and has plunged Spanish historiography into an increasingly delirious interpretation of the past because of the interdiscursive interpenetration that grows proportionally as the economic mentality becomes more influential. Let us consider, as an example, a (confessional?) text by Marcelino Menéndez y Pelayo, taken from the second volume of his *Historia de los heterodoxos españoles*:

> I understand quite well that these things will cause a piteous smile in politicians and financial experts who, seeing us poor, down, and humiliated at the end of the seventeenth century, do not find words contemptuous enough for a nation that fought against half of a conspiring Europe, and this [it was doing] neither to round out its territory nor to obtain war compensation, but for theological ideas . . . the most useless thing in the world. How much better would it have been to weave cloth and to allow Luther to come and go where he wished! . . . Never, from the time of Judas Maccabee, was there a people which for so many reasons could think of itself as a people chosen to be the sword and the arm of God; and they referred and subordinated everything, even their dreams of grandeur and universal monarchy to this supreme object: *fiat unum ovile et unus pastor* [let there be one sheep pen and one shepherd]. (2:328-29)[14]

As Emilia de Zuleta (1966) emphasized in the introduction to her *Historia de la crítica española contemporánea*, Marcelino Menéndez y Pelayo is probably "the founder of modern literary criticism in Spain for he traced its general concepts and determined its methods" (11). To this feat of Menéndez y Pelayo, generally acknowledged by the historiography of Spanish literary criticism, can be added another less obvious and perhaps less glorious one. He has left behind an ideological mark that pervades Spanish literary criticism to this day, which probably explains why it is barely visible. In Zuleta's description in the book's first chapter of the "general characteristics" of Menéndez y Pelayo's work, the author emphasizes how the "sense of unity" is its "most constant element." This sense of unity is also one of "totality" and goes well beyond his "own and personal" style to create a background against which two elements stand out.

The first unifying element in the work of Menéndez y Pelayo is his desire to determine, through literary history, a unique spiritual orientation of Spain's past. . . . According to him, the fundamental axis of this past is situated at the intersection of two integrated elements, the first being a Spanish national element and the second a Catholic traditional element. The Spanish national element was able to emerge and define itself, in spite of differences, because of the Roman imprint which provided the unifying foundations of all orders and of language in particular. This national unity will subsequently be reinforced by the unity of faith which will accomplish its highest synthesis during the Golden Age.

The second unifying element is constituted by the global sense which allowed him to consider the literary and cultural process in time as well as in space.

For Menéndez y Pelayo, the historical framework—and thus its literature—has a range far wider than the one usually attributed to it by critics and researchers. It embraces everything which at one point had been Hispanic—not only Spanish, but also Portuguese and Latin American. This enlargement of the framework directly influences his notion of Spanish literature which covers Latin, Portuguese, and Catalan literature as well as Semitic influences and Hispanic-American literature. (Zuleta 1966, 16-17)

From Roman Spain onward, then, and not only since the reunification of the Christian kingdoms (and the exclusion of other languages and cultures that co-existed in the Iberian Peninsula during the Middle Ages) by the Catholic kings at the end of the fifteenth century, we witness the formation of this nation and empire, the culture of which is unique and indivisible. One could not better define the cultural isolation to which the Inquisition and censorship condemned this nation; neither could one better pave the way for the definition of national spirit proclaimed in our time by Spanish fascism, imposed by force during the near half-century of Franco's dictatorship, and still alive even in the absence of dictatorship owing to the inertia and the unconscious dimension of ideologies.

What Emilia de Zuleta fails to mention is that Menéndez y Pelayo's work, so unitary and totalitarian, emerges from the polemical struggles against the temptations of Spanish Krausism precisely in order to esape from such an isolation and to promote an open dialogue between Spain and the world external to it, as well as between different notions of the world that, in spite of inquisitions and censorship, have always existed in Spain and confronted the Spanish. An autocritical sentence by Gumersindo de Azcárate was the pretext that allowed Menéndez y Pelayo to appear on the Spanish chess board. The ensuing polemic—his contribution to the well-known controversy on the ''Spanish science''—gave Menéndez y Pelayo the platform he needed to establish while he was still very young the intellectual profile to which he would pay tribute for his entire life. In his essay *El Self-Government y la Monarquia doctrinaria*, Gumersindo de Azcár-ate had maintained:

> According to the fact, for instance, that the state protects or denies scientific freedom, the energy of a people will in a more or less evident manner show its particular geniality in that domain and will even be able to go so far as to stifle its activity, just as was the case with Spain for three centuries. (114)

This claim, which is only the often-repeated expression of the inferiority complex of many Spanish in scientific matters and also of the attempt to preserve their genius (a genius well concealed because smothered by a lack of freedom), led to Menéndez y Pelayo's endless catalogues of the Spanish names who according to him had contributed to different fields of knowledge. This polemical disposition, an *apologetica defensio*, would thereafter animate his work, and he would bequeath it to posterity, Ramón Menéndez Pidal included. Emilia de Zuleta strove to distinguish these two men by means of their different stances toward Spain: "Master and disciple differ undoubtedly in terms of fundamental ideological notions: in the first case, that of a single Spain founded on the Catholic tradition alone; in the second case, that of two Spains, divided and often antagonistic" (197).

In comparison with the universal genius that Menéndez y Pelayo had proposed as his goal from youth onward and faced with his clerical ideology, Menéndez Pidal appears to be a specialized historian and philologist and a liberal. His work in the domain of medieval Castilian text editing and in the codification of the grammar and vocabulary of these texts (such as the *Poema de Mio Cid*) as well as his research on historical grammar constitutes scientific contributions of inestimable value that led, moreover, to the formation of a school. The cultural dynamism that informs his work, however, is not bereft of the master's nationalist premises or of the religious model, now symbolized by the "civilizing mission" of Castile: first, the notion of continuity, which confers meaning upon history while upgrading (national) values, establishes models that exclude that which they would transgress and interrupt—in short, that which would be derivative of the "other"; second, that which is specifically Spanish is reduced to the Castilian, a reduction that is supposed to constitute a synthesis of those characterisic continuities. This reduction of the Spanish to the Castilian is formulated mainly in Menéndez Pidal's *Los Españoles en la historia y en la literatura* (1951). At this point the Spain born of the "struggle against the infidels" whose momentum derives from the accomplishment of a civilizing mission coincides with the expansion of this Castile of "contempt and force" that, according to Antonio Machado's verse in *Campos de Castilla*, "enveloped in its rags / despises what it doesn't know" ("envuelta en sus andrajos / desprecia cuanto ignora").

With regard to his stance vis-à-vis the conquest of America, let us consider some of Menéndez Pidal's remarks on the (Andalusian) Padre Las Casas, taken from his "very mature work" ("máxima madurez," as Laín Entralgo put it), *El Padre Las Casas y Vitoria* (1958). As he summarizes in the first of these collected essays ("Vitoria y Las Casas") the attitude of each toward the conquest and colonization of America, Menéndez Pidal points out:

We have shown what these two illustrious Dominicans thought of Spain's activity in America. On the one hand, the Andalusian Las Casas, of an intelligence limited by his passionately blinded heart, a tireless writer of thousands of pages, pretentious, in a hurry to publish his views in the various works published in Seville. . . . On the other hand, Vitoria, that old Castilian, modest, silent, and whose contemporaries regretted his being an enemy of writing in spite of his prodigious intellectual qualities. (36)

He was earlier comparing the two attitudes to what Vitoria calls the "legitimate titles of domination" of Spain in America. In his commentary on the first of the eight titles established by Vitoria, Menéndez Pidal writes:

According to Vitoria, the first legitimate title according to which the Barbarians could be dominated by the Spanish was that of universal human society and the natural need of human beings to communicate. All nations consider inhuman the unjustified refusal to welcome guests and travelers. The right of a people, derived from natural right, allows for the establishing of free trade and communication between peoples, that is to say the *ius peregrinandi et degendi*, if no prejudice follows therefrom; the Spanish therefore have the right to travel to the Indies and to remain there. (21)

It becomes obvious, as Menéndez Pidal had asserted earlier, that Vitoria, unlike Las Casas, thinks not abstractly but within the framework of historical reality, and that, rather than emphasize the title of evangelization, he focuses on that of trade, "a title despised and rejected by Las Casas" (20-21). Regarding "other nonreligious titles," Menéndez Pidal adds:

Las Casas considered the caciques, or "kings," as he was wont to call them, as sovereigns of a state in every way comparable with that of the Catholic king; with absolute simplicity, he judged as equal the Indians and civilized peoples, whereas Vitoria . . . (27)

Especially in the second essay of this book, "Una norma anormal del Padre Las Casas," the ideological communion between master and disciple is perceived in spite of the differences that separate them. In a polemic against the "*Leyenda negra*" that troubles the history of Spain in America, Menéndez Pidal simply eliminates his first mentor, Las Casas, by declaring him mad. Here is his argument:

Exaggeration is contempt of truth, and unbridled, habitual and irrepressible exaggeration is contempt with pathological tendencies. Las Casas, while deploying monstrous quantitative hyperboles, reaches an extreme qualitative exaggeration. (32)

Even if the conclusion of this syllogism is not immediately explicit, it is clear that the modifier "perturbed" later attributed to Las Casas is a consequence of this argument. About "Las Casas y Hernando de Soto," Menéndez Pidal tells us that

the medieval hatred between two religions is implacably renewed in Las Casas's perturbed soul against Hernando de Soto, who dies while entrusting to God his soul and his position as *Adelatando* of Florida, which he had received from Charles Quint for the purpose of spreading the faith and culture of the West in the savage lands of the New World. (64)

The syntagma "spreading the faith and culture of the West" as well as the religious tone in the formulation of the defense of Hernando de Soto against Las Casas and of the legitimation of his position ("received from Charles Quint") all contradict—or at least contaminate—the secularized interpretation of Spain's presence in the Indies that Menéndez Pidal seemed to have proposed in the text cited earlier. Furthermore, this syntagma contextualizes the adjective "savage" used to qualify "the . . . lands of the New World" (a qualification that metonymically extends to the inhabitants of those lands), just as it contextualizes the substantives "Barbarians" and "Indians" ("*gentes indias*") that he opposes to "Spanish" and "civilized peoples" and just as "caciques" is opposed to "kings" (and, in particular, to the "Catholic kings") and "inhuman" to "right of the people." An entire binary system of concepts thus characterizes the oppositions that Menéndez Pidal establishes between the "Andalusian Las Casas" and the "old Castilian Vitoria," as well as between the native people and the Spanish. We thus find a Manichaean dualist vision as much on the acts of Spain in America as on the comportment of its actors and interpreters.

Chapter 9
The Emerging of a Discursive Instance:
Columbus and the Invention of the "Indian"

A personal anecdote should help us better understand the preoccupations from which this study originated. Some years ago, while traveling in Mexico, I visited the ruins of Teotihuacan. My visit coincided with the festivities of the Quetzal-coatl temple, a celebration that brings together a great number of native families. What at first seemed to be a museum thus became the gathering point of a living people. Commenting to my wife on the colors, forms, and themes of the murals of the Quetzalpapalotl palace, as well as on their similarities to the art of the aboriginal population of Canada, without realizing it I used the word "Indio" (Indian). One of the visitors politely took me to task: "Señor, nosotros no somos indios. Somos teotihuacanos. Fueron los españoles quienes nos llamaron 'indios.' " (Sir, we are not Indians. We are Teotihuacans. It was the Spaniards who called us "Indians").

I realized how much our daily language practices bear the mark of all the errors, discriminations, dominations, and destructions that have been and still are perpetrated through language and that, through a sort of cumulative sedimentation, remain with it through the centuries. Even a professional scholar of languages cannot avoid using an occasional discriminatory word—toward women, perhaps, or toward an ethnic or age group. Concerning this, Bakhtin writes:

> No member of a verbal community can ever find words in the language
> that are neutral, exempt from the aspirations and evaluations of the
> other, uninhabited by the other's voice. On the contrary, he receives the
> word by the other's voice and it remains filled with that voice. He
> intervenes in his own context from another context, already penetrated

by the other's intentions. His own intention finds a word already lived in. (Cited by Todorov 1984, 48)

It is this ideological and social mark of the "already lived in" word (in Bakhtin's sense), its emergence and its various migrations and historical developments, that constitutes the object of discursive analysis as we practice it in my research group, Marginalisation et marginalité dans les pratiques discursives (MARGES). The recent creation in Montreal of an Inter-University Centre for Discourse Analysis and Text Sociocriticism (ICDATS/CIADEST) supports our conviction that "the emergence of notions, syntagmas, idioms, compositional (argumentative, narrative) schemata, their respective evolutions, their moments of eclipse, and their resurrection within diverse conjunctures—in short, their various semantic mutations" constitute a specific field of knowledge that lies at the juncture of the various human and social sciences. The thesis shared by the center's founding members is:

That which is being said and written in a given historical moment comprises facts which "function independently" of particular applications and usages. Such facts exist "outside of individual consciousness" and are endowed with "power," stakes, and an effectiveness that render them the vehicles of "social forces." Discourses are *social facts*. Produced within language, they are yet not strictly of a linguistic order. However, as means of knowing (and unknowing) they are not "pure" gnoseological entities.[1]

Starting from the working hypothesis that our speech is always a construction on "the already-there-ness of language" or, according to Bakhtin, a repetition of a "word already lived in," in such a way that only the mythical Adam could have used a language free of all marks other than those of "his own desire," of "his own personal creation," or of "his own individual intentions," I will approach here the word *Indian*, which speaks to us even today of the *proton pseudós*, of the initial error of the so-called Discovery of the New World. This word also constitutes an aggregate, the result of a sedimentation process of all that the Western imagination has projected onto the aboriginal people of the Americas from as early as 1492 up to the preparations for the 1992 celebration of the fifth centenary of what is called "the discovery of the New World."

The title of this chapter inscribes itself in a whole series of recent studies whose titles include the word invention. As Werner Sollors (1989) emphasized in his introduction to the collective volume *The Invention of Ethnicity*, the word invention has become "a central term for our comprehension of the universe" (ix). Sollors also notes that the use of this term is no longer limited to discourses on the advances of technological progress or to the neo-Aristotelian discussion of the distinction between poetry and history or even between textual strategies and "factual" representation. He also lists a series of publications dating from 1960 to recent critical works showing that

> a variety of voices now use the word [invention] in order to describe, analyze, or criticize such diverse phenomena as the invention of culture; of literary history; of narrative; of childhood as well as the loss of childhood; of adolescence; of motherhood; of kinship; of the self; of America; of New England; of Billy the Kid and the West; of the Negro; of the Indian; of the Jew; of Jesus and Christianity; of Athens; of the modern hospital; of the museum of science; of the 1920s in Paris; of our ability to "see" photographic pictures; of the vision of the outlaw in America; or of the American way of death. (x)

Every field of study in this long enumeration corresponds to at least one title in the bibliography established by Sollors (238-39 n. 3).[2] He thus demonstrates that at the present juncture, "the category of 'invention' has been stressed in order to emphasize not so much originality and innovation as the importance of *language* in the social construction of reality." His thesis is that the word invention, which has become a buzzword, nevertheless offers "an adequate description of a profound change in modes of perception." To interpret as "invention" what had previously been understood in terms of "essentialist" categories has "resulted in the recognition of the general cultural constructedness of the modern world" (x).

Referring to Michel Foucault (1966, 1971) and Hayden White (1982), Sollors insists that the constitution of the fields of study in the humanities is a true "*poetical* act, a genuine 'making' or 'invention' of a domain of inquiry" (x). With James Clifford (1986), he wants to remind ethnographers of the rhetorical tradition of viewing texts as "composed of inventions rather than observed facts," and he agrees with Benedict Anderson (1985) on the necessity in the field of ethnography, a field of particular interest to us here, for a reflection "upon the conditions under which modern national and ethnic groups have been invented (or 'imagined')" (x-xi).[3]

In a special issue of the journal *Études françaises* dedicated to " 'Invention," Jacinthe Martel (1990) has sketched out some of the elements of a lexicological and semantic history of the concept. She traces the travels of the word invention through its various semantic transformations, most particularly the displacement of the concept in the Renaissance "from the rhetorical field toward that of the poetic," a shift that has helped to "modify its meaning in an important fashion." Moreover, because "the literature of the Renaissance rests on the theory of imitation which it elects as its main and first rule," Martel suggests that

> even if, etymologically speaking, the term invention means "action of finding, of discovering," the notion refers us back less to an invention as such of the arguments than to a discovery. . . . The task of the poet is then actually to find his poetic material in the already-there and not to invent it from scratch. In the midst of this esthetic of imitation, it is less

in terms of the novelty of the subject than in terms of its renewal (at the level of disposition and elocution) that the poetical invention can occur. (33)

From the rich polysemy of the word invention discussed by Derrida (1989), I select two meanings: the rhetorical invention (first element of the classical trilogy *inventio, dispositio, elocutio*) and the inaugural event that, through socialization, establishes for the future a possibility or power that will remain at the disposal of all. My reduction of this polysemy to only two semantic fields is in accord with the hypothesis advanced by Derrida (and confirmed by Martel) that

> within an area of discourse that has been fairly well stabilized since the end of the seventeenth century in Europe, there are only two major types of authorized examples for invention. On the one hand, people invent *stories* (fictional or fabulous), and on the other hand they invent *machines*, technical devices or mechanisms, in the broadest sense of the word. Someone may invent by fabulation, by producing narratives to which there is no corresponding reality outside the narrative (an alibi, for example), or else one may invent by producing a new operational possibility (such as printing or nuclear weaponry. (32)

I end this quotation at the point where Derrida explains the association that he draws "on purpose" between these two examples, "printing or nuclear weaponry," "the politics of invention—which will be my theme," he writes, "being always *at the same time* cultural politics and war politics." My purpose here is to show how the invention of the Indian by Christopher Columbus—and with him, by the Western world—is at the same time fable, "stories," and "new operational possibility," most particularly one of a commercial nature—without forgetting the constraints imposed by the ideological and social mark of the "word already lived in," according to Bakhtin, on all uses of language.

Christopher Columbus faces a double bind as he writes of his voyage of discovery, a story that constitutes the founding text of the invention of the "Indian." He must evoke known or recognizable socialized references to make his readers, particulary the kings of Spain, the "Catholic kings," believe the story of his invention: the reaching of the Indies by a Western route. If like the mythical Adam, Columbus bestows names on the lands that confront him along his western sea route and, through this act of naming, appropriates them and their inhabitants—not to mention the more solemn and explicit gesture of taking possession of them in the name of the Catholic kings—then the language he uses to name them constitutes an "already-there," the repetition of a "word already lived in." In addition to this double bind characteristic of all passage of desire through discourse, Columbus must face an epistemological one specific to the context in which he writes. This context imposes the necessity of evoking the written text—as an authority still in effect—and the increasingly imperious necessity of experimental knowledge for the true knowledge.

Like Don Quijote in Cervantes's novel, and a little more than a century earlier, Christopher Columbus stands as a man of the book. Consequently, he must be true to the letter that guarantees the fulfillment of his mission. Thus, if at the beginning of the *Diario* of his first voyage he speaks only of "lands," of "islands," of "la gente de aquella isla," of "aquellas gentes," soon Columbus will identify some island or other as being Cipango and its inhabitants as being "people of the Great Khan." Also, he will soon resolve to look for the city of Guisay in order to bring to the Great Khan the letters of the Catholic kings and to request the reply that he was eager to bring back to them.[4] In the short account of his voyage that we find in his letter to Luis de Santángel dated February 15, that is, some months later, however, Columbus affirms:

> Señor: Porque sé que avréis plazer de la grand victoria que nuestro Señor me ha dado en mi viaje vos escribo ésta, por la cual sabréis cómo en treita y tres días pasé a las Indias con la armada que los illustríssimos Rey e Reina, Nuestros Señores me dieron, donde yo fallé muy muchas islas pobladas con gente sin número, y d'ellas todas he tomado posesión por Sus Altezas con pregón y vandera real estendida, y non me fue contradicho.
>
> A la primera que yo fallé puse nombre Sant Salvador a conmemoración de su Alta Magestat, el cual maravillosamente todo esto a dado; los indios la llaman Guanahaní. A la segunda puse nombre la isla de Santa María de Concepción; a la tercera, Fernandina; a la cuarta la Isabela; a la quinta la isla Juana, e así a cada una nombre nuevo. (Fernández de Navarrete 1954, 167)

> [Sir: Since I know that you will be pleased at the great success with which our Lord has crowned my voyage, I write to inform you how in thirty-three days I crossed from the Canary Islands to the Indies, with the fleet which our most illustrious sovereigns gave me. I found very many islands with large populations and took possession of them all for their Highnesses; this I did by proclamation and unfurled the royal standard. No opposition was offered.
>
> I named the first island that I found "San Salvador," in honour of our Lord and Saviour who has granted me this miracle. The Indians call it "Guanahani." The second island I named "Santa Maria de Concepción," the third "Fernandina," the fourth "Isabela," and the fifth "Juana"; thus I renamed them all. (Columbus 1969, 115)]

On the one hand Columbus follows to the letter the texts of Pierre d'Ailly (*Imago mundi seu eius imaginaria descriptio* [Louvain, 1480]), and Marco Polo (*Voyages* [Venice, 1485]) to convince his readers that he has reached the Indies by a new route. On the other hand, he appropriates the already-there-ness and the already-named ("The Indians call it——") by giving it a new name, a gesture that constitutes, according to Derrida, the most radical act of violence, the "originary violence of language." Actually, commenting on the experiences with the

Nambikwara reported by Lévi-Strauss in *Tristes Tropiques*, Derrida (1974) writes:

> To name, to give names that it will on occasion be forbidden to pronounce, such is the originary violence of language which consists in inscribing within a difference, in classifying, in suspending the vocative absolute. To think the unique *within* the system, to inscribe it there, such is the gesture of the arche-writing: arche-violence, loss of the proper. (112)

Columbus is not the only individual within the Western tradition to exercise this violent form of domination through dispossession and possession by attributing a new name, by renaming. Even today, for example, we can recall the name changes to which the Inuit have been subjected, the centuries during which their language has been banned. The front page of the Montreal edition of the February 18, 1991, issue of the *Gazette* reported the case of a Canadian federal agent who thirty-four years ago registered a newborn Inuit under the name of E7-1411. "Boy's name or girl's—Hard to tell," quips the *Gazette* reporter, turning this into a trivial event.

But Columbus is not content only with renaming the lands and their inhabitants that he encounters while sailing toward the Indies on his western route. He also describes them, and to do this, he turns again to the "already-said." From biblical descriptions of paradise and of man and woman in a state of pure nature—that is, before the Fall through original sin—and from classical descriptions of the *locus amoenus* and of the goodness and natural beauty of human beings in the Golden Age (particularly in Virgil and Ovid), Columbus constructs an image of the "Indian" whose authenticity will not be questioned. This image will be accepted as the product of direct empirical knowledge and, moreover, because it confirms the expectations of all—such an image being foretold in the texts, sacred as well as classical. This image, constructed and attached by Columbus to the word "Indian," becomes this new object of knowledge that will be submitted to the theological, philosophical, judicial, and economic questioning of the time. Through the reports of those who played a part in the conquest (trader, missionaries, and others) and, above all, through the controversies that took place in the universities of Valladolid and Salamanca in the sixteenth century over "the nature of the Indians" (Ginés de Sepúlveda and Bartolomé de Las Casas) and the "legitimacy of domination titles" of Spain in America (Bartolomé de Las Casas and Francisco de Vitoria), the "Indian" (false word and false image) becomes a discursive instance, a topos on which converge all the discursive formations of the different disciplines of contemporary knowledge which each appropriate a share in the division of the discusive working .

The first description of what Columbus will later call the "Indian" as it was recorded in his *Diario* on October 12, 1492, has been submitted to many readings and uses, from Pedro Mártir de Anglería and Bartolomé de Las Casas to Menéndez Pelayo and Menéndez Pidal (see the preceding chapter). The reception of Columbus's text emphasizes two conceptual axes along which the aboriginal people of the Americas have been—and are today—named and therefore classified. As Lévi-Strauss (1962, 285) argues, "On ne nomme jamais, on classe l'autre" (One never just names, one classifies the other). Depending on whether one uses religious or secular (or even scientific) parameters, one comes to consider the "Indian" as belonging to a class of beings who live in a state of pure nature or as savages; but they are always defined, explicitly or implicitly, in terms of a lack: lack of evangelization (a Christian one) or lack of civilization (a Western one). This binary or Manichaean system has left a deep mark on five centuries of Spanish and Western historiography of the "Indies," taking in turn the form of a glorification or of a condemnation of the "savages." Thus, for Pedro Mártir de Anglería and for Bartolomé de Las Casas, it is not the law of God but cupidity, envy, and wrath that the Spaniards taught those people who, before their arrival, had lived in a state of original innocence. The October 12, 1492, description of Columbus's *Diario* affords Las Casas proof of the existence of these beings that Pliny, Pomponius Mela, Strabo, Virgil, Isidor of Seville, Boethius, and others had described as "most holy and most happy." For Hernán Cortés and for Francisco López de Gómara, on the contrary, the conquest of America represents an ("epic") gesture of "redemption of the most primitive people on earth," who until then had lived in a state of "cannibalism, polygamy, polytheism not free of cruel human sacrifices."

These two apparently irreconcilable positions do not differ on the epistemological level. Actually, they differ only in terms of their "selection" (*inventio* in the ancient rhetoric) of reported facts with regard to a specific interpretative line of argument concerning the conquest. But none of them thinks of questioning the legitimacy of this conquest, not even those who insist on drawing out its negative consequences. The second alternative will predominate in the Western world, if we put aside a certain European episode that generally covers the period of conflict between Reformation and Counter-Reformation during which the work of Bartolomé de Las Casas and especially his *Brevíssima historia de la destruición de las Indias*—which will give rise to what the Spanish have called "la Leyenda Negra" (the Black Legend)—was taken up by parts of Europe, mostly as a criticism of the Catholics' action in the New World.

Hegel (1975), to mention only one example, considers "America and its culture, especially as it had developed in Mexico and Peru," as "a purely natural culture which had to perish as soon as the spirit approached it." This "necessity" corresponds, according to Hegel, to an "inferiority" of the aboriginal people of the Americas.[5] Excluded from history, from reason, and from the spirit, this part of the world, not yet ready to assume its role in history, does not really interest Hegel, even as a "country of the future":

It is up to America to abandon the ground on which world history has hitherto been enacted. What has taken place there up to now is but an echo of the Old World and the expression of an alien life; and as a country of the future, it is of no interest to us here, for prophecy is not the business of the philosopher. In history, we are concerned with what has been and what is; in philosophy, however, we are concerned not with what belongs exclusively to the past or to the future, but with that which *is*, both now and eternally — in short, with reason. And that is quite enough to occupy our attention. (170-71)

The question of the New World in Hegel's work appears only as a brief, nine-page digression in which he moreover discusses it from a Eurocentric standpoint: "The world is divided into the Old and the New — the latter taking its name from the fact that America and Australia only became known to the Europeans at a later stage of history" (162). The discussion of the Old World, however, brings Hegel to declare *his* history "the object" of "universal history": "Putting aside the New World and whatever dreams we might build upon it, we now pass on to the *Old World*. It is essentially the setting of those events which we have to consider here, i.e., the setting of world history" (171). That such a mentality is still very much alive seems obvious when one examines the quite generalized consensus in Europe and in North America concerning the 1992 commemoration of the fifth centenary of the so-called discovery of the New World. One can also point to the celebration of the "Fiesta de la Hispanidad," also referred to as the "Fiesta de la Raza," which is celebrated each year in the Hispanic world on October 12.

A certain nostalgia remains, however, for the "dreams" that, according to Hegel, remain attached to the idea of the New World. These dreams, of which the ultimate referent is always the lost paradise, the biblical Eden, find their expression in an ethnography in the manner of Rousseau's or of Lévi-Strauss's. This redemptive ethnography appears therefore as a paradoxical blend of two elements: on the one hand, remorse in the face of the destructive intrusions perpetrated on the cultures of these "primitive" people and, on the other hand, an affirmation of the necessity of such intrusions in order to preserve in writing (as in a museum) their cultural inheritance. The redemptive ethnography thus finds itself both the agent and the main denouncer of the damage caused to these people, as Jacques Derrida (1974) pointed out. A "critical nostalgia" (Diamond) before all that remains of an authentically primitive nature and a "search for origins" (Rosaldo) constitute the main characteristics of redemptive ethnography, the last-chance rescue of the "primitive" on the part of the "civilized." In addition to this paradox, however, James Clifford (1986) suggests that ethnography's disappearing objects become a "rhetorical construct" — *inventio?* — by the very fact of their textualization:

Ethnography's disappearing object is, then, in significant degree, a rhetorical construct legitimating a representational practice: "salvage" ethnography in its widest sense. The other is lost, in disintegrating time and space, but saved in the text. . . . It is assumed that the other society is weak and "needs" to be represented by an outsider (and that what matters in its life is its past, not present or future). (112-3)[6]

The tradition of Utopian thinking has also found inspiration from Christopher Columbus's text. For example, Thomas More will locate his *Utopia* in America, and the Jesuits will carry out this project later in their *reducciones* in Paraguay, the myth serving thus as guide for reading reality and thereafter for its own realization.

Beatriz Pastor (1983, 1988) has discovered a dual "process of significant distortion" of reality in Columbus's narrative. There is first the "literary model" provided by Pierre D'Ailly, Aeneas Sylvius, Marco Polo, and Pliny (I would add the Bible, Virgil, and Ovid). According to Beatriz Pastor, this literary model informs "the fictionalization of reality one finds in Columbus's narrative." But there is another process whose "origin is not literary but economic; its historical finality consisting in a project, first veiled and then more and more explicit, of instrumentalization of the reality of the New World for strictly commercial purposes." Within this framework Beatriz Pastor interprets the descriptions and characterizations of the native people one finds in Christopher Columbus's *Diario*:

> The first three characteristic features of the Natives according to code 1 — nudity, poverty, and absence of weapon — defined them as savages and serfs. The fourth feature — generosity — sets them down as beasts on the basis of their incapacity to engage in commercial activities according to the trade law of the Western world. (1988, 55)

In Columbus's *Diario*, by November 12, a month after his first description of the "Indian" (analyzed in the preceding chapter), the "tone" of the narrative has changed in the sense described by Beatriz Pastor:

> Because I saw and recognize (says the Admiral) that these people have no religious beliefs, nor are they idolaters. They are very gentle and do not know what evil is; nor do they kill others, nor steal; and they are without weapons and so timid that a hundred of them flee from one of our men even if our men are teasing them. And they are credulous and aware that there is a God in heaven and convinced that we come from the heavens; and they say very quickly any prayer that we tell them to say, and they make the sign of the cross. So that Your Highnesses ought to resolve to make them Christians: for I believe that if you begin, in a short time you will end up having converted to our Holy Faith a multitude of peoples and acquiring large dominions and great riches and all of their peoples for Spain. Because without doubt there is in these lands a very great quantity of gold; for not without cause do these Indians that I bring with me say that there are in these islands places where they dig gold and wear it on their chests, on their ears, and on their arms, and on their legs; and they are very thick bracelets. And also

there are stones, and there are precious pearls and infinite spicery. And
in this Rio de Mares from which I departed tonight there is without
doubt an exceedingly great quantity of mastic and even greater if a
greater production is wanted, because the trees themselves, when
planted, bear quickly. And there are many and very large ones, and they
have a leaf and a fruit like the mastic tree, except that the trees, as well
as the leaf, are larger, as Pliny says, and as I have seen, [than] on the
island of Chio in the Archipelago. And I ordered many of these trees
tapped to see if they would produce resin in order to bring it; and since
it has rained during the whole time that I have been in the said river I
have not been able to get any of it, except a very little bit which I am
bringing to Your Highnesses . . .
    And there is here in the mouth of the said river the best harbor that I
have seen up until today, clean and wide and deep and a good place and
site to make a town and fort where any ships whatever can tie up
alongside the walls; and it is a very temperate land, and high, and with
good water. (Fernandez de Navarrete 1954, 143-47)

I have shown in the preceding chapter how, from the perspective of discursive
analysis, it is possible to discover in Columbus's text, in the very first words of
the admiral about the "people of this island," the continuation of a mercantil-
ization (for all purposes unconscious) of the lands, of the human beings, and of
their belongings and a plan of action for the organization of a very profitable
trade. In fact, the principal axis of Columbus's first description of the Indians
consists mostly in a narration of the exchange of material goods and (eventual)
services. In the appreciation of these goods, as the many adjectives in the text
indicate, the emphasis is more on the exchange value than on the use value, that
is, the emphasis is more on the comparison (according to profitability criteria) of
what is given with what is received. In spite of the obvious concern with evangelization, the religious discourse finds itself contaminated by an economic discourse that, at the time, is becoming more and more hegemonic in Spain as it
already is in the rest of Europe. In chapter 6 I tried to show the impact of an
economic discourse, specific to the economic (bourgeois) mentality, on the official religious discourse, specific to the theological (feudal) mentality, including
the (neo)scholastic philosophy that is the basis of the political and religious
thought of imperial Spain. This influence was making itself felt simultaneously
with an attempt to reinstate a medieval order that — as the earlier mentioned contaminations show — is already obsolete. Not even Don Quijote, despite his un-
failing idealism, can avoid the contamination of his anachronistic chivalrous discourse by reckonings of an economic nature.
    It is hardly surprising, in this context, that Pierre Vilar (1976) takes advantage
of the writings of the great Spanish theologians and moralists of the sixteenth and
seventeenth centuries, particularly those of the University of Salamanca, and includes them alongside the true *tratadistas* (*doctores* and *arbitristas*) when he

writes the history of the economic theories of the time. Because the cathedral of Seville was used as *contratación* site for the *comercio de Indias*, Vilar names its *gradas* the Wall Street of the time.

This curious mix of religious and economic interests, sometimes considered contradictory or at least conflictual, is nevertheless present in a more or less perceptible way in all the discourses produced about the "Indian." Has not economic success (like military success) sometimes constituted a sign of the divine predestination of individuals or nations? This should not be taken as a characteristic of the Spain of the Catholic kings or of the Habsbourgs, or even of medieval mentality. The whole dynamic of progress and of the expansion of the Western world (through a process of "evangelization" or of "civilization," depending on the degree of religious or secular ideology displayed by a given age) accords with the divine order received by Adam and Eve to dominate the earth, recorded in Genesis 1:26, the founding text of the Judeo-Christian tradition. For the Christian world, this first divine mission entrusted to humanity is reinforced by a second one, Christ's order to go out and preach the gospel to all nations, a mission that could perhaps explain, ideologically, the interventions of the Western world all over the planet, from Saint Paul to George Bush.

In Spain's case, the narrative of Christopher Columbus's voyage fits into the framework of the larger narrative of the identity of the Hispanic nation, of *la Hispanidad* understood as the end product of a whole series of historical actions, all interpreted as being of a religious character:

1. The eviction of the Moslems, a "holy war," a crusade against the infidels, a secular war against Islam, or a *Reconquista* (as Spanish historiography has been in the habit of calling the period preceding the unification of Spain under the crown of the Catholic kings in 1469).
2. The establishment, as early as 1478, of the Inquisition tribunal and the eviction of the Moorish people, followed in 1492 by the conquest of Granada and the eviction of the Jews by the Catholic kings in the name of the *pureza de fe* (purity of faith) of their subjects. With this mentality the Spaniards embark upon the conquest of America. They will call the temples of the natives *mezquitas* (mosques) in the chronicles of the Indies, proof of the presence, in the action of Spain in America, of the pathos of the *Reconquista* and of the religious war.
3. Publication in 1492 of the first Spanish grammar in the Castilian language (henceforth called the "Spanish language"). Its author, Nebrija, declares it "compañera del Imperio" (the companion of the empire) in his dedication to Isabella, the (Catholic) queen of Castile.
4. Extensive territorial expansion, supported by Rome and interpreted as the accomplishment of a religious mission: "the evangelization of

the savage people of Africa and America,'' a program in which the Spanish Crown will act as ''Regio Vicariato Apostólico'' (royal apostolic vicar).

It should be noted that the narrative of what I would call the Spanish autohistoriography is part (once the antinarrative called ''la Leyenda Negra,'' the Black Legend, is forgotten) of the larger narrative of the autohistoriography of the Western world. The proof lies in the celebration by the entire Western world of the fifth centenary of the ''discovery'' of the New World. The narrative of Christopher Columbus thus fits into a series of ever-larger narratives, the last of which would be the autohistory of Western (Christian) civilization. What historic irony can be read in the fate of this Jew from Genoa, who renamed himself ''Christus Ferens'' (''bearer of Christ'') and founded the Spanish-Christian ''mission'' in the New World.

Starting, then, from a memory saturated by the ''already-there-ness'' of a language and culture, and within a historical dynamic equally preprogrammed, neither Christopher Columbus nor late fifteenth-century Spain arrived at a conjuncture where the preconditions to meet the other, let alone report such an encounter, would prevail. Because of this absence of the necessary conditions of intelligibility and of the language to express it, the other will remain unknown even if appropriated through naming and through being turned into an object of knowledge and integrated within the mechanism of a religion marked with a strong commercial overtone. The invention of the ''Indian'' is therefore more an invention of itself than an invention of the other. The resulting paradox will be rational in the sense that it is founded on Western legal practices, a framework where invention is considered a source of rights (royalties, letters of patent, property rights: *res nullius primi capienti*).

Derrida (1989) suggests an alternative, the only one capable in his eyes of giving rise to a true invention free of all possible contamination by scientific, cultural, or even ''programmatic'' invention:

> The invention of the other, the incoming *of* the other, certainly does not take the form of a subjective genitive, and just as assuredly not of an objective genitive either, even if the invention comes from the other— for this other is thenceforth neither subject nor object, neither a self nor a consciousness nor an unconscious. To get ready for this coming of the other is what I call the deconstruction that deconstructs this double genitive and that, as deconstructive invention, comes back in the step— and also as the step—of the other. To invent would then be to ''know'' how to say ''come'' and to answer the ''come'' of the other. (56; emphasis in the original)

Derrida leaves one question open: ''Does that ever come about? Of this event one is never sure'' (56). I have the feeling—and some recent events seem to confirm it—that the conditions that may make such a dialogue possible are still lacking. Will our reflection at least help us understand the preconditions necessary to make visible to our culture the emergence of a discordant, of a truly heterologous voice? My intervention does not claim to do that. I hope only to contribute to a better understanding of our own language, of its constraints and of its mode of functioning when concerned with the other.

Chapter 10
The (Relative) Autonomy of Artistic Expression:
Bakhtin and Adorno

At the beginning of the century, the first attempts to go beyond traditional categories of literary research—creation (artistic or literary), originality, inventiveness (where the author is transformed into an epic hero of sorts, admirable and inimitable), influences (as sources or as effective history, the German *Wirkungsgeschichte*) and the author's subjective intentions—brought about a twofold empirical orientation. On one hand arose the study of aesthetic material, as advocated, for example, by schools of stylistics; on the other, the "abstract objectivism" (as Bakhtin judiciously put it) of Saussurean synchrony and its outgrowth, structuralism. Exploring the path forged in Germany by Wilhelm von Humboldt and followed in Russia by A. A. Potebnia, Bakhtin's circle arose from the dialectical, dialogical rejection of both orientations in the name of the sociohistorical dynamics to be found in all language activity. Thus considered, Bakhtin would be the very "dialogical space" that he postulated as fundamental to the study of any literary text considered a crossroads.[1] This is why I propose a reading of the legacy of Bakhtin's circle within the historical juncture in which it emerged and within the dialogical dynamics that characterize it.

Whether the matter at hand be an analysis of individualized stylistics (the aesthetics of personal expression in a particular work) or a systematization of general linguistic and stylistic procedures, Bakhtin reproaches Vossler and Spitzer, as well as Vinogradov and the formalists in general, for their return to an individualistic subjectivism that contradicts their postulated empirical objectivism. Furthermore, Bakhtin tells us, these schools tend to confuse the part (linguistic substance) with the whole (expression, be it literary or not): what is only the means by which intersubjective communication is achieved becomes an autonomous, self-sufficient, and autotelic entity.[2]

On the other hand, the formal method—like Saussure and the Geneva school that inspired it—works for Bakhtin only on an abstraction. General grammars indeed all tend to establish as the object of their study the system, that is, an abstract form of language elaborated by the analyst and therefore of no value other than providing a scientific simulacrum. For Bakhtin, "the speakers' collective conscience" (where Saussure situates synchrony) is but the product of theoretical reflection; accordingly, "this system does not exist in real historical time." In an extreme manifestation—which Antoine Meillet's group avoids by being more "critical" and by acknowledging the "abstract but also conventional nature of all systems of signification"—Voloshinov and Bakhtin go so far as to accuse that school of "hypostatizing abstract objectivism."[3] Within such a system, signs are related only to one another and are interpreted exclusively through the distinctive features that oppose them to and differentiate them from other signs in the same system. There is no relationship either with objective reality or with—and this is more serious for Bakhtin's group—the "intersubjective point of view," the ideology, gnoseology, and axiology that underlie every sociohistorical convention.

Because every statement is incomplete by itself, sociohistorical convention is nonetheless the *conditio sine qua non* of the effectiveness of the system in any (oral or written) language activity. It is therefore an error to isolate the statement from the enunciative situation, from the enunciative *hic et nunc* where an enunciating subject and an (at the very least anticipated) addressee have communicated (in the case of texts as document) or are communicating (in the case of the spoken word). Since any statement presupposes more than it says, Voloshinov calls the use of language an enthymeme. Indeed, each of the explicit particulars (the produced verbal part) of the use of language acts as a trigger that summons in those whom it fully reaches (whether listener or reader) an entire world of which it is a fragment, a world of images and memories shared by the transmitting and receiving subjects of the statement (the implied component). The context, then, becomes an essential part of this whole—a whole larger and more complex than the sum of phonemes, morphemes, or lexemes transmitted in the act of communication by the enunciating subject. As is the case with the context, the point of view shared by the speakers is integrated in this spatial and temporal as well as cognitive and axiological whole.[4] Considered as utterances, the word and the text become sociohistorical facts that can be analyzed not as mystical experiences or metaphysical realities (relevant only within an individualistic subjectivism), but as social phenomena. Thus simultaneously superseded are "abstract objectivism" and "individualistic subjectivism," the thesis and antithesis with which Voloshinov and Bakhtin sum up the major trends of Western (European) linguistics, whose influence in the Soviet Union was still felt when the cornerstone of analytical materialism was being laid. This is not the result of a syncretical compromise between thesis and antithesis but rather of a dialectical synthesis that destroys their common epistemological basis, that is, the consideration of individual speech acts (already a contradictio in adjecto for Bakhtin's group) as phenomena analyzable only from the point of view of the subjective psyche.

Marc Angenot (1984, 9) pointed out that the debate on *Marxism and the Philosophy of Language* "proceeds by opposing and rejecting for a double reason two linguistic ideologies deemed idealistic." He draws our attention to the similarities between this strategy and that of the traditional Marxist tract:

One begins by observing two antagonistic errors that seem, by their very antagonism, to involve the entire field of a discipline. One then interposes what must strictly speaking be called a *proscribed third party*. The third party coming to disrupt the affair is of an analytical/ materialistic nature described here in the following words: "The utterance's nature is social." This statement leads to the following equation: all language is ideology. (10)

Although I agree with Marc Angenot on the argument's style (tractlike?), I cannot subscribe to his evaluation of *Marxism and the Philosophy of Language* (Bakhtin and Voloshinov 1973) as a work that discards more than it creates.[5] What I see in that work as well as in all of the Bakhtin circle writings of that period is rather the maturing of the theoretical foundation for the aesthetics of verbal interaction—an aesthetics characteristic initially of the group and then of Bakhtin himself when he reappeared in the sixties. We should therefore examine more closely the two schools as Voloshinov-Medvedev-Bakhtin perceive them in order to understand, beyond the polemic, the dialogue that they initiated.

It should first be noted that the two antithetic trends were selected and depicted from a specific perspective: the identification and demarcation of language as the specific object of an aesthetics of verbal interaction called *metalingvistika*. Todorov (1981) translates this term as *translinguistique* (translinguistics), though he acknowledges that a term more likely to convey Bakhtin's position would be *pragmatique* (pragmatics); this would place Bakhtin at the beginning of pragmatics in the actual sense of that discipline. It is therefore not a matter of refusing other possible perspectives in the study of the same object, language. Such perspectives are legitimate only within certain limits that must necessarily be recognized: the limits of their own perspective. A science is indeed characterized not by its object (*objectum materiale*), but by the perspective from which it confronts that object (the *objectum formale* of traditional scholastics). Consequently, what Bakhtin criticizes in Saussurean linguistics (to which he opposes his *metalingvistika*) is that it presumes to have as its own perspective the only possible object of a (genuine) science of language. Without acknowledging its own limitations, it considers itself as the *only* science of language. What is censured is the fetishization of certain models and, as a corollary, the denial of other models that are just as legitimate from another point of view or from the global perspective as proposed by Bakhtin.

From the perspective of the five points in which Voloshinov and Bakhtin formulate their own proposition at the end of the chapter on verbal interaction, let us analyze the four points that summarize the two antagonistic theories.[6] We shall see that what is rejected in each point of both theories is the extreme stand in the name of which the relevance of a certain aspect of the opposite viewpoint is vindicated. With the opposition of language as a stable system (*ergon*) and language as creative activity (*energeia*), on the one hand one accepts the heuristic value of systematization, but on the other one denies to such an abstraction the capability of accurately explaining the concrete reality of language, that is, language as an uninterrupted evolutionary process achieved through the verbal interaction of speakers with the result that the process is social. The Humboldt principle of language as *energeia* is sanctioned and the principle of language as *ergon* is consequently denied. Rejected, however, is the notion that the laws governing language's creativity would be those of individual psychology (the second point of individualistic subjectivism); on the contrary, the system's internal laws are acknowledged, but without being hypostatized or isolated from the social reality that ultimately imposes on them its own incessant evolution. This principle (the third point of Voloshinov and Bakhtin's proposition) not only confirms the close connection between language activity and its contents and their ideological values, but it also insists on the specificity of the linguistic work of art, which individualistic subjectivism puts in analogical correlation with artistic creation, thereby reducing it to an individual mental creative process. The third postulate of abstract objectivism is rejected in the name of a partial acceptance of individualistic subjectivism's third postulate (which is modulated in the name of the objective specificity of the verbal communication system). Finally, in view of the fourth postulate of abstract objectivism, which maintains that the fortuitous nature of individual distortions gives way to the irrational and illogical evolution of languages, the social character of any use or abuse of speech is asserted, whereas the possibility of individual speech acts is excluded as a *contradictio in adjecto*.

The inevitable dialectical tension between system and event, norm and usage, tradition and act (in writing as well as in reading) is precisely what had escaped the two antithetical theories as well as contemporary immanentist structuralism. This is why they cannot account for what is of primary interest to Bakhtin's group: an understanding of the historical workings and changes (the realization of structural dynamics into temporal forms) and of the aesthetic effects brought about by the dialectical tension between norm and violation in any speech act and in any text not restricted to the purely mimetic reproduction of a model of verbal or discursive usage. Irony, parody, carnivalesque subversion (in the broad Bakhtinian sense of the term), as well as any use or abuse of what Bakhtin calls "the other's discourse," are understandable only within a signification process. They shatter both the system's rigidity and pure creative subjectivism because they are sociohistorical semiotic games that refer simultaneously to the history of the verbal sign in question and to its "legitimate" users within a given society and its antagonistic groups. Because society, as Bakhtin's group understands it—as Marx understands it on the base of class struggle dialectically creating a conflictive unity—is plural, or dual at the very least, because it organizes antagonistic elements and regulates their conflicting interests. Words and speech also carry the socioideological marks of the group that uses them and imposes rules and restrictions on their usage (the "discourse order" that Michel Foucault will later develop). This socioideological stamp is also that of the conflict of interests that tends to incorporate individual endeavors into the integrity and efficiency of the system—a system based on a unifying, totalitarian, *monological* coherence or truth—while at the same time bringing about the opposite result, the dialectical, dialogical "dysphonia" of the dominated versus the dominating groups, whose interests are served by that monologically absolute coherence and truth.[7]

From the preceding considerations there necessarily follows a corollary: to assert that sociohistorical semiotic games are the key to understanding the signification processes in which, according to Bakhtin, all speech acts (oral or written) are implied requires that one add the social (diastratic) dimension to the historical, temporal (diachronic), and geographical (diatopic) dimensions of the ideological sign.

Regarding the late arrival in Europe (in the Western world) of Bakhtin and Voloshinov's critique of Saussure in *Marxism and the Philosophy of Language*, Marc Angenot (1985) notes that this book could not have been read in Western Europe at the time of its publication in Russia in 1929: "Structuralist functionalism had not yet acquired a position that would have justified a refutation according to the rules and a critical Marxism would not have been heeded for lack of conditions of intelligibility." According to Angenot, the most opportune moment for the appearance of Bakhtin's text in Europe would have been thirty years later when structuralism in Western Europe converted the "pseudo Saussure" of the *Cours de linguistique générale* into a dogma of literary and social science. The French translation, however, was published in 1977, when, with few exceptions, "linguistics and, even more, semiologies, seem to have installed themselves definitively in the exclusion of history and of ideology." The time, then, is still not right for critical materialism to be taken into consideration: the challenge has been ignored, and instead an intellectual atmosphere has been created that invites semiologists "to settle into comfort and syncretism" (10).

Pierrette Malcuzynski (1984), also confronted with the "fantastic" projection of Bakhtin's person and writings on contemporary theory and criticism in humanities (along with all the misunderstandings and compromises that follow from the attempt to uncover an "acceptable" Bakhtin), advanced the following hypothesis:

It does not seem overbold to think that if Bakhtin had been translated earlier, particularly in France, the impact of structuralism and semiotics in the humanities would have taken a much different tack. In like manner and more specifically in literary theory, the migrating constellations of the notion of intertextuality would have presented other configurations. (45-46)

These observations, which refer in both cases particularly to the French world, can also be applied, *servatis servandis*, to the Federal Republic of Germany. The writings of Bakhtin first published include—as far as I know— *Literatur und Karneval. Zur Romantheorie und Lachkultur* (Munich, 1969); *Probleme der Poetik Dostoevskijs* (Munich, 1971); a summary of the study on the *chronotopos* in the novel, "Zeit und Raum im Roman," *Kunst und Literatur* 22 (1974): 1161-91; *Marxismus und Sprachphilosophie* (Frankfurt, 1975); *Aesthetik des Wortes* (Frankfurt, 1979). In 1976 Medvedev, *Die formale Methode in der Literaturwissenschaft* appeared in Stuttgart. It cannot be said that these texts have had a pronounced influence on West German literary studies or on other sectors of the humanities or *Geisteswissenschaften*. A symposium organized at the University of Constance in 1980 tried to fill this void.[8] Its focus was to have been, as Hans Robert Jauss declared in his opening words, Bakhtin's theory and, especially, the notion of "dialogy." This focus was displaced, however, when additional considerations were, explicitly or implicitly, introduced: Schleiermacher, Gadamer, and Jauss; Winnicott and Lacan; the Russian formalists and Prague structuralism, particularly Mukarovski, but also Zirmunskij and Durisin; Ingarden and Grappin—in short, the hermeneutic, psychoanalytic, or philosophical theories that deal with reception. The prehistory of reception aesthetics came to the fore, and Bakhtin found himself transformed into a reception theorist—a reception, moreover, that deals more with the direct relationship between text and reader than with the context of communication or the ideologic mediation of the changing context.[9]

Theodor W. Adorno's hypothesis in *Aesthetische Theorie* (Frankfurt, 1970) on "art's dual nature, as an autonomous and a social phenomenon" ("Doppelcharakter der Kunst als autonom und als *fait social*") as well as on its enigmatic character ("Raetselcharakter") raised anew the problems that had absorbed Bakhtin's group, although these problems are of course now articulated within the framework of the critical theory ("Kritische Theorie") peculiar to the Frankfurt school. Although the paths are different and one cannot speak of Bakhtin's influence or presence in Adorno's text, the concurrence of the results nevertheless reveals a common Marxist basis.

The problem of the literary text's polysemous ambiguity (as well as the enigmatic nature of any artistic work) has driven sociologists and philosophers to adopt two opposite but complementary positions. Historicist philologists would opt for the monosemic reduction of the text to the author's intention or message, as would also philosophers of ideology and sociologists of the subject who, although they deny authors' control over their works and their meaning, investigate the work of art and the literary text as if they were denotative historical documents. (Neo)positivists would exclude meaning as a pertinent (scientific) object of literary and, generally speaking, aesthetic studies: they would limit themselves to studying texts and works of art in general as a social phenomenon and would direct their attention to quantifiable external factors such as the typology of the work's readers, its editions, markets, and circulation; or they would deny the text (the work of art) any social substructure and limit their scientific investigation to an equally quantifiable analysis of stylistic elements such as forms, structures, and internal operating rules (stylistic and linguistic rules in the case of the text).

Although the two positions are irreconcilable, the empirical sociology of literature and art concurs here with the various immanentist formalisms and structuralisms in their (neo)positivist conception of scientific knowledge and in their exclusion of meaning from the scientific field. The two positions also concur in their (at the very least implicit) acceptance of the opposition *hors texte* (social)/ textual immanence (free of any social constraint), and in so doing they subscribe to the *Wertfreiheit* proposed by positivism's philosophy of values. Finally, both conceptions are based on the justified rejection of the ingenuousness with which historicist philologists and some analysts (who may or may not be Marxist) of subject matter reduced the literary text and the work of art in general to monosemous documents through which one purported to interpret the author, the artist's personality, or his sociohistorical environment. It was in response to that reduction that Adorno proclaimed the first principle of his aesthetics: the enigmatic, connotative, and therefore polysemous nature of the work of art.

The enigmatic nature of art, however, excludes neither the meaning nor the social character of aesthetics — on the contrary. It is precisely in dealing with this problem that Adorno contests external sociological views and immanentist formalisms: he rejects their postulates while proposing, as Bakhtin had done earlier, an aesthetics theory (a synthesis of both antithetic conceptions) that acknowledges both the relative autonomy of the artistic literary expression and the necessity of its social realization. We have here an authentic sociology of forms that insists on the specificity of art and on its participation in sociohistorical processes. In the case of literature, this twofold postulate could be conveyed, in today's terms, through the close interdiscursive relationship between communicative language (the conceptual, to use Adorno's terminology) and its ludic literary reproduction (the mimetic).

For Adorno, then, the literary text is polysemous (or connotative as opposed to denotative or monosemous) and mimetic (or fictional instead of real). It is a make-believe (*als ob*) that deals with linguistic norms as well as with the logic of reality. It is therefore a mistake to read it as a denotative text (and to consider it as a social, direct, monosemous document) or to deny it meaning and see in it only its verbal technique or a sociology of the document's production and circulation as merchandise. Subject-matter analysis and some Marxist analyses that reduce the text to the simple and direct expression of an ideology share with the various historical expressions of formalism a refusal to confront the implications that the literary text's double nature noted by both Adorno and Bakhtin presents in a truly critical study, that is, a study that takes into consideration the text's social nature and its specificity.

Epilogue

In an article in the journal *Gorn*, Tretyakov (1923, 1972) asks himself: How is it that man, who as a child draws, dances, sings, and invents "good words," as an adult is truly impoverished in his expressive faculties and is satisfied with only occasionally enjoying the creativity of an artist? Gerhard Goebel-Schilling (1988) comments on Tretyakov's question:

> As a Marxist Tretyakov knows the answer. He knows very well that if the average adult's relationship to Art has been reduced to pure consumption or to what we used to call "reception," this process is the result of the division of tasks in a society of classes and of the corresponding education. (35)

Goebel-Schilling then asks, what would everybody's relationship with all the social activities, including the artistic ones, look like in a society where the division of tasks were no longer consolidated in a system of classes? He reminds us of the passage from *German Ideology* in which Marx, apparently joking about a naive vision of the socialist utopia, describes a society that would not confine people to a monolithic formation but would allow everyone to "do this or that, go hunting in the morning, fishing in the afternoon, take care of the animals in the evening, and be a critic after the meals, just as I wish to and without becoming therefore a hunter or a fisherman, a shepherd or a critic" (Marx and Engels 1966, 1:97).
Goebel-Schilling goes on to remark on the practice of writing:

> We are used to seeing the historiography of literature being based on the myth and reality (because it is not only a myth) of a vocational or at

least professional delegation of this art to certain creative individuals who are surrounded by more or less faithful followers or, in the terrible but pertinent terminology of the German *Rezeptionsästhetik*, by "receivers." (35)

For a new conception of the literary text and a new literary history, Goebel-Schilling proposes getting back to the "games of conversation that can be transformed into games of writing," in line with the title of the fifth essay in his book, "An Alternative Way: Writing Socialized by the Game." What he is proposing is not new. Rolf Kloepfer has also experimented with the production of literary texts for teaching foreign languages at universities and schools, and we find the theoretical foundation of this experience in his *Poetik und Linguistik*. For Kloepfer poetic competence should not be considered a separate faculty to be added, in some privileged cases, to the linguistic competence that he calls "normal"; on the contrary, poetic competence is an integral part of what he calls "the capacity of semiosis," which not only implies using the language but also "innovating the language" (1975, 30ff., 81ff.). The socialization of literature by games proposed here implies two things:

1. The defetishization of the author as creative genius by a generalization of literary activity that places it within the social activities of every subject, independent of the social division of work.
2. A conception of literary activity as working on language rather than as simply using it in a mimetic way.

In most cases our speech acts are indeed limited to the simple mimetic reproduction of accepted models in our social repertoire, according to a ritual ordered by different circumstances or situations. The social interaction that implies the use of any oral or written language is possible only within preestablished functions for a predetermined type of text, as in the case of performatives. Researching other forms of social interaction through linguistic communication, Siegfried J. Schmidt and Harald Weinrich, for example, discovered the existence of structurally preestablished communicative formulas that also have the sociocommunicative function of binding users. Such formulas are interiorized by members of every society, who use them constantly while respecting the rules of both their functioning and their pertinence. These communicative acts therefore always function in accordance with a sort of precise ritual. Actually, every discursive formation functions as a socially adjusted practice within a given community, producing a ritualized organization of verbal signs. Literary communication does not escape Michel Foucault's "ordre du discours" (order of discourse), even if it does not always respect constraints and if it develops within an institutionalized modality of paradoxical communication where the code of the reader is not necessarily any longer the author's own, the author being also a reader of discursive and textual practices.

Because the literary text does not necessarily respect the constraints of discursive formations used or abused by the composition of the text, the literary text is oriented in two ways: toward the system or subsystem of which it has been a part and toward the sociolinguistic processes in which (*nolens, volens*) it participates.

Let us recall that my hypothesis from the beginning was that only the existence of an interdiscursive corelation in the Spain of its time could explain the eruption in *Lazarillo de Tormes* of the autobiographical fiction characteristic of the picaresque novel; as long as both the communicative circuit that frames this discourse and its nature (its lexicon and its narrative program) aim at a practice of confession, I oriented my research to document the existence of such autobiographical confessional practices.

The structure of the picaresque text appears now to be a copy of that of the spiritual confessions and the autobiographical demonstrations demanded by the Inquisition. The author of *Lazarillo* assumes that certain readers have a curious familiarity with these practices, but *Lazarillo*'s discursive mask is worn so naturally that readers might have difficulty recognizing a travesty. Indeed, the naive reader has traditionally seen in *Lazarillo* the authentic confession of a town crier of Toledo supposedly called Lázaro. Is my thesis the product of a researcher's fantasy, or does a conscious reader historically exist? One of these readers seems to have been Cervantes, and we find the proof in chapter 22 of the first part of *Don Quijote*, where the communicative situation of Lazarillo and its narrative program is reproduced in a highly original way.

Defining itself as a simple parody of the chivalric novel, *Don Quijote* is an authentic *Literaturroman* that included the entire contemporary literary repertory: epic and popular epic, picaresque and courteous novel, Byzantine, Moresque, and so on. Cervantes thus incorporates all literary forms of his time, and other discursive forms through frequent discursive transfers, into the material of his novel. Consequently, he goes further than the ceremonial communication that actualizes predetermined signs to attract the reader's attention to the process of communication itself and to the laws of functioning characteristic of every discursive formation or genre, which makes *Don Quijote* a true dialogical space, where—as in *Lazarillo*—we find a testimony about the way a text reads discursive history and inserts itself into it.

Jorge Luis Borges skillfully captured this dimension of Cervantes's novel in the story of Pierre Menard, who not only represents the double constraint every subject has to confront when desiring to communicate, but above all a double mimetic reproduction of *Don Quijote*. Pierre Menard's utopian acquisition of the Spanish language of the seventeenth century, reviving the Catholic beliefs and appropriating the details of the style typical of Cervantes's idiolect in order to be able to express himself like Cervantes, strikingly resembles Don Quijote's pathologically deformed reading of chivalry novels that motivates his anachronic epic project and the archaic language in which it is realized. When "reading" *Don Quijote*, Borges follows literally Cervantes's process in "reading" the chivalry novels, by interposing a person—Pierre Menard. Pierre Menard thus becomes the Don Quijote of our times in his transhistoric "homosemantism," and Borges becomes a second Menard (or second Cervantes?) whom he demands as a necessary condition for the reconstitution of the first Menard. Also, the relation between Borges and Menard is not too different from the relation between Cervantes and the supposed author of *Don Quijote*, Cidi Amete Benengeli.

Like Don Quijote in Cervantes's novel, and a little more than a century before Cervantes, Christopher Columbus is a man of the book who would be loyal to the "letter" that guarantees the accomplishment of his "mission." In order to make credible the alien experiences of his voyages of discovery, Columbus has only to evoke known and recognizable (socialized) references to describe his "invention": the arrival at the Indies by a western route. Even if, with Adamic arrogance, he gives names to the lands he "discovers" in his maritime route from the West to the Indies—and by the act of naming these lands appropriates them and their inhabitants—the language that articulates the naming is an "already-there," therefore a repetition of words "already inhabited."

But Columbus is not satsfied with naming the "discovered" lands and their inhabitants. He also describes them. And to do this he again uses the already-said. Drawing upon both the biblical description of man and woman in the state of pure nature and the classical description of *locus amoenus* and the Golden Age, Columbus gives us an image of the "Indian" whose authenticity is not questioned. This image was received as the fruit of direct experimental knowledge that confirmed what was expected because the way had been prepared by sacred and classic texts. This constructed image, attached by Columbus to the word "Indian," soon becomes a new object of knowledge subjected to the theological, philosophical, judicial, and economic interrogations of the time. The "Indian" (wrong name and wrong image) therefore becomes what I call a discursive instance, a common place (*topos*) in which all the instituted discursive formations of the era converge within their division of discursive work.

My preoccupation—like that of Bakhtin and his circle in the Soviet Union of the 1920s and 1930s, as well as that of Adorno and the Frankfurt school—is the socialization of forms of expression and of communication, including literary ones, avoiding (if possible) a new form of fetishism: "creation," even if it is now accessible to everybody, as seems to be the case with Goebel-Schilling and Kloepfer's propositions about the games of writing.

Invited by the Royal Society of Canada to present my reflections on the future of literary studies at the colloquium "The Humanities in the Eighties" in Montreal in 1980, I proposed to reintegrate, in a literary history still to come, the interaction of four elements that constitute the literary fact: context, author, text, reader (see Gómez-Moriana 1980b). These four elements, or instances of the literary fact, have so successfully preoccupied literary studies that paying attention to one means forgetting the rest. If tradition studies cultivated a fetishism of the creator in the historic person of the author, the first steps of socializing literary production created a new fetishism at the same time that it dispossessed the author: that of the socioeconomic or historicocultural context from which the work arose as a necessity, determined by historic imperatives (deterministic sociocriticism). The orientation of literary studies toward the research of data relating to authors or their geographic and historic space could demonstrate the erudition of the author, the sources of inspiration of certain elements or isolated details of his or her work, his or her originality, the spirit of the time, his or her ideology, and so on. But this orientation resulted in ignoring the text as a totality organized by certain principles of composition. This ignoring of traditional literary studies explains the violent reaction of structuralism toward historicism, to which it opposed a purely immanent study of the literary work, thus creating a third fetishism: that of the text as the only pertinent object of the literary study. This approach should actually be called achronic instead of synchronic because it locates the text in an atemporality and refuses to consider other systems of signification related to the text, whether as contexts of production or as contexts of different readings or receptions through time and space.

These days, a whole series of studies more or less directly related to the *Rezeptionsästhetik* developed by the Konstanzer Schule are about to make the receiver (the reader and the act of reading) the new object of exclusivity in the study of the literary fact. Thus arises the fourth fetishism of literary studies: that of the reader, or subject of the reception of the text. The text has now been transformed into a conglomerate of ''stimuli,'' into pure ''potentiality'' that needs ''realization'' by the reader to become a ''work.'' Readers give the text its sense by connecting and structuring the series of sentences and the empty spaces that constitute their own verbal materiality. The reader has thus become the true creator of the literary work, both on the aesthetic level (as the subject of the aesthetic enjoyment of the text) and the semiotic level (by giving sense to the text).

By integrating the four elements as inseparable dimensions of the same phenomenon, the literary fact, I intend not only to overcome each of the four fetishisms of literary criticism, but I try also to integrate literary fact into both discursive and cognitive histories. Consequently, when we contextualize the text in relation to its discursive surroundings, as well as to its production and its reception, and when we measure its intervention in language and in the collective imaginary, we discover in the interaction between author and reader a new dimension: the process of consciousness. It is in relation to this process that I define the sociocritical dimension of aesthetics.

From this postulate then, my explications proceed simultaneously from the text *Lazarillo de Tormes* and from the emergence in sixteenth-century Spain of the picaresque autobiography as a genre, starting with the model subverted in the autobiographical confession of Lázaro de Tormes: the autobiographic confessions directly or indirectly related to the Inquisition and realized under its command. I risk stating that *Lazarillo* is to the picaresque novel what the signaled inquisitional practices are to *Lazarillo*, a discursive model that has been transgressed. A rupture at the same time destructive and creative (*Umbau*) thus gives rise to a new model of a whole series of texts, the so-called picaresque novel. Cervantes—and Borges after him—reduces the authority of the text to the grotesque, which guided the process and the accounts of Columbus's travels, as well as those of Don Quijote, and which Martínez Bonati calls the "critic of poetic reason." Indeed, in *Don Quijote* Cervantes uses a whole series of proceedings of discursive experimentation, an indication that literary practices, especially in a period of crisis, participate in a process of consciousness that gives them critical position toward both the nonliterary and the literary, because the different literary proceedings are also part of the discursive system of the society in question.

If I insist on the socioesthetic value of this intervention, sometimes rupture, always within the use of established models, it is to show clearly that its study does not signify a return to erudite positivism. Besides the pleasure that erudition produces by revealing the origin of something (a purely historicist pleasure that characterizes the traditional search for sources), we are dealing here with an authentic liberation—as much in the effect of the text itself, as in its archeological reconstruction or contextualization by means of the *mise en série* with other discursive practices of Spain that produce and receive these texts.

I have thus produced—against the fetishizing isolation of the text that praises the aesthetic autonomy of literature—its *mise en série* within textual and discursive contexts. Considering the proper marks of every particular discursive field in its relative autonomy (following Bakhtin and his circle and also Adorno and the Frankfurt school), I have examined the points of contact and exchange, of use, abuse, and interaction (by usurpation or by contamination) of one discursive field by another. I have thus violated the boundaries of disciplines and discursive practices usually studied in isolation from one another as a result of the work division in our society. This order moves, as I have shown, by the playful intervention of jokes (the lowest level of literature) and of literary transgressive practices. We have here the linguistic and social functions of literary practices. By their ludic, more or less transgressive imitations of the socially regulative uses of language, they work also on the collective imagination.

Notes

Introduction: Semiotics and Philology in Text Analysis

1. In 1927, Juri Tynjanov and Roman Jakobson denounced Saussurian synchrony as an "illusion" (see Matleika and Pomorska 1971, 80), and one year later Jakobson (1962, 1-2) proposed a reorganization of historical phonetics—Saussure's and neogrammarians' "phonetic laws"—into a chronology of phonemic systems, a project that was carried out later by André Martinet (1955). But it was neither this branch of linguistics nor its echo in Prague structuralism that inspired anthropological, literary, and even linguistic structuralism in the rest of Europe and the United States. In the Western world, synchrony continued to mean a *static* reality and the only one perceivable as a "system" by the collective conscience.

2. Examples of research inspired by nationalism are the works by Th. Braga, A. Farinelli and Mario Penna, Gendarme de Bévotte, Victor Said Armesto, and Ramón Menéndez Pidal on the origins of the "convidado de piedra" and through them, of the Don Juan legend. Each participant in the controversy discovered new sources in his own country, documenting (provisionally) the "nationality" of the legend.

3. See A. Gómez-Moriana (1980b, 1982a, 1985).

4. See M. Bakhtin and V. N. Voloshinov (1973), particularly the third part, chapters 8 through 11.

1. The Subversion of Ritual Discourse

1. At the Eighth Congress of the Canadian Association of Hispanists (McGill University, June 1972), I put forward this working hypothesis in a paper whose summary was published in the *Boletín de Filología Española* (1972): 54-56. A grant by the Canadian Arts Council subsequently allowed me to confirm my hypothesis by consulting various collections in archives and libraries, particularly the records of the Inquisition, which are kept in the Archivos Históricos Nacionales de Madrid.

2. "Tu cabeza es hermosa, pero sin sexo" in lieu of "Tu cabeza es hermosa, pero sin seso (but

brainless)," which translates La Fontaine's verse in *Le renard et le buste*: "Belle tête, dit-il, mais de cervelle point." Following the Spanish text:

Dijo la zorra al busto después de olerlo:
Tu cabeza es hermosa, pero sin seso.
Como éste hay muchos,
Que, aunque parecen hombres,
Sólo son bustos.

3. *The Pleasaunt Historie of Lazarillo de Tormes. Drawen out of Spanish by David Rouland of Anglesey* (1586; reprint, Oxford: Basil Blackwell, 1924), 19. Further quotations in the text are from this edition, with page numbers in parentheses.

4. Quoted by E. Cros (1976, 21) from the Spanish edition of *Obras completas de Vives*, vol. 1 (Madrid: Editorial Católica, 1947), 1395.

2. Intertextuality, Interdiscursiveness, and Parody

1. In his introduction to Clásicos Planeta's anthology of the picaresque novel (vol. 1, Barcelona, 1967), Francisco Rico speaks of Jauss's and Baumanns's "preposterous views" (xlvi), which indicates, among other things, that he did not understand that Baumanns's article is a rebuttal of Jauss's views.

2. *Moniciones* are the repeated warnings that the inquisitors directed as general invitation (*edicto de gracia*) or to those accused in the first three hearings so that they might search their memories and examine their consciences. The response was a voluntary, "spontaneous" confession, a prerequisite for mercy. Otherwise, the inquisitors proceeded *conforme a justicia* ("in accordance with the laws of justice"). See Juan Antonio Llorente, 1967, 207ff: "Explicación de las palabras y frases técnicas que se usaban en el Santo Oficio".

3. The reconciliation (*reconciliación*) follows the general life confession (*declaración indagatoria*) that the "suspect" presents to the experts (*calificadores*) who make a first (prima facie) evaluation of each case. More than once, such a reconciliation served the accused well, as happened to Teresa of Avila. Quite a few contemporary autobiographies—like her *El libro de su vida*—have their origin in this practice and are therefore linked to the inquisitorial practices.

4. The soliloquies of Fray Pedro Fernández Pecha (ca. 1400), founder of the Hieronymites of Spain, were published in the journal *Ciudad de Dios* (175 [1962]: 710-63) by Angel Custodio Vega, who states in his introduction that these soliloquies, modeled on Augustine's *Confessions*, constitute "the most common form of prayer in all the Middle Age centuries, from the time of the holy Bishop of Hipona to the sixteenth century" and defines them as the "soul's confession to God in his presence." The *Confesión de un pecador delante de Iesuchristo, redentor y juez de los hombres, compuesta por el Doctor Constantino* corresponds to this definition. Its second edition surfaces in Evora in 1554, the year *Lazarillo*'s three earliest-known editions appear. This same type of discourse is found in the *Opúsculos literarios*, published by Paz y Meliá in *Bibliófilos españoles*. In the Siglo de Oro's lyrical poetry, especially sonnets, we also observe this type of contrite confession, addressed to a "thou" (probably Jesus crucified, before whom these sonnets would be declaimed as a prayer). Some spiritual autobiographies from assorted periods have been published in Juan Flors's collection, *Espirituales españoles*. Finally, the inquisitorial confessions have been printed as parts of specific trials, for example, those of Luis Vives's mother (Madrid-Barcelona: Instituto Arias Montano, 1964); Brocense (published by Antonio Tovar and Miguel de la Pinta Llorente, Madrid, 1941); and Archbishop Carranza (published as *Proceso inquisitorial del Arzobispo Carranza* by Ignacio Tellechea Idígoras, Madrid: Real Academia de la Historia, 1962). In 1974 Haim Beinart began publishing the records of the trials of *judaizantes* (practitioners of Jewish customs) in *Records of the Trials of the Spanish Inquisition in Ciudad Real*, vol. 1, 1483-85 (Jerusalem, 1974); vol. 2, 1494-1512 (Jerusalem, 1977).

5. About the epic "I," see Zimmermann (1971).

6. Compare, for example, Lázaro's comments in the first chapter on Zaide's robberies ("Let us never therefore marvell more at those which steale from the poore, nor yet at them which convey from the houses they serve, to presente therewith whome they love, in hope to attayne thereby their desired pleasure, seeing that love was able to encourage this poore condman or slave to doe thus", [9]) and those in the second chapter about the stinginess of the cleric from Maqueda ("I know not if it were of his own, or if he had acquired it along with his clerical robes" [25]) with his statement in the first chapter about the bump on his head against the stone bull of Salamanca given him by the blind man, which indicates a change of attitude in the very instant of the act: "It semed then immediatly that I awaked out of simplicitie, wherein I had of long time slept like a child, and I said to my self, my blind master hath good reason, it is ful time for me to open mine eyes, yea, and to provide and seeke mine owne advantage, considering that I am alone without helpe" (11). "For I being examined of the deede' after much thretning was constrainned as a childe, for feare, to discover the whole matter" (9) says Lázaro about his attitude to Zaide's robberies, removing himself from this attitude of those days. The commentary about his disillusion upon seeing through the Toledo squire's pretences demonstrates again an attitude concurrent with the one of the time of writing: "God knoweth that when I met with any of his estate, being of like gravitie, pace and countenance, hove I pitied them, thimking' that they did endure that which I did see him daily suffer" (48). But his attending the squire did not arise from precisely that attitude.

7. On the book title and chapter epigraphs and its narrator, see Jean Claude Simard (1978). On the correlation of the Alcalá edition and the Burgos and Antwerp editions and on the role of the Alcalá interpolations, see José Varela Muñoz (1977), who perceives two levels of consciousness in the Burgos and Antwerp text: they depict Lázaro as the town crier proclaiming his own dishonor ("pregonero de su propia deshonra"). The Alcalá interpolations, by obliterating that difference, remove the paradox as a structural technique of Lázaro's tale: Lázaro now knows as much as the implicit author. My characterization of the text differs from that of Simard and Varela Muñoz but does not contest it: on the contrary, I believe that the three views are complementary.

8. On the term double bind, see Watzlawick, Beavin, and Jackson (1967), especially chapter 6.

9. "Vuestra Merced escribe se le escriba y relate el caso por extenso" literally translates as: "Your Worship commands that the case be written and reported to him at length."

10. Session 14 (November 25, 1551), *Doctrina de sacrameneto poenitentiae.* See especially chapter 6: "De ministro huius sacramenti et absolutione," and canon 9: "Si quis dixerit, absolutionem sacramentalem sacerdotis non esse actum iudicialem . . . A[nathema]. S[it]." The Council of Trent's definition evidently corresponds to an already-established practice.

11. The *edicto de gracia* created a grace period during which those who voluntarily (spontaneously) identified themselves to the inquisitors as repentant heretics soliciting absolution without public penance would be absolved secretly (see Juan Antonio Llorente, 1967, 207ff.: "Explicación de las palabras y frases técnicas que se usaban en el Santo Oficio"). Hence the term [confesión] espontánea and the verb espontanearse. In reality, once entered nobody escaped the Inquisition that easily.

3. Autobiography and Ritual Discourse

1. "Quisiera yo que, como me han mandado y dado larga licencia para que escriba el modo de oración y las mercedes que el Señor me ha hecho, me la dieran para que muy por menudo y con claridad dijera mis grandes pecados y ruín vida . . . Suplico [al Señor] me dé gracia para que con toda claridad y verdad yo haga esta relación que mis confesores me mandan" (T. de Jesús [1979], 117).

2. "Written by Mother María Antonia after numerous requests from her confessor, Father Joseph de Jesús María, divided into sections and chapters by himself" (M. A. de Jesús [1961], 57).

3. " This I do, because Your Grace has expressly requested this act of obedience" (Vela y Cueto [1961], 307).

4. "Up until the age of twelve, I shall have to write of childish things; for so earnestly has Your Grace entreated me not to omit anything that I might remember" (Carvajal y Mendoza [1966], 132).

5. "Quede[n] por memoria todos mis hechos e milagros que la Virgen Sancta María me mostró [de modo que] todas las criaturas que estuvieran en tribulación sean ciertas . . . que si se encomiendan de corazón a la Virgen Sancta María, que ella las consolará y acogerá como me consoló a mí" (Córdoba [1883], 35).

6. "Para que naide pierda de sus inmensas misericordias [de Dios] la confianza que se debe tener, cuyos efectos habemos, mientras habemos vivido en el mundo, no solamente entendido y creído, pero casi palpado y experimentado" (Ayala, *Discurso de la vida del Ilustríssimo y Reverendíssimo Señor Don Martín de Ayala, . . . escrito por sí mesmo*).

7. "Yo digo lo que ha pasado por mí, como me la mandan, y si no fuere bien, romperálo a quien lo envio, que sabrá mejor entender lo que va mal que yo. A quien suplico, por amor del Señor, lo que he dicho hasta aquí de mi ruín vida y pecados lo publiquen. Desde ahora doy licencia, y a todos mis confesores que así lo es a quien esto va. Y si quisieren, luego en mi vida" (T. de Jesús [1979], 117).

8. See Watzlawick, Beavin, and Jackson (1967).

9. The consequence that may be inferred from this intention, the functional ordering of the account that has personal identity give way before functional identity, is what motivates Plato's well-known lamentation about the Sophists: "In courts, no one is interested in establishing the facts objectively, but rather in persuading, and persuasion is a question of likelihood rather than a question of truth." *Lazarillo* seems to censure this possible rhetorical discursive manipulation by loading the autobiographical discourse with folkloric elements, and by giving it at the same time such coherence as to make it seem likely. See Gómez-Moriana (1980a).

10. "Just as there is within the tale an important functional exchange (shared by a giver and a recipient), homologically, the tale itself is an object of communication: it implies a giver of the account and a receiver," states Roland Barthes (1966, 18). This conception of the narrative in which the account becomes an object to be offered implies the narrator-donor's authority over it. Nevertheless, by returning to the original participant-role schema—that is, to Tesnière's didactic observation of the role distribution in the "spectacle" of language in which Greimas (1966, 173) was so interested—we shall also have to submit this donor-subject in his subject position to the reduction operated by the addresser. It follows that the corrected framework we propose in schema 2 pertains not only to autobiographical writing but to all language acts, as long as the spectacle that *homo loquens* presents to himself is considered as enunciation and reception, instead of being confined to the syntax of what is enunciated.

11. The preterit always indicates a temporal distance between the enunciation's present and the enunciated act's past, although when it is the case of a statement in the first person, it seems that both temporal dimensions are blurred in the personal pronoun I, and consequently so are the referring and the referred "I"'s.

4. Narration and Argumentation in Autobiographical Discourse

1. Compare Benveniste's complementary distribution of verb tenses with Harald Weinrich's, which was carried out at the same time. Weinrich (1964) distinguishes between tenses of the commented world (*besprochene Welt*) and tenses of the narrated world (*erzählte Welt*). The most frequently used tenses in the register of the commented world are the present, future, and compound past; in the register of the narrated world, the imperfect, simple past, pluperfect, and conditional. In a later work in which he returns to this topic, Weinrich (1979) again proposes this binary distribution as a possible basis for the literary distinction between the nonnarrative and the narrative. Both history and autobiography enter into Weinrich's "narrative," whereas they are separated by Benveniste. It is this concept of narrative that determined the first component of my title for this chapter, though I added a second component (argumentation) in order to insist also on the discursive dimension of autobiography. Note that I am dealing with two dimensions of the text and not with the typological or

taxonomic distinction that is the case for both Benveniste and Weinrich. Compare also the distinction established by Todorov (1966) between "reported events," which he calls history, and "the way by which the narrator lets us know them," which he calls discourse. I believe that all narration is in fact argumentative, and on this axiom I base my thesis that sociohistorical conditioning determines changes of perspective in the selection and strategic ordering of the narrative material in all historical narration and in particular the autobiographical.

2. Benveniste continues: "The fundamental tense is the aorist, which is the tense of the event outside the person of a narrator" (208).

3. Oswald Ducrot (1980) insists on the need to admit that "utterances are produced, in other words, that there are moments when they do not yet exist and moments when they no longer exist." "What I need,'" Ducrot again insists, "is that one take into consideration among the historical facts the emergence of utterances (énoncés) at different points of time and space. The speech act itself (énonciation) is this emergence" (34). In this way Ducrot introduces a collective volume on French expressions that reveal what he calls "a saying hidden behind what is said" (34).

4. Mieke Bal (1985) distinguishes the following three dimensions in the narrative: fable (logical and chronological sequence of events), history (its presentation), and text (the narrator's work).

5. Thus Frank Bowman compares Ignacio de Loyola's *Relato* with Henry Suso's, who writes of his life in the third person as "the Servant of Eternal Wisdom" (not unlike the popes who refer to themselves as "servant of the servants of God"). On this form of autobiographical writing, see Philippe Lejeune (1980); on the various forms in which the autobiographical genre crystallizes, see Elizabeth Bruss's *Autobiographical Acts: The Changing Situation of a Literary Genre* (1976), and Robert Elbaz (1988).

6. This hypothesis refers to the notion of rhetoric in its first stages, with the Greek Sophists, which would give rise to the Latin oratorical tracts and reappear in the *ars dicendi* that becomes in Europe the Jesuit school of sacred oratory (but also of apologetic theology), and in the treatises of argumentation that proliferate in the sixteenth and seventeenth centuries, what Perelman (1977) calls "L'empire rhétorique. Perelman speaks of the "decline of rhetoric" toward the end of the sixteenth century as "due to the rise in bourgeois thought that widened the role of evidence, of the personal evidence of Protestantism, of the rational evidence of Cartesianism or of the sensory evidence of empiricism" (21).

7. "Ynformacion de Miguel de Cerbantes de lo que ha seruido a su magestad y de lo que a hecho estando captiuo en Argel y por la certificacion que aqui presenta del duque de Sesa se vera como quando le captiuaron se le perdieron otras muchas ynformaciones fées y recados que tenia de lo que hauia seruido a su magestad" (Archivo General de Indias, Patronato Real, legajo 253). See transcription and English translation in the Appendix to the second volume of Hispanic Issues, *Autobiography in Early Modern Spain*, ed. Nicholas Spadaccini and Jenaro Talens (Minneapolis: The Prisma Institute, 1988), 247-85.

8. In the "Prologue to the Reader" of his edition of *Ocho comedias y ocho entremeses nuevos nunca representados* (Madrid: Viuda de Alonso Martín, 1615), Cervantes writes: "In the theatres of Madrid *Los tratos de Argel* was put on, as well as *La destrucción de Numancia* and *La batalla naval*, where I dared to reduce the comedies to three days, from the original five; I showed, or better, I was the first to represent the imaginations and the hidden thoughts of the soul, bringing out moral figures in the theatre to the general and hearty applause of the listeners; I composed during that time up to twenty or thirty comedies, all of which were recited without the audience offering either cucumbers or other throwable objects: the plays ran their course without whistles, shouts or jeers. I had other things to work on, I left the pen and the comedies, and along came that monster of nature, Lope de Vega."

5. Evocation as a Literary Procedure in *Don Quijote*

1. During the sixteenth century, theologians and spiritual authors (Melchor Cano, Esbarroya,

Malon de Chaide, Teresa de Avila) as well as humanists (Huarte de San Juan, Pérez de Moya, Alonso Fuentes, Alonso López Pinciano) often condemned novels of chivalry; in 1555, the Valladolid courts demanded their prohibition. The *Entremés de los romances*, by parodying the romances, becomes the *Quijote*'s literary antecedent (see Menéndez Pidal [1920]).

2. This play of fiction within fiction, of the representation's representation, of the process's own novelistic production, has brought about comparisons between the *Quijote* and Velázquez's *Meninas*. See, for example, E.C. Riley (1962) and Michel Foucault (1966). Helmut Hatzfeld (1952, 1966) compares Cervantes to Velázquez in a different sense.

3. Thus, in chapter 72 of the 1615 *Quijote*, in an interesting dialogue with Don Alvaro Tarfe (a character of Avellaneda's *Quijote*), Don Quijote and Sancho demonstrate that they are authentic and that "all other don Quixote and all other Sancho Pansa are but dreames, fopperies, and fables" (*The History of Don Quijote of the Mancha*, translated from the Spanish of Miguel de Cervantes by Thomas Shelton 1612, 1620. Reprint. New York: AMS Press, 1967), 4:257. Further quotations in the text are from this edition, with volume and page number in parentheses.

4. In this respect, Michel Foucault (1966) states: "Cervantes's text withdraws into itself, sinks into its own depths, and becomes the object of its own story. The first part of the adventures takes on in the second part the role that chivalresque novels played at the beginning. Don Quijote must be true to this book he has actually become." Foucault considers *Don Quijote* "the first modern work," because in it, truth resides no longer in the relationship between word and object but in "that thin and constant relationship that verbal markings weave between themselves" (62). See also Gérard Bucher (1980) on this matter.

5. Textual linguistics has insisted on the text's internal links, while maintaining its immanence. On the basis of certain semantic principles already drafted in his *Linguistik der Lüge* (1966), Harald Weinrich (1969) explains the difference between the definite and the indefinite article: he attributes to the first the function of connection with the preceding context (*anaphora*) and to the second the function of connection with the following context (*cataphora*, in ancient rhetoric). In this way a noun's polysemy is reduced to what is concretely signified in a sentence, and the texture is guaranteed. In the revised edition of *Tempus, Besprochene und erzählte Welt* (1971), Weinrich insists again on this distinction, which he extends to other elements comparable to the article: possessive and demonstrative pronouns, numeral adjectives (28-33). All this, however, supposes that the text is a closed system. This is why what I have called "transtextual anaphora" in the first chapter cannot be explained within this theory. At the very beginning of *Don Quijote*, we have a determiner without any preceding information to serve as intratextual context: "A Yeoman of their calling that use to pile in their hals old Launces, Halbards, Morrions and such other armours and weapons" (1:23). "A yeoman of their calling" has not been mentioned in the preceding text. *Their* is therefore a deictic that points to an extratextual referent, folkloric figures or a reality in the reader's daily experience. I say that they usually refer to another utterance in the text itself to break away from the immanence of the text fostered by structuralism and textual linguistics. On this point see Gómez-Moriana (1980b), 171-85.

6. Joseph Kestner (1977) prefers to reserve the term Urtext for novels of chivalry, especially *Amadís de Gaula* that, according to him, takes on the paradoxical trait of reality. By ascribing it the quality of mediator, René Girard (1976) also makes of the *Amadís* the Urtext of the *Quijote* in a certain way. Perhaps that term should be reserved for Cidi Hamete's "text," fictionally recuperated and elaborated by Cervantes. But in Cervantes's second *Don Quijote*, that is, the 1615 novel, the first *Don Quijote*, the 1605 novel, acts as Urtext. This brings Michael McCanles (1976) to state: "We have, then, the remarkable example of a heterocosmos, a novel that contains a second world that in turn contains part of itself" (279).

7. Marthe Robert (1963) insists on the "theatricality" of *Don Quijote*, a trait she considers the source of the difficulties in adapting the novel to the stage itself. Similarly, Cesare Segre (1974, 213) explains: "The theatrical metaphor dominates all of the second part of the novel." I do not understand why he limits this image to the novel's second part, for I believe that the text is an authentic mise-en-scène of a ritual act supposedly known and understood by the text's addressees in which

autonomous elements converge as is the case, for example, with the beggars that reenact Leonardo da Vinci's *La Cena* in Buñuel's film *Viridiana*.

8. As an example, we have Don Miguel de Unamuno's (1958) very brief comment on that chapter: "Here Cervantes inserts the chapter VI in which he relates 'the pleasant and curious search and inquisition made by the Curate and Barber of Don Quijotes Library,' all of which is literary criticism and of little import to us. Books and not life are its concern. We shall disregard it" (40). Also, Montherlant (1962) states in his preface to *Don Quijote* that Cervantes ignored the most relevant reality of his time—the Inquisition.

9. Other critics who adhere to these traditions include Américo Castro (1935), Helmut Hatzfeld (1966), Angel Rosenblat (1971), E. C. Riley (1962), and Paul Decouzis (1966).

10. See Miguel de la Pinta Llorente (1953, 1958); Bartolomé Bennassar (1979), especially chapter 8 by Jean-Pierre Dedieu on "Le modèle religieux: Le refus de la Réforme et le contrôle de la pensée."

11. Referring to Pottier's *situation de communication*, Krysinski (1975) adds: "It is within this framework that our expression 'referential sign' has a certain relevance. To create or to read the novel from the standpoint of a perfect communication situation, is to acknowledge that the more one immerses oneself in the context, the more one is surrounded by references" (75). By "perfect communicative situation" or "absolute context," Krysinski means the "perfect harmony between the author's onomasiology and the reader's semasiology," which necessarily implies a "maximum of information about the theory and the reality as well as about novelistic signs."

12. See Ernst Cassirer, *Philosophie der symbolischen Formen* (Darmstadt: Wissenschaftliche Buchgesellschaft, 1964).

13. Unamuno is even more audacious when he compares Ignacio de Loyola to Don Quijote, a comparison that can be made because Ignacio de Loyola's biographer, Padre Rivadeneira (1945), writes the saint's life as a "godly" adventure of chivalry.

14. This is the Council of Trent's definition in session 7 (*De Sacramentis*), March 3, 1547: "Si quis dexerit, per ipsa novae legis sacramenta ex opere operato non conferri gratiam, A[nathema]. S[it]" (canon 8). The same session of Trent that thus described the effects of sacraments also defined the conditions under which they are to be administered in general, especially those referring to baptism (matter, form, minister, and subject). In the succeeding sessions, the council turned its attention to each of the other sacraments and also to the so-called sacramentals.

15. On the initiatory rite and its possible connection with the novel, see Simone Vierne (1973); on the subjects' *raréfaction*, see Michel Foucault (1971).

16. Regarding the allusions to the Council of Trent by *Don Quijote*, cf. Helmut Hatzfeld (1966), chapter 3, "Los medios estilísticos al servicio de la ideología del tiempo" (131ff.), and Paul Decouzis (1966). Both authors cite the overbearing presence of the council's canons in *Don Quijote* without attaching much importance to the distortions affecting them.

17. Inquisition file 4470 in the Archivos Históricos Nacionales de Madrid includes various copies of the instructions for visiting libraries. All agree on the necessity of accomplishing the visit in one day, "comenzándola muy de mañana, por el daño que de tener cerradas las tiendas se puede seguir a estos libreros" (no. 6: *Visitas de librerías públicas y privadas*). According to the instructions of the Inquisitor General dated June 25, 1618, friar Antonio Pérez of Saint Benedict's order is instructed to visit "las tiendas de libreros desta corte de manera que en la prosecución deste mandato no hay ruido ni estruendo alguno"; rather, it is recommended that "poco a poco vaya viendo y reconociendo los libros que en cada dellas hubiere." In the execution of his task, the friar can count on the secular arm: "y que para la ejecución desto acudan los alguaciles del Consejo y familiares a lo que por él se le ordenare en razón de las obras vistas." The document is signed by Sebastián de Huerta, secretary of the tribunal. The visiting of private libraries, most often triggered by the death of their owners, was regulated by similar laws. In this case, speed was recommended because the heirs might distribute the books among themselves before they could be scrutinized.

18. A similar displacement is encountered at the end of Cervantes's *Casamiento engañoso*, in the words of Alférez Campuzano presenting the *Coloquio de los perros* "written and commented" by him: "Puesto caso que me haya engañado y que mi verdad sea sueño y el porfiarla disparate, ¿no se halagará vuestra merced, señor Peralta, de ver escritas en un coloquio las cosas que estos perros, o sean quien fueren, hablaron?" (*Obras completas de Cervantes* [Madrid: Aguilar, 1965], 997).

19. I am reminded of Bakhtin's (1978) description of "plurilinguisme" in the novel: "The author more or less draws away from that language, he objectivizes it by distancing himself from it, by refracting his intentions through public opinion (always superficial, often hypocritical), which are embodied in his language" (123). The novel thus becomes "the expression of a Galilean linguistic conscience that denies the absolutism of a sole and unique language; the former will no longer consider the latter as the ideological world's only verbal and semantic nucleus; and it acknowledges that the multitude of national and above all social languages are as likely to become 'languages de vérité' as relative, objective, limited languages. . . . The novel presupposes the verbal and semantic decentralization of the ideological world" (183). Bakhtin quotes English (Fielding, Smollet, Sterne, Dickens, Thackeray), German (Hippel, Jean-Paul Ritcher) and Russian authors (Dostoyevski). Cervantes as well as Mendoza, Grimmelshaussen, Rabelais, and Le Sage are Bakhtin's "foremost models," forerunners who "saw light in the course of a process of parodic destruction of the old novelistic worlds" (130). If the thesis I propose in this work is valid (that is, that the *Don Quijote* recalls or evokes various ritual discourses prevailing at that time, including the imputative discourse), Bakhtin's diagram should be corrected in order to place the *Don Quijote* as "plurilingual" or "polyphonic novel."

6. Discourse Pragmatics and Reciprocity of Perspectives

1. See Oswald Ducrot (1984), especially chapter 8, "Esquisse d'une theorie polyphonique de l'enonciation" (171-233).

2. Here is Musil's text: "There was a depression over the Atlantic. It was travelling eastwards, towards an area of high pressure over Russia, and still showed no tendency to move northwards around it. The isotherms and isotheres were fulfilling their functions. The atmospheric temperature was in proper relation to the average annual temperature, the temperature of the coldest as well as of the hottest month, and the a-periodic monthly variation in temperature. The rising and setting of the sun and of the moon, the phases of the moon, Venus and Saturn's rings, and many other important phenomena, were in accordance with the forecasts in the astronomical yearbooks. The vapour in the air was at its highest tension and the moisture in the air was at its lowest. In short, to use an expression that describes the facts pretty satisfactorily, even though it is somewhat old-fashioned: it was a fine August day in the year 1913." (1953, 1:3).

3. For those who find this rapprochement of *Don Quijote* and the *Manifesto* too daring, Karl Marx in the first book of the *Capital* claims that the "error" of Don Quijote was "to believe that the errant chivalry was compatible with all forms of society" (*Marx-Engels Werke* [Berlin: Institut für Marxismus-Leninismus, 1974] 23:96).

4. In modern editions, as well as in the English translation, this multiplication error has been corrected. See Martín de Riquer's note on the subject in his edition of *Don Quijote* (1971), 64.

5. See Blanca González de Escandón (1938) and Antonio García Berrio (1978). On the degraded society that makes Don Juan's acts of mockery possible, see Mercedes Sáenz-Alonso (1969) and Serge Mausel (1971).

6. In session 6 (*Decretum de iustificatione*), chapter 10 ("De acceptae iustificationis incremento"), Trent proclaims: "Sic ergo iustificati . . . euntes de virtute in virtutem, renovantur de die in diem, hoc est, mortificando membra carnis suae et exhibendo ea arma iustitiae in sanctificationem per observationem mandatorum Dei et Ecclesiae: in ipsa iustitia per Christi gratiam accepta, cooperante fide bonis operibus crescunt atqne magis iustificantur." In the De iustificatione canons of the same section 6 we read again: "Si quis dixerit, iustitiam acceptam non conservari atque etiam non augeri coram Deo per bona opera, sed opera ipsa fructus solummodo et signa esse iustificationis

adeptae, non etiam ipsius augendae causam: A[nathema]. S[it]'' (canon 24). Canon 32 talks as well of meriting the ''augmentum gratiae . . . atque etiam gloriae augmentum.'' On the diffusion that these doctrines attained in seventeenth-century Spain, see José Antonio Maravall (1955).

7. The Antimodernization of Spain

1. In their *Dialektik der Aufklärung*, Adorno and Horkheimer (1947) show this permanent autodestruction inscribed in the aporia that includes in its critical premises the project of the Enlightenment—a project with which the successes and also the errors of so-called modernity have been identified. The critiques of modernity could, however, obey entirely different motives: whereas Habermas, for instance, tries to go beyond such a project with his own postulates by declaring it incomplete, other thinkers of postmodernity are opposed to this project in the name of a nostalgic return to the ''values'' of a tradition that such a project negates. See Hall Foster (1983).

2. We are dealing here with the epistemological base of the fragmentation of the modern world and the relativization of values that follows from the refusal to refer to the real (*Wertfreiheit*). It is against this conception that the traditional Spanish doctrine of truth fights, a heritage of the Aristotelian-Thomist scholasticism that has recently been restored by Opus Dei without an awareness of the fact that the *Wertfreiheit* is the base of the market-oriented economy—the economic system to which, incidentally, the Opus Dei adheres.

8. Narration and Argumentation in the Chronicles of the New World

1. ''Assi que, después de repurgada la cristiana religion, por la cual somos amigos de Dios, o reconciliados con él; después de los enemigos de nuestra fe vencidos por guerra y fuerça de armas, de donde los nuestros recebian tantos daños y temian mucho maiores; después de la justicia y essecución de las leies que nos aiuntan y hazen bivir igualmente en esta gran compañia que llamamos reino y república de Castilla; no queda ia otra cosa sino que florezcan las artes de la paz. Entre las primeras, es aquélla que nos enseña la lengua.''

2. Jean-Jacques Chevallier (1969) has summarized this process as follows: ''En dépit des survivances de Cités-états, aux dimensions petites mais a la puissance commerciale et politique appréciable, en dépit des velléités ou des réalisations éphémeres d'Empires démesurés, on voit émerger irrésistiblement, de la fin du Moyen Age au début des temps modernes (Renaissance et Reforme), les grands États-Nations de forme monarchique: France, Angleterre, Espagne. La notion de souveraineté, doctrinée par Jean Bodin, deviendra leur robuste armature juridicopolitique. Souveraineté du roi, en Parlement ou non, et souveraineté de l'État tendront à l'identification'' (50).

3. In his *Historia de la bula de la cruzada en España*, José Góñiz Gaztambide equates the terms Reconquest and Crusade within the context of the Spanish Middle Ages. He points out the traditional idea of the ''struggle against the infidel'' in terms of the eight centuries of the Arabic presence in the Iberian Peninsula, although he is content with affirming that the word crusade already appears in the first half of the thirteenth century'' (151). This comment, I believe, confirms my thesis that Pope Innocent III put forth this idea at the beginning of the thirteenth century.

4. For more on the titles of the Spanish kings and their missionary activities, see Egaña (1958) and Rouco-Varela (1965).

5. Paraphrasing Ovid, Pedro Mártir de Anglería spoke of the natives in the following terms in his *De orbe novo* (1530): ''Without laws, without books, without judges, they naturally did right . . . content with nature's bounty . . . as is said of the Golden Age'' (''Sine legibus, sine libris, sine iudicibus suapte natura rectum colunt . . . sylvestribus fructibus contentos . . . uti legitur de aurea aetate''). The words by Columbus that we will comment on in the pages that follow echo similar classical texts as he describes the conditions of the ''Indians.''

6. Gonzalo Fernández de Oviedo transcribes and comments on the text of the *requerimiento* in book 29, chapter 7 of his *Historia general y natural de las Indias* (1959, 3:227ff.). The unlikely anecdote is found in Picón Salas (1969, 44).

7. This polemical vision still predominates in our time. Even Todorov (1982) could not escape it.

8. I cite from Columbus's *Diario*, as compiled by Bartolomé de Las Casas, in Fernández de Navarrete's *Colección de los viajes y descubrimientos que hicieron por mar los españoles desde fines del siglo XV*, and currently available in Fernández de Navarrete (1954), 1:86ff., hereafter *Diario*. Hernando Colón (1984) echoes Columbus's text, as does Columbus himself in his correspondence, especially in the "Letter to Luis Santángel, February 15-March 14, 1493" ("Carta a Luis de Santángel de 15 de febrero-14 de marzo de 1493"), in which we find a description of the "Indians" using the terminology of the *Diario*. This letter can be found in Fernández de Navarrete (1954, 167ff.).

9. "Esto que sigue son palabras formales del Almirante, en su libro de su primera navegación y descubrimiento de estas Indias. 'Yo [dice él], porque nos tuviesen mucha amistad, porque conoscí que era gente que mejor se libraría y convertiría a nuestra Santa Fe con amor que no por fuerza, les di a algunos de ellos unos bonetes colorados y unas cuentas de vidrios que se ponían al pezcuezo, y otras cosas muchas de poco valor con que hobieron mucho placer, y quedaron tanto nuestros que era maravilla. Los cuales después venían a las barcas de los navíos adonde nos estábamos, nadando, y nos traían papagayos y hilo de algodón en ovillos y azagayas, y otras cosas muchas y nos las trocaban por otras cosas que nos les dábamos, como cuentecillas de vidrio y cascabeles. En fin, todo tomaban y daban de aquello que tenían de buena voluntad. Mas me parecio que era gente muy pobre de todo. Ellos andaban todos desnudos como su madre los parió, y también las mujeres, aunque no vide más de una farto moza y todos los que yo vi eran todos mancebos, que ninguno vide de edad de más de treinta años; muy bien hechos, de muy fermosos cuerpos, y muy buenas caras; los cabellos gruesos cuasi como sedas de cola de caballo, e cortos; los cabellos traen por encima de las cejas, salvo unos pocos detrás que traen largos, que jamás cortan; dellos se pintan de prieto, y ellos son de la color de los canarios, ni negros ni blancos, y dellos se pintan en blanco y dellos de colorado, y dellos de lo que fallan, y dellos se pintan las caras, y dellos todo el cuerpo, y dellos sólo los ojos, y dellos sólo el nariz. Ellos no traen armas ni las cognocen, porque les amostré espadas y las tomaban por el filo, y se cortaban con ignorancia. No tienen algún fierro; sus azagayas son unas varas sin fierro, y algunas de ellas tienen al cabo un diente de pece, y otras de otras cosas. Ellos todos a una mano son de buena estatura de grandeza, y buenos gestos, bien hechos; yo vide algunos que tenían señales de feridas en sus cuerpos, y les hice señas qué era aquello, y ellos me amostraron cómo alli venían gentes de otras islas que estaban acerca y les querían tomar, y se defendían; y yo creí, e creo, que aquí vienen de tierra firme a tomarlos por captivos. Ellos deben ser buenos servidores y de buen ingenio, que veo que muy presto dicen todo lo que les decía, y creo que ligeramente se harían cristianos, que me pareció que ninguna secta tenían. Yo, placiendo a nuestro Señor, levaré de aquí al tiempo de mi partida seis a V.A. para que desprendan fablar. Ninguna bestia de ninguna manera vide, salvo papagayos en esta isla.' Todas son palabras del Almirante."

10. "A las dos horas después de medianoche pareció la tierra. . . . Amañaron todas las velas . . . temporizando hasta el día viernes que llegaron a una isleta de los Lucayos, que se llamaba en lengua de indios Guanahani. Luego vieron gente desnuda, y el Almirante salió a tierra en la barca armada, y Martín Alonso Pinzón y Vicente Anes, su hermano, que era capitán de la Niña. Sacó el Almirante la bandera real. . . . Puestos en tierra vieron árboles muy verdes y aguas muchas y frutas de diversas maneras. El Almirante llamó a los dos capitanes y a los demás que saltaron en tierra, y a Rodrigo Descovedo, escribano de toda la armada, y a Rodrigo Sánchez de Segovia, y dijo que le diesen por fe y testimonio como él por ante todos tomaba, como de hecho tomó, posesión de la dicha isla por el Rey e por la Reina sus señores. . . . Luego se ayuntó allí mucha gente de la isla."

11. "El Almirante, viéndolos tan buenos y simples, y que en cuanto podían eran tan liberalmente hospitales, y con esto en gran manera pacíficos, dióles a muchos cuentas de vidrio y cascabeles, y a algunos bonetes colorados y otras cosas, con que ellos quedaban muy contentos y ricos."

12. "Pero el deseo que tenemos al servicio de Dios e celo a su santa fe católica, nos face po-sponer todos los intereses y olvidar los trabajos e peligros continuos que por esta causa se nos rec-rescen. Y podiendo, non solamente guardar nuestros tesoros, mas aún haber otros muchos de los mo-ros mesmos, que muy voluntariamente nos los darían por la paz, negamos los que se no ofrescen y derramamos los nuestros, solamente esperando que la santa fe católica sea acrescentada y la Cris-tianidad se quite de un tan continuo peligro como tiene aquí a las puertas, si estos infieles del Reino de Granada no son arrancados y echados de España." For other documents from this period, see *Tratados internacionales* (1952).

13. "Pues esta Corona gasta sus tesoros y emplea todas sus fuerzas en defensa de la fe, y ha dilatado nuestra sagrada Religión por tantos reinos y provincias tan extendidas, trayendo la nación española otros nuevos mundos a la obediencia a la Sede Apostólica."

14. "Yo bien entiendo que estas cosas harán sonreir de lástima a los políticos y hacendistas, que, viéndonos pobres, abatidos y humillados a finales del Siglo XVII, no encuentran palabras de bastante menosprecio para una nación que batallaba contra media Europa conjurada, y esto no por redondear su territorio ni por obtener una indemnización de guerra, sino por ideas de Teología . . . la cosa más inútil del mundo. Cuánto mejor nos hubiera estado tejer lienzo y dejar que Lutero entrara y saliera donde bien le pareciese! . . . Nunca, desde el tiempo de Judas Macabeo, hubo un pueblo que con tanta razón pudiera creerse el pueblo escogido para ser la espada y el brazo de dios; y todo, hasta sus sueños de engrandecimiento y de monarquía universal, lo referían y subordinaban a este objeto su-premo: *fiat unum ovile et unus pastor*."

9. The Emerging of a Discursive Instance

1. Marc Angenot (McGill University), Antonio Gómez-Moriana (Université de Montréal), and Régine Robin (Université du Québec à Montréal), *The Inter-University Centre for Discourse Analysis and Text Sociocriticism* (Montreal: CIADEST, 1991), 3-4.

2. If *La invención de América* by Edmundo O'Gorman (1957) is fully in line with Sollors's approach, Thomas Hunt King's doctoral thesis, *Inventing the Indian: White Images, Oral Literature, and Contemporary Native Writers* (1986) is not. For example, the first part ("The Period of Explo-ration") of King's first chapter is summarized at the beginning of the second part ("The Period of Colonization") of the same chapter: "While the language of exploration contained exaggeration and while it fostered a view of the Indian as an inferior being, it had also been reasonably honest and objective. The explorers were keen observers. . . . As settlement replaced the visit, the European reaction to the Indian intensified, and the language used to describe the Indian changed. . . . Where explorers saw a new man in a New World, colonists, particularly the Separatists and the Puritans, saw a wild beast in a howling wilderness . . . unlike the direct reports of the explorers, the image of the Indian when filtered through the minds of the colonists, was more dramatically colored" (14-15).

3. Concerning this matter, see also Edward Saïd, *Orientalism* (1978), subtitled in the French translation by Catherine Malamud *L'Orient créé par l'Occident* (Paris: Éditions du Seuil, 1980).

4. Columbus, *Diario*, Sunday, October 21, 1492, 103.

5. "Culturally inferior nations such as these are gradually eroded through contact with more advanced nations which have gone through a more intensive cultural development" that renders them "physically and spiritually impotent" (Hegel [1975], 163). "The American continent had in some respects outlived itself when we [*sic*] first came into contact with it, and in other respects, it is still not yet fully developed" (170).

6. See also by the same author, *The Predicament of Culture: Twentieth-Century Ethnography, Literature, and Art* (Cambridge, Mass.: Harvard University Press, 1988).

10. The (Relative) Autonomy of Artistic Expression

1. I am using here the accepted synecdoche wherein the name Bakhtin implies his whole circle,

particularly Voloshinov-Medvedev-Bakhtin. I am thus avoiding the problem of the authorship of each text, a problem in any case not very relevant in such a coherent corpus and one so well marked by its underlying historical circumstances.

2. In accordance with the previous note, I shall refer indiscriminately to works on formal method, poetics, and linguistics, on the Marxism and philosophy of language, on the theory of the novel (including Dostoyevski and Rabelais), and on the aesthetics of verbal expression without necessarily indicating the author or authors. The themes more specifically developed here can be found in Voloshinov (1981).

3. See in particular Voloshinov (1983b). For studies on the formal method that focus on the same problem, see Medvedev (1983); Bakhtin and Medvedev (1978); Bakhtin and Voloshinov (1973) and Bakhtin (1978).

4. See particularly Voloshinov (1983a). The same issue is also the subject of Voloshinov's studies on literary stylistics (English version in *Bakhtin School Papers*, 93-152) and of Bakhtin's "Le problème des genres discursifs" and "Le problème du texte dans la linguistique, la philologie et les autres sciences humaines," both in *Esthétique de la création verbale* (Bakhtin 1984).

5. Here are Marc Angenot's (1984) words: The critical and polemic value of *Marxism and the Philosophy of Language* is stronger, we have to admit, than that of its alternative theoretical construction" (11). On the rhetoric of the tract, see Angenot (1982). Tractlike or not, I would like to underline here the argument's dialectical organization adopted by Marx from Hegel (assertion—denial—denial of the denial or *Aufhebung*).

6. The expression of the two antagonistic theories reduced to four antithetical points can be found first in "The Most Recent Trends in Western Linguistics" (Voloshinov [1983b], 33, the thesis on individualistic subjectivism; 34, the thesis on abstract objectivism) and again in chapter 4 of *Marxism and the Philosophy of Language* (Bakhtin and Voloshinov 1973).

7. This twofold social dynamism has given rise to two antagonistic trends in social theory: the functionalist (unitary) and the dialectical (dualist). About these two trends and their actual assessment, see chapter 4 ("La nature du lien social: l'alternative moderne") in Jean-François Lyotard (1979), with a selected bibliography on the two trends.

8. See Renate Lachmann (1982), proceedings of the symposium of Constance, July 8-11, 1980.

9. For a critical analysis of the reception theory in that sense, see Gómez-Moriana (1980b, 1982a).

Works Cited

Abrams, M. H. 1953. *The Mirror and the Lamp*. New York: Oxford University Press.

Adorno, T. W. 1970. *Aesthetische Theorie*. Frankfurt: Suhrkamp.

Adorno, T. W., and M. Horkheimer. 1947. *Dialektik der Aufklärung: Philosophische Fragmente*. Amsterdam: Querido.

Aldea, Quintín. 1961. "Iglesia y Estado en la España del siglo XVII." *Miscelánea Comillas* 36: 143-354.

Alemán, M. 1962-67. *Guzmán de Alfarache*. Ed. Samuel Gili y Gaya. Clásicos Castellanos, vols. 73, 83, 90, 96, and 114. Madrid: Espasa Calpe.

Alfonso X el Sabio. 1555. *Las Siete Partidas*. Ed. Gregorio López. Salamanca: A. de Portonaris.

Amadís de Gaula. 1960. *Los cuatro libros del invencible caballero Amadís de Gaula*, in *Libros de caballerías españoles*. Ed. Felicidad Buendía. Madrid: Aguilar.

Anderson, B. 1985. *Imagined Communities: Reflections of the Origins and Spread of Nationalism*. London: Verso.

Angenot, M. 1982. *La parole pamphlétaire: Contribution à la typologie des discours modernes*. Paris: Payot.

_____. 1984. "Bakhtine, sa critique de Saussure et la recherche contemporaine." *Bakhtine*, special edition of *Études Françaises* 20(1): 7-19.

_____. 1985. *Critique de la raison sémiotique*. Montreal: Les Presses de l'Université de Montréal.

Angenot, M., A. Gómez-Moriana, and R. Robin. 1991. *The Inter-University Center for Discourse Analysis and Text Sociocriticism*. Montreal: CIADEST. Originally published as *Constitution d'un "Centre Interuniversitaire d'Analyse du Discours et de Sociocritique des Textes" (CIADEST)* (Montreal: CIADEST, 1990).

Anglería, P. M. de. 1530. *De orbe novo*.

Apuleius. 1929. *The Golden Ass: Apulei Metamorphoseon libri XI*, ed. Caesar Giarratano. Augustae: Paraviae.

Aristotle. 1911. *Ars Poetica*. Oxford: Clarendon Press.

Aubrun, C. 1957. "Le *Don Juan* de Tirso de Molina: Essai d'interprétation." *Bulletin hispanique* 59: 26ff.

163

Augustine, Saint. 1934. *Confessiones*. Leipzig: Teubner.

Austin, J. L. 1962. *How to Do Things with Words*. Cambridge, Mass.: Harvard University Press.

Ayala, Martín de. *Discurso de la vida del Ilustríssimo y Reverendissimo Señor Don Martín de Ayala, Arçobispo de Valencia, hasta quatro días antes que Dios Nuestro Señor le llevase consigo, escrito por sí mesmo*. Biblioteca Nacional de Madrid, Ms. 1881, fol. 62ff.

Azcárate, G. de. 1877. *El Self-Government y la monarquía doctrinaria*. Madrid: A. de San Martín.

Baader, H. 1964. "Noch einmal zur Ich-Form im *Lazarillo de Tormes*." *Romanische Forschungen* 76: 437-43.

Bakhtin, M. 1978. *Esthétique et théorie du roman*. Paris: Gallimard.

———. 1981. *The Dialogic Imagination*. Trans. Caryl Emerson and Michael Holquist. Austin: University of Texas Press. Originally published Moscow, 1975.

———. 1984a. *Problems of Dostoevsky's Poetics*. Trans. Caryl Emerson. Minneapolis: University of Minnesota Press. Originally published Leningrad, 1929.

———. 1984b. *Rabelais and His World*. Trans. Hélène Iswolsky. 1968. Reprint. Bloomington: Indiana University Press. Originally published Moscow, 1965.

———. 1986. *Speech Genres and Other Late Essays*. Trans. Vern W. McGee. Austin: University of Texas Press.

Bakhtin, M., and P. M. Medvedev. 1978. *The Formal Method in Literary Scholarship*. Trans. A. J. Wehrle. Baltimore: Johns Hopkins University Press.

Bakhtin, M., and V. N. Voloshinov. 1973. *Marxism and the Philosophy of Language*. Trans. L. Matejka and I. R. Titunik. New York: Seminar Press. Originally published Leningrad, 1929-30.

Bakhtin School Papers. 1983. Ed. Ann Shukman. *Russian Poetics in Translation* 10.

Bal, M. 1985. *Teoría de la narrativa*. Madrid: Cátedra.

Barthes, R. 1966. "Introduction à l'analyse structurale des récits." *Communications* 8: 1-26.

Bataillon, M. *Erasme et l'Espagne*. 1937. Paris: Droz.

———. 1962. "Des historiettes au roman autobiographique." *La vie de Lazarillo de Tormes*. Trans. A. Morel-Fatio. Paris: Aubier-Flammarion.

———. 1954. *El sentido del Lazarillo de Tormes*. Paris: Librairie des Éditions espagnoles.

———1968. *Novedad y fecundidad del Lazarillo de Tormes*. Salamanca: Anaya.

Baumanns. P. 1959. "Der *Lazarillo de Tormes*, eine Travestie der augustinischen *Confessiones*?" *Romanistisches Jahrbuch* 10: 285-92.

Beaujour, M. 1977. "Autoportrait et autobiographie." *Poétique* 8: 442-58. (Reprinted in *Miroir d'encre* [Paris: Seuil, 1980].)

Belic, O. 1969. "Los principios de composición en la novela picaresca." In *Análisis estructural de textos hispanos*. Madrid: Prensa Española.

Bennassar, B. 1979. *L'Inquisition espagnole. XV–XIX siècles*. Paris: Hachette.

Benveniste, E. 1966. *Problèmes de linguistique générale*. Paris: Gallimard. Translated by M. E. Meek as *Problems in General Linguistics*. Coral Gables: University of Miami Press, 1971.

Bruss, E. 1976. *Autobiographical Acts: The Changing Situation of a Literary Genre*. Baltimore: Johns Hopkins University Press.

Bucher, G. 1980. "La logique de la reconnaissance dans le texte évangélique." *Le Vraisemblable et la Fiction: Recherches sur le contrat de véridiction*, 26-44. Colloque de Montréal, October 24-26, 1974. Montreal: Université de Montréal.

Carvajal y Mendoza, Luisa. 1966. *Autobiografía*. Vol. 20 of *Espirituales Españoles*. Barcelona: Juan Flors.

Casalduero, J. 1958. "El desenlace de El Burlador de Sevilla." *Studia Philologica et Litteraria in Honorem L. Spitzer*. Reprinted in *Estudios sobre el teatro español* [Madrid: Gredos (1967), 126-42.]

———. 1970. *Sentido y forma del Quijote*. Madrid: Insula.

Casas, Bartolomé de las. 1981. *Historia de las Indias*. Ed. Augustín Millares Carlo. 3 vols. Mexico: Fondo de Cultura Económica.

Cassirer, E. 1964. *Philosophie der symbolischen Formen*. Darmstadt: Wissenschaftliche Buchgesellschaft.

Castro, A. 1925. *Pensamiento de Cervantes*. Madrid: Hernando. Reprinted Madrid: Noguer, 1972.

––––––. 1935. "Perspectiva de la novela picaresca." *Revista de Archivos, Bibliotecas y Museos*, 12: 123-38. Reprinted in *Hacia Cervantes* (Madrid: Taurus, 1957).

––––––. 1948. Prologue, *Lazarillo de Tormes*. Ed. E. Hesse and H. Williams. Madison: University of Wisconsin Press, 1948. Reprinted in *Hacia Cervantes* (Madrid: Taurus, 1957).

––––––. 1957. *Hacia Cervantes*. Madrid: Taurus.

Cervantes Saavedra, M. *Obras completas*. Recopilación, estudio preliminar, prólogo y notas por Angel Valbuena Prat. Madrid: Aguilar, 1965.

––––––. [1612, 1620] 1967. *The History of Don Quijote of the Mancha*. Translated from the Spanish of Miguel de Cervantes by Thomas Shelton. 2 vols. Reprint. New York: AMS Press.

––––––. 1971. *Don Quijote de la Mancha*. Ed. M. de Riquer. Barcelona: Juventud.

Chabás, J. 1953. *Nuevo manual de historia de la literatura española*. 2d ed. Havana: Cultural.

Chandler, F. W. [1899] 1961. *Romans of Roguery*. Vol. 1: *The Picaresque Novel in Spain*. Reprint. New York: B. Franklin.

Chevallier, J.-J. 1969. *L'Idée de Nation*. Paris: Presses Universitaires de France.

Cicero, M. T. 1889. *Tusculanae diputationes*. In *M. Tullii Ciceronis scripta*. Leipzig: Teubner.

Clifford, J. 1986. "Introduction: Partial Truths" and "On Ethnographic Allegory." In *Writing Culture: The Poetics and Politics of Ethnography*, ed. J. Clifford and G. E. Marcus. Berkeley: University of California Press.

––––––. 1988. *The Predicament of Culture: Twentieth-Century Ethnography, Literature, and Art*. Cambridge, Mass.: Harvard University Press.

Colón, H. 1984. *Historia del Almirante: Crónicas de América*. Vol. 1. Ed. Luis Arranz. Madrid: Historia 16.

Columbus, C. (Cristóbal Colón). 1954. *Diario*. Compiled by Bartolomé de Las Casas. In *Colección de los viajes y descubrimientos que hicieron por mar los españoles desde fines del siglo XV, Obras de Don Martín Fernández de Navarrete*. Ed. Carlos Seco Serrano. Biblioteca de Autores Españoles, vol. 75. Madrid: Atlas. 86ff.

––––––. 1954. *Carta a Luis de Santángel*, Fernández de Navarrete. Vol. 75. 167-70.

––––––. 1969. *The Four Voyages of Christopher Columbus*. Ed. and trans. J. M. Cohen. Harmondsworth: Penguin Books.

––––––. 1989. *The diario of Christopher Columbus's First Voyage to America. Abstracted by Fray Bartolomé de las Casas*. Transcribed and trans. O. Dunn and J. E. Kelley, Jr. Norman: University of Oklahoma Press.

Córdoba, Leonor de. 1883. *Relación de su vida*. Madrid: Miguel Ginesta.

Council of Trent. 1955. *De Sacramentis* (session 7); *Doctrina de sacramento poenitentiae* (session 14). In *Enchiridion Symbolorum*, ed. H. Denzinger. Fribourg: Herder.

Cros, E. 1975. *L'Aristocrat et le Carnaval des gueux: Étude sur le "Buscón" de Quevedo*. Montpellier: C.E.R.S.

––––––. 1976. "Le folklore dans le *Lazarillo de Tormes:* nouvel examen. Problèmes méthodologiques." *Picaresque européenne: Actes du Colloque de Montpellier*. Montpellier: C.E.R.S. 9-24.

––––––, and A. Gómez-Moriana. 1984. *Lecture idéologique du Lazarillo de Tormes*. Montpellier: C.E.R.S.

De Certeau, M. 1975. *L'écriture de l'histoire*. Paris: Gallimard.

Decouzis, P. 1966. *El 'Quijote' y el Concilio de Trento*. Vol. 1 of *Cervantes, a nueva luz*. Frankfurt am Main: Vittorio Klostermann.

Dedieu, J. P. 1979. "Le modèle religieux: Le refus de la Réforme et le controle de la pensée." In *L'Inquisition Espagnole: XV-XIX siècles*. Ed. Bartolomé Bennassar. Paris: Hachette. 269-311.

Denzinger, H. 1955. *Enchiridion Symbolorum: Definitionum et declarationum de rebus fidei et morum*. Fribourg: Herder.

Derrida, J. 1967. *De la Grammatologie*. Paris: Minuit.

———. 1974. "The Violence of Letter: From Lévi-Strauss to Rousseau." In *Of Grammatology*, trans. G. Chakravorty Spivak. Baltimore: Johns Hopkins University Press. 101-40.

———. 1989. "Psyche: Inventions of the Other." In *Reading de Man Reading*, ed. L. Waters and W. Godzich. Minneapolis: University of Minnesota Press. 25-66.

Dubois, J. 1978. *L'institution de la littérature*. Brussels: Nathan-Labor.

Ducrot, O. 1980. *Les mots du discours*. Paris: Minuit.

———. 1984. *Le dire et le dit*. Paris: Minuit.

Eagleton, T. 1976. *Marxism and Literary Criticism*. Berkeley and Los Angeles: University of California Press.

Egaña, A. 1958. *La teoría del regio vicariato español en Indias*. Rome: Pontif. Gregorian University.

Elbaz, R. 1988. *The Changing Nature of the Self*. London: Croom Helm.

Felman, S. 1980. *Le scandale du corps parlant: Dom Juan avec Austin ou la séduction en deux langues*. Paris: Seuil. Translated by C. Porter as *The Literary Speech Act: Don Juan with J.L. Austin, or Seduction in Two Languages*. Ithaca, N.Y.: Cornell University Press, 1983.

Fernández de Avellaneda. 1934. *Segundo tomo del ingenioso hidalgo Don Quijote de la Mancha, que contiene su tercera salida . . .* Madrid: Librería Bergua.

Fernández de Navarrete, M. 1954. *Obras de Don Martín Fernández de Navarrete*. Ed. Carlos Seco Serrano. Biblioteca de Autores Españoles, vols. 75-77. *Colección de los viages y descubrimientos que hicieron por mar los españoles desde fines de siglo XV*. Madrid: Atlas.

Fernández de Oviedo, G. 1959. *Historia general y natural de las Indias*. 3 vols. Ed. Juan Pérez de Tudelan Bueso. Biblioteca de Autores Españoles, vols. 117-21. Madrid: Atlas.

Fernández Enciso, M. 1519. *Suma de Geografía*. Seville.

Fernández Pecha, Fray P. 1962. *Soliloquios*. Ed. Angel Custodio Vega. *La Ciudad de Dios* 175: 710-62.

Fontanier, P. 1977. *Les Figures du discours*. Ed. Gérard Génet. Paris: Flammarion.

Foster, H., ed. 1983. *The Anti-Aesthetic: Essays on Postmodern Culture*. Port Townsend, Wash.: Bay Press.

Foucault, M. 1966. *Les Mots et les Choses: Une archéologie des sciences humaines*. Paris: Gallimard.

———. 1969. *L'Archéologie du Savoir*. Paris: Gallimard.

———. 1971. *L'Ordre du discours*. Paris: Gallimard.

———. 1975. *Surveiller et Punir: Naissance de la prison*. Paris: Gallimard.

Foulché-Delbosc, R. 1900. "Remarques sur le Lazarillo de Tormes." *Revue Hispanique* 7: 81-97.

Friedrich, H. 1976. *Structures de la poésie moderne*. Paris: Denoël/Gonthier.

García Berrio, A. 1978. "Tipología textual de los sonetos clásicos españoles sobre el *carpe diem*." *Dispositio* 3: 243-93.

Gilman, S. 1970. "Los inquisidores literarios de Cervantes." *Actas del Tercer Congreso de la Asociación Internacional de Hispanistas*. Mexico: El Colegio de México.

Girard, R. 1976. *Critique dans un souterrain*. Lausanne: L'Age d'homme.

Goebel-Schilling, G. 1988. *La littérature entre l'engagement et le jeu: Pour une histoire de la notion de littérature*. Marburg: Hitzeroth.

Gómez-Moriana, A. 1972. "Sobre la función del 'yo' narrante en el *Lazarillo de Tormes*." *Boletín de Filología Española* 42-45: 54-56.

———. 1980a. "Procédés de véridiction dans le roman picaresque espagnol." *Le Vraisemblable et la Fiction: Recherches sur le Contrat de véridiction*, 12-25. Colloque de Montréal, October 24-26, 1974. Montreal: Université de Montréal.

———. 1980b. "Spécificité du texte vs vocation universelle de la littérature." *Mémoires de la Société Royale du Canada*, 4th series, 18: 171-85.

_____. 1980c. "La subversión del discurso ritual: una lectura intertextual del *Lazarillo de Tormes.*" *Revista Canadiense de Estudios Hispánicos* 4 (Winter): 133-54.

_____. 1982a. "L'histoire littéraire. Ses rapports avec la pragmatique du discours." In *Renouvellements dans la théorie de l'histoire littéraire: Actes du Colloque International de Montréal.* Ottawa: S.R.C. and A.I.L.C.

_____. 1982b. "Autobiografía y discurso ritual. Problemática de la confesión autobiográfica destinada al tribunal inquisitorial." *L'autobiographie en Espagne: Actes du Deuxième Colloque International de la Baume-les-Aix* (May 23-25, 1981), 69-94. Aix-en-Provence: Université de Provence. French transl. in *Poétique* 56 (1983): 444-60.

_____. 1982c. "La evocación como procedimiento en el *Quijote.*" *Revista Canadiense de Estudios Hispánicos* 6 (Winter): 191-223.

_____. 1985. *La subversion du discours rituel.* Longueuil: Le Préambule.

_____. 1987a. "Entre la philologie et la stylistique (Espagne)." *L'Enseignement de la littérature dans le monde,* special edition of *Études Françaises* 23: 1-2.

_____. 1987b. "Hacia una reintroducción de la dimensión diacrónica en el análisis del texto." *Dispositio* 12: 213-26.

_____. 1988. "Discourse Pragmatics and Reciprocity of Perspectives: The Promises of Juan Haldudo (*Don Quixote* I, 4) and Don Juan." *Sociocriticism* 4: 87-109.

_____, and C. Poupeney-Hart, eds. 1990. *Parole exclusive, parole exclue, parole transgressive. Marginalisation et marginalité dans les pratiques discursives.* Longueuil (Quebec): Les Editions du Préambule.

Góñiz Gaztambide, J.1958. *Historia de la bula de la cruzada en España.* Vitoria.

González de Escandón, B. 1938. *Los temas del "carpe diem" y la brevedad de la "rosa" en la poesía española.* Barcelona: Universidad

Greimas, A. J. 1966. *Sémantique structurale,* Paris: Larousse.

_____. 1980. "Le contrat de véridiction." *Le Vraisemblable et la Fiction: Recherches sur le contrat de véridiction,* 1-11. Colloque de Montréal, October 24-26, 1974. Montréal: Université de Montréal.

Grivel, C. et al. 1979. *Écriture de la religion. Écriture du roman. Textes réunis par Charles Grivel.* Groningen: Centre Culturel Français—Presses Universitaires de Lille.

Guillén, C. 1957. "La disposición temporal del *Lazarillo de Tormes.*" *Hispanic Review* 25: 264-79.

Hatzfeld, H. 1952. "Artistic Parallels in Cervantes and Velázquez." Vol. 3 of *Estudios dedicados a Menéndez Pidal.* Madrid.

_____. 1966. *El "Quijote" como obra de arte del lenguaje.* Madrid: Insula.

Hegel, G. W. F. 1975. *Lectures on the Philosophy of World History: Introduction.* Trans. H. B. Nisbet. Cambridge: Cambridge University Press.

Instrucciones para las visitas de librerías y de bibliotecas públicas. Inquisition file 4470, Archivos Históricos Nacionales de Madrid.

Jakobson, R. 1962. *Retrospect: Selected Writings, 1.* The Hague: Mouton.

Jauss, H. R. 1957. "Ursprung und Bedeutung der Ich-Form im *Lazarillo de Tormes.*" *Romanistisches Jahrbuch* 8: 290-311.

Jesús, María Antonia de. 1961. *Edificio Espiritual.* Vol. 5 of *Espirituales Españoles.* Barcelona: Juan Flors.

Jesús, Teresa de (Teresa de Avila). 1979. *Libro de su vida.* Ed. Dámaso Chicharro. Madrid: Cátedra.

Kestner, J. 1977. "Les trois *Don Quichotte.*" *Poétique* 8: 20-27.

King, T. H. 1986. *Inventing the Indian: White Images, Oral Literature, and Contemporary Native Writers.* Ph.D. diss., University of Utah.

Kloepfer, R. 1975. *Poetik und Linquistik.* Munich: Fink.

Kristeva, J. 1968. "Problèmes de la structuration du texte." In *Tel Quel: Théorie d'ensemble.* Paris: Seuil. 297-316.

_____. 1969a. "Le mot, le dialogue et le roman." In *Séméiotiquè: Recherches pour une sémanalyse*. Paris: Seuil. 143-73.

_____. 1969b. "Le texte et sa science." In *Séméiotiquè: Recherches pour une sémanalyse*. Paris: Seuil. 7-26.

_____. 1970. *Le texte du roman: Approche sémiologique d'une structure discursive transformationnelle*. Paris: Mouton.

Kruse, M. 1959. "Die parodistischen Elemente im *Lazarillo de Tormes*." *Romanistisches Jahrbuch* 10: 292-305.

Krysinski, W. 1975. "Roman et signes de référence." *Canadian Journal of Research in Semiotics* 3(Winter): 65-83.

Labertit, A. 1972. "Le prologue du Lazarillo de Tormes." In *Introduction à l'étude critique*, S. Saillard, C. Marcilly, A. Labertit, and E. Cros. Paris: Armand Colin. 147-81.

Lachmann, R. 1982. *Dialogizitaet*. Munich: Fink.

Lázaro Carreter, F. 1966. "La ficción autobiográfica en el *Lazarillo de Tormes*." In *Litterae Hispanae et Lusitanae*. Munich: Huber. 195-213. Reprinted in *Lazarillo de Tormes en la picaresca*. 11-57.

_____. 1969. "Construcción y sentido del *Lazarillo de Tormes*." *Abaco* 1: 45-134. Reprinted in *Lazarillo de Tormes en la picaresca*. 59-192.

_____. 1970. "Para una revisión del concepto de novela picaresca." *Actas del Tercer Congreso de la Asociación Internacional de Hispanistas*. Mexico: El Colegio de México. Reprinted in *Lazarillo de Tormes en la picaresca*. 193-229.

_____. 1972. *Lazarillo de Tormes en la picaresca*. Madrid: Ariel.

Lejeune, P. 1975. *Le Pacte autobiographique*. Paris: Seuil.

_____. 1980. *Je est un autre*. Paris: Seuil.

Lévi-Strauss, C. 1962. *La pensée sauvage*. Paris: Librairie Plon.

_____. 1968. *Tristes Tropiques*. Paris: Librairie Plon.

Lida de Malkiel, M. R. 1962. *La originalidad artística de La Celestina*. Buenos Aires: Editorial Universitaria.

Llorente, J. A. [1812] 1967. *La Inquisición y los españoles. Memoria*. Ed. Valentino Fernández Vargas. Madrid: Ciencia Nueva.

López de Gómara, F. 1946. *Historia general de las Indias*. Biblioteca de Autores Españoles, vol. 22. Madrid: Atlas.

López Pinciano, A. 1973. *Philosophía antigua poética*. Ed. Alfredo Carballo Picazo. Madrid: C.S.I.C.

Lyotard, J. F. 1979. *La condition postmoderne: Rapport sur le Savoir*. Paris: Minuit.

McCanles, M. 1976. "The Literal and the Metaphorical: Dialectic or Interchange." *PMLA* 91: 279-90.

Machiavelli, N. 1979. *The Prince*. Trans. George Bull. New York: Penguin.

Mainer, J.-C., ed. 1971. *Falange y Literatura: Antología*. Barcelona: Labor.

Malcuzynski, M.-P. 1984. "Critique de la (dé)raison polyphonique." *Bakhtine*, special edition of *Études Françaises* 20(1): 45-46.

Maravall, J. A. 1955. *La philosophie politique espagnole au XVIIe siècle dans ses rapports avec l'esprit de la Contreréforme*. Paris: Librairie philosophique J. Varin.

Marni, A. 1952. "Did Tirso de Molina Employ Counterpassion in His *Burlador de Sevilla*?" *Hispanic Review* 20: 123-33.

Martel, J. 1990. "De l'invention: Éléments pour l'histoire lexicologique et sémantique d'un concept." *L'Invention*, special edition of *Études Françaises* 26(3): 29-49.

Martinet, A. 1955. *Economie des changements phonétiques*.

Martínez Bonati, F. "Cervantès et les régions de l'imagination." *Études littéraires* 8 (1975): 304-43 (Spanish version *Dispositio* II, 1, 1977).

Marx, K., and F. Engels. 1954. *The Communist Manifesto*. Introduction by S. T. Possony. Trans. Samuel Moore. Chicago: Henry Regnery.

———. 1966. "Die deutsche Ideologie." In *Marx/Engels Studienausgabe*. Ed. Irving Fetscher. Frankfurt am Main.

Matleika, L., and K. Pomoroska, eds. 1971. *Readings in Russian Poetics*. Cambridge, Mass.: MIT Press.

Mausel, S. 1971. *L'univers dramatique de Tirso de Molina*. Poitiers: L'Université.

Medvedev, P. M. 1983. "The Formal (Morphological) Method, or Scholarly Salierism." In *Bakhtin School Papers*, 51-64.

Menéndez y Pelayo, M. 1956. *Historia de los heterodoxos españoles*. 2 vols. Madrid: La Editorial Católica.

Menéndez Pidal, R. 1920. *Un aspecto en la elaboración del "Quijote"*. Madrid: Ateneo científico, literario y artístico.

———. 1951. *Los Españoles en la historia y en la literatura*. Madrid: Espasa-Calpe.

———. 1958. *El Padre Las Casas y Vitoria con otros temas de los siglos XVI y XVII*. Madrid: Espasa-Calpe.

Minguet, C. 1970. *Recherches sur les structures narratives dans le "Lazarillo de Tormes."* Paris: Centre de Recherches Hispaniques.

Molina, Tirso de. *El burlador de Sevilla y convidado de piedra*. Ed. Xavier A. Fernández. Madrid: Alhambra, 1982.

Montherlant, H. de. 1962. Préface à *Don Quichotte*. Trans. Francis Miomandre. Paris: Livre de poche.

Morris, C. W. 1938. *Foundations of the Theory of Signs*. Chicago: University of Chicago Press.

Moser, W. 1985. "La Mise à l'essai des discours dans *L'Homme sans qualités* de Robert Musil." *Canadian Review of Comparative Literature* 12: 13-45.

Müller-Bochat, E. 1973. "Tirsos Themen und das Ende Don Juans." In *Spanische Litteratur im Goldenen Zeitalter, Fritz Schalk zum 70. Geburtstag*. Frankfurt am Main: Klostermann. 325-37.

Musil, R. 1953. *The Man without Qualities*. Trans. Eithne Wilkins and Ernst Kaisser. London: Secker and Warburg.

Nebrija, Antonio de. [1492] 1969. *Gramática Castellana*. Facsimile. Ed. R. C. Alston Menston. Scholar Press.

Nerlich, M. 1977. *Kritik der Abenteuer-Ideologie. Beitrag zur Erforschung der bürgerlichen Bewusstseinsbildung 1100-1750*. 2 vols. Berlin: Akademie-Verlag.

O'Gorman, E. 1957. *La invención de América*. Mexico: Fondo de Cultura Económica.

Pastor, B. 1983. *Discurso narrativo de la conquista de América*. Havana: Casa de las Américas.

———. 1988. *Discursos narrativos de la conquista: Mitificación y emergencia*. Hanover, N.H.: Ediciones del Norte.

Paz y Meliá, A. 1892. *Opúsculos literarios*. Madrid: Bibliófilos Españoles.

Perelman, C. 1977. *L'Empire rhétorique: Rhétorique et argumentation*. Paris: J. Vrin.

Picón Salas, M. 1969. *De la conquista a la independencia*. Mexico: Fondo de Cultura Económica.

Pinta Llorente, M. 1953, 1958. *La Inquisición española y los problemas de la cultura y de la intolerancia*. 2 vols. Madrid: Ediciones Cultura Hispánica.

Pitollet, C., ed. 1949. Foreword, *Lazarillo de Tormes*. Paris: Aubier.

Plato. 1867. *Sophistes: The Sophistes and Politicus of Plato, with a revised Text and English Notes*. Ed. Lewis Campbell. Oxford: Clarendon Press.

The Pleasaunt Historie of Lazarillo de Tormes. Drawen out of Spanish by David Rouland of Anglesey. [1586] 1924. Reprint. Oxford: Basil Blackwell.

Ponce de la Fuente, Constantino. 1547 (anonymous). *Confession de un pecador delante de Jesu Cristo, redentor y juez de los hombres, compuesta por el Doctor Constantino*. Seville. Also published Evora, 1554; Antwerp, 1556.

Proceso inquisitorial contra la familia judía de Juan Luis Vives. 1964. Ed. Instituto Arias Montano, Madrid: C.S.I.C.

Proceso inquisitorial del Arzobispo Carranza. 1962. Ed. Ignacio Tellechea Idígoras. Madrid: Real Academia de la Historia.

Proceso inquisitorial del Brocense. 1941. Ed. Antonio Tovar and Miguel de la Pinta Llorente. Madrid: Instituto Antonio de Nebrija.

Propp, V. 1970. *Morphologie du conte*. Paris: Gallimard.

Records of the Trials of the Spanish Inquisition in Ciudad Real. 1974, 1977. Ed. H. Beinart. 2 vols. Jerusalem: Hebrew University.

Quevedo, F. de. 1965. *La vida del Buscón llamado Don Pablos*. Ed. Fernando Lázaro Carreter. Salamanca: University de Salamanca.

Rico, F. 1967. Introduction to *Antología de la novela picaresca*. Ed. Francisco Rico. Barcelona: Planeta.

———. 1970. *La novela picaresca y el punto de vista*. Barcelona: Seix Barral.

———. 1971. Introduction, *Lazarillo de Tormes*. *Biblioteca Básica Salvat*. Madrid: Salvat and Alianza Editorial.

Ricoeur, P. 1969. *Le Conflit des interprétations. Essais d'hermeneutique*. Paris: Seuil.

Riley, E. C. 1962. *Cervantes' Theory of the Novel*. London: Oxford University Press.

Rivadeneira, P. 1945. *Vida de los Padres Ignacio de Loyola, Diego de Laínez, Alfonso Salmerón y Francisco de Borja. . . .* Madrid: B.A.C.

Robert, M. 1963. *L'Ancien et le Nouveau: de Don Quichotte à Kafka*. Paris: Grasset.

Rojas, F. de. 1969. *La Celestina: Tragicomedia de Calisto y Melibea*. Ed. Dorothy S. Severin. Madrid: Alianza Editorial.

Romain, T. 1967. Introduction to Lesage, *Gil Blas*. Paris: Aubier.

Rosenblat, A. 1971. *La lengua del Quijote*. Madrid: Gredos.

Rouco-Varela, A. 1965. *Staat und Kirche im Spanien des 16. Jahrhunderts*. Munich: Hueber.

Sáenz-Alonso, M. 1969. *Don Juan y el donjuanismo*. Madrid: Guadarrama.

Saïd, E. 1978. *Orientalism*. New York: Vintage.

Schizzano-Mandel, A. 1980. ''Le procès inquisitorial comme acte autobiographique: Le cas de Sor María de San Jerónimo.'' *L'autobiographie dans le monde hispanique: Actes du Colloque International de la Baume-les-Aix* (May 11-13, 1979), 155-69. Aix-en-Provence: Université de Provence.

Schmid, W. 1973. *Der Textaufbau in den Erzählungen Dostojewskijs*. Munich: Fink.

Schmidt, S. J. 1973. ''Texttheorie und Pragmalinguistik.'' In *Lexikon der germanistischen Linguistik*. Tübingen: Niemayer. 223-44.

———. 1974, 1976. *Pragmatik*. 2 vols. Munich: Fink.

Segre, C. 1974. ''Construzioni rettilinee e construzioni a spirale nel Don Chisciotte.'' In *Le Strutture et il Tempo*. Turin: Einandi. 183-219.

Simard, J.-C. 1978. ''Los títulos de los tratados en el *Lazarillo de Tormes*.'' *Revista Canadiense de Estudios Hispánicos* 3 (Winter): 40-46.

Sollors, W. 1989. *The Invention of Ethnicity*. New York: Oxford University Press.

Starobinski, J. 1970. ''Le style de l'autobiographie.'' *Poétique* 1: 257-65.

Talens, J. 1975. *Novela picaresca y práctica de la transgresión*. Madrid: Ediciones Júcar.

Tarr, F. C. 1927. ''Literary and Artistic Unity in the Lazarillo de Tormes.'' *PMLA* 42: 404-21.

Tellechea Idígoras, I. 1968. *El Arzobispo Carranza y su tiempo*. Madrid: Ediciones Guadarrama.

Thibaudet, A. 1938. *Réflexions sur le roman*. Paris: Gallimard.

Todorov, T. 1965. *Théorie de la littérature: Textes des formalistes russes réunis, présentés, et traduits par Tzvetan Todorov*. Paris: Seuil.

———. 1966. ''Les catégories du récit littéraire.'' *Communications* 8: 125-51.

———. 1971a. ''L'héritage méthodologique du Formalisme.'' In *Poétique de la prose*. Paris: Seuil. 1-9.

———. 1971b. "Introduction au vraisemblable." In *Poétique de la prose*. Paris: Seuil. 92-99.

———. 1981. *Mikhail Bakhtine: Le principe dialogique: Suivi des Ecrits du Cercle de Bakhtine*. Paris: Seuil.

———. 1982. *La Conquête de l'Amérique: La question de l'autre*. Paris: Seuil, 1982. Translated by R. Howard as *The Conquest of America: The Question of the Other*. New York: Harper and Row, 1984.

Tratados internacionales de los Reyes Católicos con algunos textos complementarios ordenados y traducidos por José López de Toro. Vols. 7, 8 in *Documentos inéditos para la historia de España*. Madrid: Imprenta Góngora.

Tretyakov, T. 1972. *Die Arbeit des Schriftstellers*. Ed. H. Boehncke. Reinbek: Rowohlt.

Truchet, J. 1979. "Pastiches, parodies, contrafaçons de discours religieux dans la littérature française du dix-septiène siècle." *Écriture de la religion: Écriture du roman. Textes réunis par Charles Grivel*. Groningen: Centre Culturel Français—Presses Universitaires de Lille. 29-40.

Tynjanov, J. 1965. "De l'évolution littéraire." In *Théorie de la littérature: Textes des formalistes russes réunis, présentés, et traduits par Tzvetan Todorov*. Paris: Seuil.

Unamuno, Miguel de. 1958. *Vida de Don Quijote y Sancho según Miguel de Cervantes Saavedra, explicada y comentada por Miguel de Unamuno*. 11th ed. Madrid: Espasa-Calpe.

Valbuena Prat, A. 1958. *Antología de la novela picaresca*. Madrid: Aguilar.

Vance, E. 1973. "Le moi comme langage: Saint Augustin et l'autobiographie." *Poétique* 4.

Van Dijk, T. A. 1980. "El procesamiento cognoscitivo del discurso literario." *Acta Poetica* 2: 3-26.

Varela Muñoz, J. 1977. "El *Lazarillo de Tormes* como una paradoja racional." *Revista Canadiense de Estudios Hispánicos* 1 (Winter): 153-84.

Vega, A. C. 1962. "Los soliloquios de Fray Pedro Fernández Pecha (+ca 1400), fundador de los jerónimos de España: Texto y estudio introductorio de Angel Custodio Vega." *La Ciudad de Dios* 175: 710-62.

Vela y Cueto, D. M. 1861. *Autobiografía*. Vol. 7 of *Espirituales Españoles*. Barcelona: Juan Flors.

La vie de Lazare de Tormes et ses fortunes et adversités. 1978. Trans. Maurice Molho. *Romans picaresques espagnols*. Bibliothèque de la Pléiade. Paris: Gallimard.

Vierne, S. 1973. *Rite. Roman. Initiation*. Grenoble: Presses Universitaires de Grenoble.

Vilar, P. [1962] 1976. "Les primitifs espagnols de la pensée économique. Quantitativisme et bullionisme." *Bulletin Hispanique: Mélanges Marcel Bataillon*, 261-84. "Los primitivos españoles del pensamiento económico: Cuantitativismo y bullionismo." Translated by P. Vilar, *Crecimiento y Desarrollo*. Barcelona: Ariel, 1976. 135-62.

Vives, J. L. 1973. *De subventione pauperum*. Ed. Armando Saitta. Florence: La Nuova Italia. Translated as *Obras completas de Juan Luis Vives*. Madrid: Aguilar, 1947-48.

Voloshinov, V. N. 1981. "Les frontières entre la poétique et la linguistique." In *Mikhail Bakhtine: Le principe dialogique*. Ed. T. Todorov. 243-85. Originally published in Leningrad, 1930.

———. 1983a. "Discourse in Life and Discourse in Poetry: Questions in Sociological Poetics." Trans. John Richmond. In *Bakhtin School Papers*, 5-30. Originally published in 1926.

———. 1983b. "The Most Recent Trends in Western Linguistics." In *Bakhtin School Papers*, 31-49. Originally published in *Literatura i Marksizm* 5 (1928).

Walter, M. 1977. "Don Quijote: Vom Ritterbuch zum realistischen Roman." *Realismus in der Renaissance: Aneignung der Welt in der erzählenden Prosa*. Ed. Robert Weimann. Berlin: Aufbau. 622-718.

Watzlawick, P., J. H. Beavin, and D. D. Jackson. 1967. *Pragmatics of Human Communication: A Study of Interactional Patterns, Pathologies, and Paradoxes*. New York: Norton.

Weinrich, H. [1964] 1971. *Tempus: Besprochene und erzählte Welt*. Stuttgart: Klett. Rev. ed., Stuttgart: Kohnhammer.

———. 1966. *Linguistik der Lüge*. Heidelberg: L. Schneider.

———. 1969. "Textlinguistik: Zur Syntax des Artikels in der deutschen Sprache." *Jahrbuch für Internationale Germanistik* 1: 61-74.

_____. 1976. *Sprache in Texten*. Stuttgart: Klett.

_____. 1979. "Les temps et les personnes." *Poétique* 10: 338-52.

White, H. 1982. "Foucault Decoded: Notes from the Underground." In *Tropics of Discourse: Essays in Cultural Criticism*. Baltimore: Johns Hopkins University Press.

Zamora Vicente, A. 1962. *Qué es la novela picaresca*. Buenos Aires: Editorial Columba.

Zimmermann, F. W. 1971. "Episches Präteritum, episches Ich und epische Normalform." *Poetica*, 3: 306-21.

Zuleta, E. de. 1966. *Historia de la crítica española contemporánea*. Madrid: Gredos.

Zumthor, P. 1976. "Le carrefour des rhétoriqueurs: Intertextualité et rhétorique." *Poétique* 7: 317-37.

Index

Compiled by Hassan Melehy

Antonio Gómez-Moriana is professor of comparative literature and Hispanic studies at the University of Montreal. He has published several books and articles in Spanish, German, English, and French on philology and social change, literary history, and semiotics. He is the founder and director of the research group "Marginalisation et marginalité dans les pratiques discursives" (MARGES) and cofounder and codirector of Montreal's Inter-University Centre for Discourse Analysis and Text Sociocriticism (ICDATS/CIADEST). He also founded and directs the monographic series *L'Univers des discours*.